THE DEVIL AND MISS JONES

THE DEVIL AND MISS JONES

The Twisted Mind of Myra Hindley

JANIE JONES
with Carol Clerk

SMITH GRYPHON
PUBLISHERS

First published in paperback in Great Britain in 1994 by
SMITH GRYPHON LIMITED
Swallow House, 11–21 Northdown Street
London N1 9BN

First published in hardback in 1993
Copyright text © Janie Jones 1993

ISBN 1 85685 060 9

A CIP catalogue of this book
is available from the British Library

Printed in Great Britain by
Cox & Wyman Ltd, Reading

This book is dedicated to my dear sister Beatrice who died of cancer and to Theo Saunders who was a devoted friend throughout my prison sentence and thereafter

CONTENTS

ACKNOWLEDGEMENTS

I owe a special thank you to my mother for putting up with me and standing by me throughout everything. Many thanks also to: my family of brothers and sisters; my solicitor, father figure and best friend, John; my solicitor O. K. Goldman for his assistance with this book; composer Tony Waddington for his song 'A Letter to Joe'; Eric, a true, loyal and trusted friend to this day; Joe Strummer for 'House of the Ju Ju Queen' and for 'Janie Jones' on the 1977 album *The Clash*; my dear friend Denise for helping me restore my house when I came out of prison; my actress friend Claire Gordon, ex-wife of Henry Root; Sister Jean Frazer for her friendship in Holloway Prison hospital; Cousin Muggins; my hairdresser, Mostafa, and his wife, Rita, from Kensington Church Street; and Carol Clerk for her great efforts with this book.

Janie Jones

Carol Clerk would like warmly to thank Nigel O'Brien for his invaluable assistance and encouragement throughout this project, specifically his hours spent on transcription, editorial research and administration. Thanks also to Mat Smith, Norman McLeod, Neal Townsend, Keith Simpson, Ted Mico, Allan Jones and Christina Melagrana for their practical help and support.

The author and publisher would like to thank the following people and organizations for permission to reproduce photographs in which they hold the copyright. Express Newspapers: p. 7 (both); p. 8 (right and bottom left); p. 11 (bottom); p. 14 (top); p. 15 (top and bottom left). John Frost: p. 9 (both); p. 11 (top left and centre). Press Association: p. 8 (below right); p. 10 (all); p. 12 (both); p. 13 (below); p. 15 (centre right); p. 16 (top). Syndication International: p. 16 (bottom). All other photographs are reproduced courtesy of Janie Jones.

CHAPTER ONE

The Devil in Disguise

We knew she was coming on to our block well beforehand. The screws told us. She was going to be transferred from Holloway Prison's E wing to D wing, where we were. Nobody wanted to believe it would happen. We'd all been saying, 'Oh, my God, she can't be . . . .' But she was. And even though the screws hated her, absolutely detested her, they insisted: 'You've gotta see her as a number. If you don't, you'll be in trouble. She's like all the rest of you. She's paying for the crime.'

At the time, I was going back and forth between my wing and the downstairs hospital. I'd been under such personal strain that my weight was going down, and I was constantly tired. I wouldn't take any medication because I was terrified I'd turn out like some of the other prisoners who were wandering around like a lot of zombies and junkies, and the hospital staff felt I should be kept under observation in a cell of my own from time to time. I spent a few months there, all told.

One day while I was in the hospital wing, I went outside on exercise with some of the nurses, and I noticed a prisoner on the other side of the lawn with a couple of officers. She kept staring over and trying to smile, grinning at me like a Cheshire cat. I didn't smile back. I never smiled at any of them because there were a lot of mentally disturbed patients down there, and you had to be careful.

I asked, 'Who is she? Is it me she's smiling at?'

'Oh, it's you, all right,' answered one of the nurses. 'But if I tell you who it is, you're not to start any trouble or violence. You've told me a load of times what you'd do if you got hold of the woman, but it's not worth it. You wouldn't be able to come out on exercise, and you'd lose remission.'

I said, 'OK, who is it?'

'Well, that's Myra Hindley.'

I couldn't believe it. I'd never have guessed it in a million years. 'How dare she smile at me!' I yelled. 'Smile at me? I'll cut her in half. I want to go back in. If I stay out here, I will not be responsible for my actions. I don't even want to breathe the same air.'

Myra Hindley looked nothing whatsoever like her famous photograph, the tarty-looking picture with the white-blonde hair and the big, bulging eyes, the evil Moors Murderess. She seemed timid, with a shy, little-girl-lost manner that I was reminded of, years later, by Princess Diana. Hindley really didn't look capable of the gruesome child killings that had sent her to prison. She was tall and slender, with brownish-red hair, wearing jeans and a top, and when she walked, she sort of glided along.

As a first impression, when I got closer, I was struck by her eyes. They were eagle-shaped, a greeny colour, and they were penetrating, quite powerful. Other than that, I saw nothing particularly attractive about her. She had thin, mean lips and a strange nose, with a hump on the bridge and a sideways bend at the bottom, although it's different now that she's had plastic surgery. I made a more favourable impact on her, though. In the days following that first encounter, I had women telling me, 'Myra talks a lot about you, she thinks you're wonderful.'

This was probably because she knew who I was. She may have seen something glamorous in the fact that I was a show-business celebrity and a so-called 'vice queen', jailed just a short while before, in the spring of 1974, for controlling prostitutes. The newspapers went wild with headlines about king-size beds, two-way mirrors, orgies and kinky aristocrats. Certainly, I kept up appearances in prison, the make-up always in place and the hair always blonde to the roots. But it was just as likely that Myra Hindley was interested in me because I was in the public eye and might be able to do her some good in the future, maybe help campaign for her.

I wanted nothing to do with the woman, so when I heard about all the compliments she was paying me, I sent messages back, describing what I'd like to do to her, which would all reach her. I'd say, 'Yeah, she might think I'm wonderful, but she is the scum of the scum, she's a murdering bastard, I'd really love to get a vat of hot fat that's been boiling for twenty-four hours and, from a great height, drop her in it, because no pain is enough for what she did to those innocent little kids. But maybe that's too quick. Maybe even hanging would be too good. Maybe she should stay here and suffer for a long time, because she deserves it.'

After I came out of the hospital and was back upstairs, sharing a cell with a friendly woman called Jenny, I started bumping into Hindley, who had eventually been moved on to D wing as we'd been warned. I usually saw her while I was going to and from the kitchen collecting food, but there was no more smiling from her because she'd got my messages. She would stare down at the ground, look nervous, even scared of me, and I'd glare at her before turning my eyes in the opposite direction. I couldn't bear to look at her for more than an instant.

This carried on for weeks, and, by now, I'd rejoined the other convicts in the machine-room, sewing. There was a smaller room off one side where three or four prisoners were working on a tapestry, including a tiny woman called Mary, who was in her late fifties. She was an educated person, and she was in for fraud. I liked her very much indeed, and she was working on the tapestry alongside Myra Hindley.

Mary eventually invited me to come and have a look at what they were doing. I said, 'No, because I can't stand that Hindley, and she's in the room.' It didn't encourage me that they had scissors in there for cutting the threads!

I kept hearing about this tapestry from Mary, that it would end up as a carpet, which would be sold in America for fortunes. She told me, 'Hindley's brilliant at it.'

My reply was: 'I'm not interested in what she's good at. I don't want to hear anything about her, so let her know that.' I used to get uptight at any mention of her name.

Then, after a week or so, my curiosity got the better of me. Mary said, 'Just come in and have a look. Don't worry about Hindley – she's at one side of the room, and I'm at the other.' So I went in, and I looked at the tapestry, and it was really fantastic. On my way out, I couldn't resist sneaking a look at what Hindley was doing. I had to turn my head upside down to see her part properly, as from where I looked it was a gargoyle. An horrific gargoyle. But it was exceptionally well done.

Later, Mary asked me my opinion. 'It's excellent. Very clever indeed,' I answered.

She prodded: 'What did you think of the part Hindley was working on? I did see you glance at it.'

I said, 'It's wonderful – for a self-portrait!'

That remark was reported back to Hindley and I was told she roared with laughter until she cried, almost. Mary said Myra had been entranced that I'd even walked into the room.

Meanwhile, other inmates on the wing were getting used to the idea of Hindley being there and trying to persuade me to give her a chance. My cell-mate Jenny protested, 'Oh, don't be hard. The poor woman's been inside for all these years, and she's been attacked over and over again.'

I said, 'I keep thinking about the poor little kids on the moors.'

And Jenny countered, 'Yes, but what can *you* do? You're a number, too. We're all numbers.'

I really liked Jenny – I still do – but it took more than her words to soften me up. There was extra persuasion from Anna Mendleson, an Angry Brigade terrorist, who was on D wing with her fellow-bomber Hilary Creek. Anna said, 'I once shared a cell with Hindley and, look, she's doing a sentence – she'll be in for life. What she did has nothing to do with you. You've got to feel very sorry for her.'

'Sorry for her?' I raged. 'Are you sick in the head or something?'

'She's got to live with it for ever,' Anna carried on. 'You don't know what she's suffered. You don't understand. Believe you me, you've really got to feel sorry.'

I said, 'No, I can't.'

Anna wouldn't give up: 'You have to see her. We're friends with her. She'll come in the cell when you're in there with us, and then what are you going to do?'

'Well, I think I'll walk out.'

'Janie, you might be on the wing a long time, and so might she.'

I liked Anna, we used to get on well. She played the guitar, and we'd all sing along, but that still didn't mean I was going to make an effort to be friendly to Hindley. The day came, though, when I was in Anna's cell with a couple of others, and Hindley walked in. They started talking. It was a perfectly normal conversation, and Hindley asked, 'Would you like me to go down and get some hot water for you, Anna?' Myra seemed nice and down-to-earth, if a bit distracted.

I didn't talk to her, didn't say anything at all. Anna said to me, 'Look, don't be embarrassing, don't walk out of the cell.'

Then Myra Hindley turned to me. 'I was highly amused by your joke about the gargoyle and the self-portrait,' she said.

'That's exactly how I feel,' I replied. 'But I seem to be forced to mix with you and see you as a number, so that's what I'm going to do, even though I don't want to. Let's just put it like that.' She looked quite happy to hear it, although it took me quite some time before I could be civil to her and longer still to become friendly. Yet, against all the odds, that's what happened within the next six months, and the 'gargoyle' comment became a standing joke between us.

It was a friendship that developed guardedly on my part. I gradually started to feel sorry for Hindley. She was a bag of bones, and she was a bit pathetic. She was always at church. I began to believe that in other circumstances, I would have found her quite a nice person. Yet I couldn't stop thinking how I'd love to get inside of her twisted mind. What made her do it? What made her get involved with somebody like Ian Brady, the one who actually killed those young people with his own hands?

As time went by, she did confide in me, and the more she did, the more I believed her. She told me everything – her whole story of the moors and her claims, later proved false, that she never witnessed any murder, that she was only a party to the aftermath of one of them and how much she regretted that. She came across as a sweet, helpless girl-next-door, someone who wouldn't harm a fly but who had been mesmerized, then obsessed and controlled, by a violent and terrifying man.

Jenny and I would sit together, and I'd say, 'Christ, something wants me not to believe it, but, at the same time, something else tells me there's a slight possibility this could be the truth she's telling me.' Hindley was very, very convincing – tears and the whole thing – talking about all the hurt over the years, and in the end I believed her 100 per cent. She had this charm and this power – I just don't know what it was – which eventually won me over, and we became friends.

She said I was the only person she could trust and talk to properly. We spent hours together, and it wasn't long before her feelings started to run riot. Myra Hindley fell madly in love with me. She wrote me romantic poetry, which I've kept; she threw tantrums if I were away from her for too long; and when we were in each other's company, she never took her eyes off me. I could feel them burning into me.

I never responded in the same way. Contrary to the sensational claims in some newspapers, I never had an affair with Myra Hindley, but I remained her friend, even after I returned to freedom. We wrote to each other, I went to see her on visits, and I supported her case for parole on various television programmes.

When she finally confessed her full part in the Moors Murders, ten years after I'd left prison, I was devastated. I'll never forgive her. But at least I can see her now for what she is: a pathological liar. She's very intelligent, very clever, very cunning, very hypnotic. She's brilliant with words, brilliant at manipulating people, and she's utterly ruthless – a devil in disguise. She should never be released.

CHAPTER TWO

In Search of Stardom

Obviously, a life involving sex, violence and prison was the last thing I imagined for myself when I arrived in London in the late 1950s, a naïve northern teenager determined to find a future in entertainment. I was compulsively drawn to the lights of the West End, where I was sure I'd discover everything I longed for – night-life, glamour and show business. I loved to have an audience; I could sing, I could dance, and I could make people laugh. I could be a star.

I was a natural performer. Even as a little kid in Seaham, Co. Durham, where I was born and bred, I had to have my stage. I was friendly with a girl whose mother made dresses for us out of black-out curtains, and we'd get up on top of the air-raid shelters and put on concerts. I remember my father being so proud of me.

I would listen to the radio all the time, singing along at the top of my voice and taking off the people I heard. I'd spend sixpence every week going to the Cozy cinema – I'd watch the film, and then I'd come back and impersonate the star. One week I'd be Veronica Lake, the next I'd be Carmen Miranda or James Cagney. I had a wild imagination. I'd be forever going off into a fantasy world of my own. Another thing I was born with was a funny, if naughty, sense of humour. For as long as I can remember, I've had people in fits of laughter, and I was forever making up filthy rhymes. I used to get a good hiding for that, but I was just always really devilish.

From the age of four, I went to dance school, learning tap, ballet and clog-dancing. I was very good. My mother used to go mad about my shoes, though. I'd be lucky if they lasted two weeks, because I'd tap the bottoms through. There would be big holes in the soles, and she'd make me wear them to school. I'd have to put cardboard in them. By the time I was fourteen, I'd won all my medals and diplomas, and Professor Elwood, whose dancing school I attended in Hexham, included me in shows and concerts. He put me up against my own teachers in dance championships at the Queen's Hall, Hexham, and I came by with flying colours. I beat the whole lot of them. He would say to me, 'You've got the gift, definitely,' and he told me I'd do well if I kept it up. But there was no way I could do that in the north, because there was nothing there. Nevertheless, his words stuck in my mind.

I left school at fourteen and ran a dancing class twice a week in a local miners' hall. The next year, I started work as a machinist in a factory, but the factory closed down shortly afterwards. I could see no future for myself, apart from other factories.

The women in that environment, a working-class, coal-mining community, used to age before their time. These were depressed days, money was short, and there were often a lot of children in each family. My mother had eight of us, four boys and four girls. I was the seventh. She was a seventh child, too, and this is where I believe I inherited the psychic powers that have given me sudden premonitions at various times throughout my life.

I was actually a surprise baby. My mother was in her late forties, and she thought she'd been through the change. One day she went to the doctor and told him she had a pain. He said, 'I'll be delivering the pain in a couple of hours.' Then of course I came along, and she needed me like Custer needed more Indians. But it wasn't over yet. A year or so later, my sister Valerie was born.

So my mother had this whole squad, and yet she still took in my grandfather when my grandmother died. There was lots of love and affection in our house in Queensberry Road, but we were very, very poor. My father would be down the mines, and my eldest sister Beatrice would take care of me while my mother washed clothes, scrubbed floors and did all the work in the house.

My parents never had much of a life, they never went on holiday, but they were quite happy with their lot. It wasn't for me, though. Even from a very young age I knew there was no way I was going to stay there and live like that. And, by the time the factory closed, I had another reason for leaving home: there was no prospect of stardom in the north!

I started to look for jobs in London, but my father tried to put his foot down. He said, 'You'll get murdered. There are a lot of funny people down there.'

I replied, 'Well, that's just too bad, it's part of life, and I have to learn for myself, so I want to go.'

His final word was, 'No.'

Regardless, I began to send off applications for jobs in nursing. I'd always been interested in people and how the mind works, so I was thrilled to be offered a position as a nurse at the Three Counties Hospital, a mental home in Bedfordshire. I moved down with my friend Kathleen who was desperate to get away from an unhappy life up north. Kathleen was a lovely girl, and she started work with me at the same hospital, first in a cleaning job and then in the laundry.

My duties were in the wards, dealing with everything from bedpans to bookwork. I was taking a nursing course as well. But the most rewarding work was with the patients themselves. I'd spend hours with even the most difficult people, talking to them, hearing the details of their personal lives and finding out what was causing them to behave the way they did. The doctors were amazed at how I could manage to get through to them. They said I had some sort of magic.

Our accommodation was in a nurses' home, and for someone as innocent as I was at the time, it was a real eye-opener. There were a lot of French and German nurses at the residence, and they used to take a bus and go to the dances at nearby American camps. Then they'd bring the men back, and they'd leave their used contraceptives lying around all over the grounds.

One day I went to the ironing room and found two German girls having it off in there. One was beautiful, with long hair, and the other one looked just like a man, with short blonde hair. I couldn't believe it. I still don't know whether they were doing it for real or as a joke – 'Let's wait until somebody comes along and give them shock treatment.' Well, they gave me shock treatment all right!

Meanwhile, I was carrying on with my dancing. I'd started giving tap lessons twice a week in a local village hall. And one of the highlights of my time at the hospital was the pantomime I put on for the nurses and staff. It got written up in the local paper. The cast included doctors and one of the sisters as Prince Charming.

Another doctor, Dr Russell, eventually offered me a job away from the wards. He needed a nursemaid for his two children who were little rascals, and he asked me if I'd like to do it part-time. I said, 'Yes, but I'd have to rule them with a rod of iron.' I was always a strict mistress! The kids and I got on really well, but after some time a government ruling came through which meant that as a nursemaid at the doctor's flat, I was no longer entitled to live at the home for the hospital nurses. If I'd stayed, they would have had to kick me out. As I'd been in Bedfordshire for about eighteen months, and I was getting a bit fed up with it all, I thought, Well, here's a chance for me to make a break and go to London to see if I can make my dreams come true.

Kathleen wanted to come with me as she'd had enough of the hospital too. Before we left, however, I did one thing. I worked out a song-and-dance act with a piano player. I believed it was my ticket to fame and fortune.

By the time we arrived in London, my sister Beatrice, the one who'd been so like a mother to me, was living there with her husband. They lived in Maida Vale. Later, I would stay with them for a short time, but for now my first home was anything but a place of cosy domesticity.

It was here, sharing a flat with Kathleen in Ladbroke Grove, that I was introduced to a permissive and sometimes bizarre world, which I never knew existed. We had a gay queen, Angel, living in the basement flat. He looked fantastic. He had long, black hair and a face like the angel he was named after. He would've put any beautiful girl to shame. He used to keep asking me if he could borrow a bra, just to see my face when I'd say, 'No.'

He was always three or four weeks behind with his rent, and then he'd have to go and earn some money by playing the piano and sketching portraits in clubs. He took me along once to a 'near beer' club in Soho, a clip-joint where the hostesses drank glasses of coloured water dressed up to look like cocktails, and the male customers would be charged the earth for these and their own glasses of shandy. I didn't like it. I saw men who'd come down from the north being conned rotten, along with a few rich Americans.

Some of the things I witnessed with Angel were quite shocking, even frightening, for a young and inexperienced girl. He took me to one incredible and exclusive place in Chelsea where they locked the doors after the spectators had gone in. There was one room set up like a court with a judge, a jury, the defence, the prosecution, the wigs, the whole lot. They had a woman on trial for cruelty to a man, who was sitting by her feet with a chain around his neck, eating out of a dog bowl. Every so often, she'd kick him in the arse and beat him around.

They heard the evidence absolutely seriously, like in a real court. The woman was found guilty, the man carried on eating out of the bowl, and then all of a sudden, it was madness. The judge got up on the table and did a tap-dance, and everybody else was going mental, all out of their minds on drink. Angel said he once attended one of their murder trials where the defendant was found guilty, the judge put on a black cap and sentenced him to death, and they staged a hanging scene.

I was frightened out of my wits just by what I'd seen myself, so when Angel asked me if I wanted to go back there, I had to decline. But it made me wonder, Well, who is really normal? What is normality?

After a few months out of town, working as a waitress here and there, I was taken on at the prestigious Windmill Theatre. Of course, I had to do nude work every now and again. Everyone did there. I used to think,

There I was with drawers down to my knees in the north. Now here I am in London with no drawers on at all. When my mother found out, it was the end of the world. She thought it was terrible. I was only ever at the back, though, on a pedestal. The taller girls were placed at the front.

It was hellish hard work. I did five shows a day, and then there were rehearsals in between. We performed on a glass stage, and we had comedy and tap routines, fan dance, ballet and different little scenes with excellent choreography. I was once in an underwater piece. It was all very sophisticated, the closest thing to the Folies in Paris. One of the rules of the fan dancing was that you had to be completely still, like a statue, while you stood on the pedestal. I used to be up there cracking gags to the other girls, and they'd be giggling and wobbling all over the place like jellies. The owner, a Mr van Dam, would go absolutely spare and tell me off after the show.

We got a load of nutters in there, jumping over the tops of seats. They used to be told over the public address system to sit down. That sort of behaviour just was not the thing at the Windmill. There was a great deal of wealth around the club. You'd see the customers arriving in Rolls-Royces, and they'd send us bouquets and cards. Many of them would come round to the stage door, and a lot of the girls married men they met backstage. There were also some beautiful women working there who could've had any men they wanted, yet were only interested in other girls.

We were all instructed to use the theatre's own canteen, not the café next door where male customers would wait hopefully to see girls from the show. But quite a few of us loved to defy the ban, and it was in this café that I met my first real boyfriend, an American marine called Carl who took me out regularly and then asked me to marry him. I accepted. It was a real love affair. It was all roses and candlelight and kisses, and it was totally pure. There was no sex involved.

He came from Buffalo, just outside New York, and he intended to take me back there with him at the end of his three years in Grosvenor Square, London. But after we'd been engaged for a year, I realized that I didn't really want to go to America. I had my career over here. Besides, I was getting a bit bored, so I broke it off with him. He was heartbroken. In retrospect, I think he was probably the big love of my life, he was 99 per cent of the 100, but it would never have worked out. And that was the only marriage proposal out of several I received around that time that I ever gave any real thought to.

It was also during my time at the Windmill that I suffered one of the biggest traumas of my life: the death of my father from silicosis, through working in the coal-mines and constantly inhaling dust. He was still a relatively young man, in his fifties. As a child, I had felt sorry for him when he came home at nights. He'd been down in the bowels of the earth, he hadn't seen the light of day, he'd been crawling along a pit line, and he'd be jet black. There was always the possibility that a prop could collapse, so he faced the constant danger of death. It was a very hard life.

I went back up to Seaham to visit him before he died. I got hold of his hand, and I was looking at him, stroking his hair, and I said, 'You can't speak, but you can hear me,' and he'd be nodding his head. But before he died, he managed to sing the Lord's Prayer from beginning to end. I was hysterical. I didn't want to believe he'd gone. I thought I'd come back one day, and he'd still be there.

I idolized my mother and father. I remember being about three or four, and my father sitting me on his knee. I'd say, 'You've got beautiful hair and lovely blue eyes, and I love you, Dad.' And he'd say, 'Oh, God, what are you after?' I was always trying to get him to tell me he loved me just a scrap more than he loved the others. And he was a very, very strict man, but he did love all of us. He used to say, 'I wouldn't take a gold pig for any of you.'

I think of him now, and I think of his dominoes and his racing pigeons, which he adored. I saw him crying over them. He had about thirty or forty, and he used to call them all by name. If one of them broke a leg, he'd set it with a matchstick and wind this cotton round it, and he'd get it flying again.

Life went on back in London, although the Windmill eventually closed in the face of competition from various new strip clubs where the girls were allowed to move about rather than stand like statues. It didn't take me long to find more work. I had already started tap-dancing and singing, wearing a top hat and tails, at the Panama Club, right opposite the Windmill. I could've been sacked for this because our contracts with the Windmill were supposed to be exclusive, but I went ahead anyway and continued when the Windmill shut down.

I was also employed by another club, the Latin Quarter, and then by the Gargoyle Club too, which was owned by Michael Klinger, the British producer, whose films included *Repulsion*, *Cul de Sac* and *Get Carter*. Quite a few of the girls who had worked at the Windmill ended up at the Gargoyle, another club which specialized in big productions, with shows upstairs and cabaret downstairs. It was there that I started taking lead roles in the cabaret, and I became involved with a lot of the upstairs choreography, too, which presented me with certain problems I hadn't anticipated. Quite a few of the girls were doing strips, and one of them used to come to work with whiplashes all over her back. I asked her, 'What the hell are those?' 'Oh, I enjoy it, the boyfriend did that,' she replied.

I said, 'I don't care what you enjoy. It's ridiculous.' I didn't give a damn what she did in her own time, but I didn't want her coming into my dance routines covered in marks, which the audience could see.

In addition to my own obligations to the Gargoyle, I'd stand in if anyone else were taken ill. I'd come on-stage and do something off the top of my head. I was always cracking gags, and I'd often have the place in an uproar. Even in a routine that wasn't meant to be funny, I'd get the comedy in somehow. Really, though, I was a complete slave in that club. I was run off my feet. Even when I had laryngitis, they would say, 'Oh, you'll be able to do it,' and somehow I would.

When I did manage any time off, I'd relax by going to a hairdresser's in Soho with the local whores. I used to love chatting to them about their profession. I was endlessly fascinated by what made them do it. They always said it was for the money, but I wasn't satisfied with being told that. I would want to get to the very heart of it all.

At this time I was still innocent sexually, although it wasn't for the lack of admirers. I used to laugh and tell the men, 'You may gaze upon my beauty,' and I'd say to my friends, 'I don't know what it is, but they're all mad about me, the fools,' and that became my catchphrase. As a young girl, I'd truly believed in the knight in shining armour, but when I came to

London and found myself surrounded by men who were only after one thing, I realized there was no such person. I was very, very disappointed. Nevertheless, I thought it was about time to broaden my experience of men, and I picked a chap who regularly came into the Gargoyle. His name was David, he was from a rich Jewish family, which owned men's clothes shops all over London, and he drove a beautiful handmade sports car. He'd been taking me out for a year, and he wanted to marry me. I liked him very, very much. He was a lovely person, whom I found most attractive. Shortly after I celebrated my twenty-first birthday at the Gargoyle, I went to a party he gave in Hampstead; I had a lot to drink, and I went to bed with him. I was the one who instigated it. He was saying, 'Oh, let's wait until we're married,' while I was insisting, 'No, let's see how we get on now.'

It was a painful and horrible experience. I could not believe that this was what everybody talked so much about. Throughout my whole career in the clubs, I'd been hearing the girls going on about their sex sessions and their orgasms and how wonderful it all was, and how the earth moved. I thought, Christ, there's no earth moving, it's one big nothing, this just is not for me. Needless to say, I decided then that I wasn't in love with David, and I have to state, though, as a postscript, that my views on sex have not changed dramatically since then. Nobody has really made the earth move for me, maybe because I've never found anyone I loved madly enough. I admire beauty, be that a beautiful work of art or a beautiful person, but it doesn't do anything for me physically.

All this may be due to my father's influence from way back. He used to tell me constantly, 'Men are only after one thing and when they get it, that's the end of that, they'll have no respect for you.' That became embedded in my mind. My mother never, ever saw my father naked, and he never saw her naked either. I've discussed this with her. She told me that he'd come in drunk and all of a sudden another kid would be on the way. It was the old Victorian ethic, and I think it must have put me off considerably. Certainly, it helped to shape my thinking about the opposite sex.

The sixties were really swinging in London. Beatlemania had arrived, colourful new pop groups were springing out of nowhere every week, Carnaby Street was jam-packed with boutiques and teenagers spending money like it had gone out of fashion, and the clubs were full of party-goers and celebrities. I was gripped with all the excitement. I loved the mini-skirts, and I wore loads of make-up on my eyes, although I never followed the trend for bouffant hairstyles. I always stuck to my own.

Everything was 'way out', a laugh and a joke, a world away from the life I'd known in Co. Durham. I could feel a big high all the time. These were glamorous days, brilliant fun, and there were fantastic parties every night, but at the same time there was a complete innocence about it all, which is why that era could never be recreated. The sixties were simply the best.

I'd built up a reputation in cabaret, and I was spreading my wings in all the major West End clubs. The Pigalle, the Stork Club, Quaglino's and the Georgian Club are just a few of the names which spring to mind. The Georgian, in St James's, was a very exclusive hostess drinking club with waitresses dressed in cat outfits. It attracted quite a few well-known personalities. One of the hostesses there was Zelda Plum, who'd also worked at the Stork as an entertainer and would later develop a famous dance with a chinchilla on her head.

My younger sister Valerie had moved to London by now and she worked in Whiteleys department store as a fashion buyer. She was staying with me at my flat in Westbourne Court, Bayswater. She'd worked in amateur shows in the north, and I formed a double act with her, which we performed at the Georgian with the resident musical trio. It was the first cabaret they'd ever had in the club. As part of the act, Valerie and I would do a Carmen Miranda number wearing hats laden with imitation fruit and a real banana at the front. We'd look out at the audience each night to see who we'd take the banana to, and I'd always pick somebody who looked quiet and shy. On this particular night, I went over to a balding man in his thirties, whom I now know as Eric, later to become one of the most important characters in my life.

The spotlight went on him, and he started protesting, 'Ee, no, no.'

I kept saying, 'Please take a bite of the banana,' and he kept refusing. I put down the microphone, and I said, 'If you don't take a bite of this banana, I'll put it right down your throat.' He nearly swallowed it.

A couple of nights later, the head waiter came over to Valerie and me. He said, 'There's a man over there who would like you to have dinner with him.' It was Eric.

We went over, and Eric said, 'Ee, I hope you don't get the wrong idea, it's the first time I've ever spoken to two girls.'

'I hope *you* don't get the wrong idea,' I replied. So we had this dinner, and it turned out that Eric was on a fortnight's holiday from Southport, where he lived. He came to the club to see us every night for the rest of his stay in London.

Coincidentally, we were booked to appear in cabaret at Southport's Kingsway Casino a week or two later, and he suggested we could stay with him and his mother. I said to Valerie, 'Well, he's harmless, he's very nice, very sweet. We could go and see how we feel, and if we don't think we're going to be comfortable, then we'll go to a hotel.'

His mother was a tiny woman, very jolly, and she ordered Eric around like a little boy. 'Eric, do this, Eric, do that.' She was absolutely astonished that he'd approached us at the Georgian because he was so shy and introverted he never usually spoke to anyone. He felt he was in the way all the time. He wouldn't even go into a shop. His mother did everything for him, but *everything*. She told us that when Eric was young, he never mixed with other children. He used to follow his father around all the time, and when his dad died, Eric lost nearly all of his hair with the shock. His sisters couldn't do anything with him. I was the first and only person after that who was able to get him chatting and bring him out of his shell.

Valerie and I stayed with them for the whole two-week residency in Southport, and once again Eric came to the show every night. His mother would be saying, 'You don't want to go again, Eric! But if you have to, don't be gawking at the girls putting their stage make-up on!' When we returned to London, he phoned regularly and came on visits. Eventually he would move down south and into my home. His life would never be the same again.

It was 1964. My sister and I had been all over England and Europe with our act. We were stars in Spain. And we were about to make our first big splash in the British press with what was to be my first of many outrageous escapades. It came about when Michael Klinger asked us to the world première of his film *London in the Raw*. He'd invited countless show-business celebrities and beautiful girls, and, remembering the publicity stunts I used to set up for the Gargoyle, he wanted me to think up something special for this event.

I said to my sister, 'We'll go topless.'

She answered, 'Never.'

I persisted, 'If we do that, I guarantee we'll steal the limelight.' I talked her into it eventually, and I told Michael Klinger.

He said, 'That would be dynamic. I'll pay for everything – the Rolls, the dresses, the furs, just anything you want to wear.'

The evening arrived and we got into the Rolls in our beautiful, long, topless dresses and fur wraps. The streets outside the theatre were jam-packed, and Valerie was scared stiff. I got out first, and of course I opened my coat. I was posing for the cameras and the whole bit, while my sister followed, hesitantly. Before I knew it, next thing, we were done for indecency and exposure at a world première. I think we went down in the history books for that one.

Naturally, the photographs were all over the papers. So were the reports of the court case, which was hilarious, a big send-up. We emerged from that with a conditional discharge. Valerie and I were subsequently offered lots of money to do our act topless, but we would not. The première incident was a one-off, a joke, but we'd always been serious about the act. It was brilliant, we had fantastic voices, and we were very powerful. At the same time, Valerie was still furious with me: 'This is ridiculous, you got me into all of this, you're too outrageous.'

We decided to split the act so that she could concentrate quietly on her songwriting. I carried on in cabaret alone, making strides into more new clubs. I starred at Le Prince, which later became the Revolution, a favourite haunt of show-business personalities, and it was while working there that I became friendly with Jimmy Sangster, whose screenwriting credits for Hammer include *The Curse of Frankenstein* and *Dracula*, and Michael Carreras, who produced and directed many Hammer films, as well as being Managing Director of Hammer Films.

Then there was the Astor, a hang-out for villains like the Kray twins, where I was billed as 'glamorous songstress/*comedienne* Janie Jones'. That's where I became friendly with celebrities like Bruce Forsyth and Max Bygraves. I used to see and hear everything that went on in there. I once came across people writing out hundreds of 'viewers votes' to send in to disrupt the outcome of television talent programme *Opportunity Knocks*. I worked at the Astor Club a million times, and the owner Bertie Green used to ask me to help him audition the dancers and singers.

However, it was when I began work at a club called the Don Juan Casanova that I started mixing in really exclusive circles. I became very friendly with the world-famous shipping tycoon Aristotle Onassis, who used to come in sometimes with the opera singer Maria Callas. On occasions, he would come into the club and pay the manager to release me for the night and then take me to another high-society club, Churchills. He liked me because I used to make him laugh, and I'd tease him about the girls he always surrounded himself with. He'd tell me how he started in the shipping lines, and he'd chat about his life. He was a lot of fun, but I think he was a very lonely person, for all the money he had.

I would often sit down for a chat with one of Princess Margaret's escorts, Billy Wallace. He had a bad heart, Billy, and he'd tell me all about his health problems. At other times, he'd sit for hours and talk about Princess Margaret. He worshipped her. A week later, I'd see them together in the club, the princess never without her long cigarette-holder.

George Peppard was another one I used to like. One night he organized a surprise for Henry Fonda's birthday. We held a special party at the Don Juan Casanova, but Henry left early because he'd been at the première of *How the West Was Won*, and he was exhausted. George paid two beautiful girls at the club to follow him back to his hotel, strip off their clothes and sing 'Happy Birthday' to an amazed actor. I went with them and, after their performance, I enjoyed a performance of my own with George, who became my lover for a brief time.

I used to spring surprises on all sorts of people. Michael Klinger once encouraged me to play a trick on his film director friend Roman Polanski who'd just arrived in London. We gave a party for Polanski, and I'd set up two girls to start an argument in front of him. They were slapping each other round the face, ripping each other's clothes off, and Polanski didn't know what to say, because he could hardly speak English. He ended up sleeping with one of the girls, a beautiful blonde model, who later went out with the club owner, Victor Lowndes. Polanski once asked me if I would go out with him – would I hell!

I spent most of my social life as well as my working hours in clubs – gay and lesbian clubs because they continued to fascinate me, theatres where I would see all the visiting shows, and night-clubs because I enjoyed the company. I'd make genuine friends there, like Nicholas Freeman who was in later years the MP for Kensington. I went out with him a good few times. The Saudi Arabian King Faisal and his son, the prince, also used to come in. They'd treat me to dinner and take me out gambling. The King would say, 'There's £1000 to play the tables.' It seemed a terrible waste, so I used to put some of it away and gamble the rest. Yet for all the riches in places like the Don Juan Casanova, not all of the customers were so generous.

Charlie Clore, who owned Selfridges department store in Oxford Street, was one of the wealthiest – and one of the meanest – men in the country. He never asked anyone to join him for dinner – except me. Even then, he made it clear that champagne was not included, and he once refused to pay the price of a cigar. He ordered half a cigar, and the embarrassed waiter ended up giving him a whole one on the house. I had originally been so taken aback to be invited to Charlie's table that I told him straight off, 'If you think you're going to get any hi-diddle-diddle off me, you're mistaken, so you may as well save the price of the dinner.' He started roaring with laughter, and once he realized I wasn't prepared to sleep with him for the sake of his wallet – or the lack of it! – we got on like a house on fire.

He once told me, 'There's something very magnetic about you, and I don't know what it is, but you should flaunt it.' I didn't say so at the time, but I was already quite aware of my power over men. And I was using it unashamedly.

It was a happy new year for me in 1966. That January, I added another string to my bow: I became a pop star. During the time I'd been working at the Astor, I'd been doing a bit of recording in a studio at the back of Oxford Street. At the end of the sessions, I threw in a song called 'Witch's Brew', one of Valerie's compositions. It was the sort of number I'd use in cabaret, a novelty, but my record company insisted they wanted to put it out as the A-side of a single.

I said, 'Oh, my God, I don't believe this. It's all right for a B-side maybe, but it's a lot of crap compared to the others I've done – the brilliant ballads with the big orchestra.' After taking advice from two other record companies, who also liked 'Witch's Brew', I reluctantly agreed that HMV could release it. The next thing I knew, it zoomed right up the charts, and all of a sudden I was in the papers and on television.

I appeared on *Top of the Pops*, *Thank Your Lucky Stars*, *The Mike and Bernie Winters Show*, *Time for Blackburn*, *Five O'Clock Club* and lots of children's programmes. Obviously, through this, I met numerous stars, people like Lulu, Dusty Springfield, Manfred Mann, Alan Price, Dave Dee, Cliff Richard, Kenny Lynch, Ed Stewart and Mary Quant.

I released a succession of singles after 'Witch's Brew'. They included 'Gunning for You', another comedy-type song of Valerie's that came out on Pye, 'Charlie Smith the Lighthouse Keeper', also on Pye, a cover of Jim Webb's beautiful 'Girls Song', on Major Minor, and 'Back on My Feet Again' on President. None was the smash hit that 'Witch's Brew' had been, but the records continued to attract publicity, which added to the demand for my appearances in cabaret. I was quite happy about this. I was making very good money out of the clubs, and it wasn't just for a song and a dance.

CHAPTER THREE

The Naked Truth

I first began to realize how to work my powers on men when I sat on my father's knee as a young girl. I would charm him into giving me money for my dancing school and my tap shoes. Later on, as I grew into my early teens, I found out just how much I could twist boys of my own age around my little finger. I used to go to the cinema with the good-looking lads, the ones I knew the other girls were mad about, and wind them up, just to show that I could do it. There wasn't any particular reason for it. I think it was just the mischief in me.

But it wasn't until I came to London and started at the Windmill that I discovered exactly what this power could do, and the extent to which a beautiful woman could use it to manipulate men. We showgirls were always receiving great big boxes of chocolates and flowers from the customers. The same men would offer to buy you dinner in the club or pay you to join them at their table as an escort. I had them coming in and handing me bundles of cash just to sit there talking to them, sometimes every evening for one or two weeks at a time.

I used to say, 'You can buy the dinner and the champagne if that's your thing, but I'm not going anywhere with you.' I'd get that straight from the beginning. They had so much money they'd throw it about. It meant nothing to them. Fifty pounds meant as much as five pence.

And I used to attract them like a magnet. Rico, the owner of the Don Juan Casanova and Le Prince society clubs, would say to me, 'Whatever you've got, you should bottle it. You'd make a fortune. These men are mad about you.' I knew I had 'it', I knew the effect I had on men, and I used it to the best of my ability.

Part of the fascination was that I amused them. I was very witty, cracking gags and sometimes coming out with a few outrageous one-liners for a bit of shock treatment. I was also a very good flirt, an expert. I'd look them in the eyes and give them the come-on, letting them think, *Maybe the next time*. And I'd always wear low-cut clothes, because that would get them really worked up – crazed, some of them. Then again, I was careful never to go anywhere I would be alone with them, because that would have been asking for trouble. Sex causes so much trouble it's unbelievable.

That's where the obstacle race used to come in, because no matter how much money they offered me, they would never get me into the bed. That intrigued them; they thought that in time they would, that they would win me over, but I was like the Rock of Gibraltar, and they did not. Once they'd been with a girl from the show, then they'd get bored and go on to the next girl, the next conquest. But something that they couldn't have, they wanted, and that was my secret weapon.

I didn't have a great deal of respect for these men. Some of them I liked on a personal level, but most of them I couldn't stand. I had to sit with them, though, because it was club policy. The majority were married. It used to sicken me. They'd come in with their wives to begin with, and then they'd start arriving alone, looking for girls. It was like they were having the same dinner every day of the week – then they wanted something different, and they could afford to buy it. Some of the wives were stunning, the most beautiful women you've ever seen, but their husbands were running around behaving like Hollywood stars, chasing every glamorous girl they saw. I watched that pattern repeat itself over and over again during my years in the clubs.

Yet I never lost sight of the fact that there is such a thing as two people falling in love and staying together. If you find that, then you really want to hang on to it – lock, stock and barrel. My mother and father adored each other; they were honest and hard-working, they were happy and that was that.

I loved the people of the north, and I was never ashamed of my background, unlike some of the girls in the clubs. There was one who was very attractive but a bit of a 'cor blimey', and she'd tell the customers her father was a rich dentist. I never heard such crap. I went to elocution lessons, and I could put on a bit of an accent if I wanted to, but when anybody, be that a celebrity or an aristocrat, ever asked me, 'Where are you from?', I'd say, 'The north of England, and my father's a coal-miner.' I was tremendously proud of it, and I still am.

At the back of my mind, I used to feel very guilty about the fact that my father used to sweat in a coal-mine and be in water up to his knees, listening to the creak of the pit props and knowing he could die at any moment. The sweat of his brow was the money that meant all the world to me for my dancing schools. He gave me what he'd worked for, and he loved me very much. That meant far more to me than any amount of money these rich men were throwing at me in the West End of London.

Listening to the prattlings of all the titled people in the society clubs, I realized that money can buy anything, money can get you out of anything, and money can speak all languages. There's one law for the rich and one for the working class, and that will never, ever change. I'd think back to our first family home in Australia Street, Seaham, where we didn't have a bathroom, just a tap outside in the street, and to how my daily job was to bring in a little pail of water. I'd remember going out with my mother and my sisters to buy clothes from the second-hand woman. I'd feel terrible that my father could be working for peanuts and that what he might earn in five weeks, these men would blow in one night on a dinner with caviare.

So no matter how exclusive the club or the company I was in, I'd always think, Coal-miners, back there slaving for a few quid, while these men are chucking money around. And I took advantage of it.

One man in the Gargoyle used to send me lilies all the time, masses and masses of lilies. I told Michael Klinger, 'I'm getting paranoid. Lilies are for funerals.'

He disagreed; 'No, lilies are for purity'.

I had to chuckle at that. I said, 'Ah, well, he's got the right one here!' Yet although I was still a very young woman, I had reached the point where nothing could have shocked me. Nothing. The girls used to come into the clubs every night talking about the men they'd been with and the fetishes that they had, and I used to think, You don't get any of that in the north, with the working class. I began to wonder about people and what they wanted, just as I've wondered about the many nutters I met in those days.

There was one chap who used to come to the Georgian in a Rolls, and all he ever wanted to do was to find a girl with a big bust. Then there was a colonel who paid girls from the Don Juan Casanova and Le Prince to sit on his back as though astride a horse and lash his arse with a big riding-crop. One regular at the Don Juan used to say: 'I want ten of the young ladies from the show to come back to my mansion.' When they got there he'd make them strut around in a ring with feathers stuck up their bottoms shouting, 'Cock-a-doodle-doo.' That was all they had to do, and they got £100 each for it.

Another customer used to take girls home and get them to bend over, naked. He'd yell, 'Charge!' and go running up to grab them, shouting as though he were in a bullfight. He never did anything more intimate, he just charged and grabbed.

The Don Juan was full of unusual men. There was one who came in sometimes with his gorgeous wife but more often turned up on his own. He'd pay a fortune for girls to sit with him and have dinner, as hostesses. But they'd always come back crying. One night this happened with a girl called Sonia. I asked her, 'Why are you so upset?'

She said, 'He sat insulting me all night long. He said I had a big nose and I was ugly.' She did have a sort of biggish hooter, Sonia, but she had lovely eyes and was very attractive. I found out from several other girls that the man called them sluts and whores, which they weren't. These particular girls were hostesses only.

Rico, the owner, told me, 'They've got to put up with it, because that's his thing, and they do get the money.'

One night, this man asked for me to sit with him. He started with the insults, telling me that I was arrogant. I said, 'Look, you've had a lot of girls crying here, but anything you say to me will be like water off a duck's back. You can insult me as much as you like. It won't upset me because I know you're getting your kicks out of it.' I had a feeling that he had some personal trouble, which made him do it, and I told him so.

He said, 'Yes, you're right. You're the first one I've told. I've got problems with my wife, and the things I'm saying to these girls are the things I'd love to say to her but daren't, because she's got all my money in her name.' After that, he used to ask for me quite often. It was because I used to take the time to talk to people, and was interested in what made them tick, that I was popular among the customers and girls alike.

One of the hostesses in the Don Juan in my time was Christine Keeler, who later became notorious as a prostitute in the Profumo scandal. She was a beautiful girl. I put her up for a few days in a flat I was renting in Frampton Street, off Edgware Road, and we got on well. The most scandalous thing she ever did in front of me was to burn a hole with her cigarette in the back seat of my first car, a brand-new Ford Capri. I gave her a hell of a bollocking.

Some of the customers, for all of their various weaknesses, were really very likeable. I was fond of Bob Geddes. I used to see him around a lot of the clubs because he was a journalist who specialized in show-business reviews. He was tall, dark-haired with glasses, and quite shy. I once asked him, 'Why don't you ever go home with any of the girls you sit with?' He told me that he was only interested in buying their knickers and sniffing them. He'd pay £50 a time. He had thousands of pairs.

Bob lived near the Cumberland Hotel in Marble Arch; he had a beautiful flat there, and he used to invite me over as a friend. He was very proud of his bar; he said it was the greatest in London. It was stocked with drinks from all over the world. He had his fetish, Bob, but he was harmless, and he was a really nice man to sit and chat to. A sweetheart. So was Eric Muller, who owned Muller Shipping Lines. He used to flip-flop around the Don Juan with his slippers on, and he'd pay a lot of the girls to go back to his big house in Marylebone's Mansfield Street and just make a fuss of him. He was quite lonely.

Another of our favourite characters was Eamonn Waters. We

nicknamed him the Sky's the Limit, because that's what he was always saying. He was so generous. He'd buy champagne and dinners all round in the Don Juan and Le Prince, and he'd pay the girls £100 each just to sit with him. He once gave me a beautiful diamond watch. He used to like having three or four girls around him all the time, and he had a wonderful personality. He used to make everybody laugh.

Eamonn came from Ireland and had a big estate up in Newcastle upon Tyne. He owned a lot of shares in a very big oil company. He was in his late fifties, bearded and a dead ringer for James Robertson Justice. He used to give autographs, pretending to be him. He was married but separated, with a daughter, and he had heart trouble.

He used to treat his favourite girls to dinner at the Kensington Royal Garden Hotel, where he'd book himself a whole suite. One night, there were six of us in the hotel restaurant with him. He left the table to go to the men's room, and he was impeccably dressed as usual. But he mustn't have fastened his trousers properly, because when he came back out, they fell down, and he was wearing these hilarious jockey-shorts. The waiters didn't know where to look.

Some people call them perverts. Other people, myself included, have come to regard many odd habits and requirements as a simple fact of life. There was, for instance, the millionaire who had a thing about me. I met him in the Gargoyle and went out with him a few times. He was very good to me and bought me some beautiful things. He had a place in Chelsea, and he used to invite me over to listen to church music with him. Sometimes we'd have dinner there, and at other times we'd go out.

If I had specially dressed up, he'd stop the car at a roadside café. He used to like the excitement of us looking immaculate in the midst of all the big, burly workmen. When it came to ordering, he'd always say, 'Oh, no, no, no, I'm not having anything, I can't afford it.' And he'd eat the scraps I'd leave on my plate. The workmen used to look at him in disbelief. Then when I'd be casually dressed, in jeans and a top, he'd take me to very smart places. That gave him a thrill. When it came to sex, though, he never wanted to go to bed with a woman. He wanted to be chastised by a strict mistress with the hair all up on top of the head. He got his jollies out of discipline. He loved to be dominated, tied up and punished. He used to say, 'Please, I want you to punish me,' and he'd ask me to cane him. It didn't turn me on in the least, but I did do it for him. He was begging me to.

Some of the other girls, the hostesses, used to be always tying up and punishing men who liked to be on racks and all that. And it always seemed to be the rich ones with the strict, boarding-school background, or the public-school education, or the nannies who used to whack them to the point where they started enjoying the punishments.

I also came across a lot of men who liked to be dominated as slaves to varying degrees. I never, ever thought of women as slaves, I couldn't stand that idea, but men, yes. In my own life, I could never bear a man who told me what to do. All right, I could get into romance, and I could get into candlelight, but I had to have total power and domination over the man. If I fancied someone, and I wanted to go with him sexually, it would be my way, not his, and then I sometimes wouldn't want to know any more. Just as men have traditionally used women, I've used men like that, and I haven't been able to get rid of them in the end.

Another familiar form of domination was humiliation. I came across men who liked to be pissed over – and worse. I'll never forget the story I was told by an Astor hostess called Anne. She had an arrangement with a man who paid her to visit his home. He would lie down with a glass plate on his face, and she would have to defecate on the plate.

I said, 'Oh, my God, how can you just do that?'

She replied, 'Well, he lets me know a day before.'

I suggested that on her next visit, she should tell him she couldn't manage it, just to see what would happen. A couple of nights later, she came into the club screaming with laughter. She said, 'I did tell him that, just for a laugh, and he burst into tears. He was crying his eyes out. He said "You've been unfaithful to me"!'

It was while I was working in Le Prince that I met the Colonel. He was about sixty. He used to come in quite a lot because his wife had died, and he was very lonely. He had a big countryside estate near Oxford, he lived very well, and he used to pay the club girls £100 each to go and spend the weekend with him there. He wasn't interested in sex. He was an alcoholic, absolutely past everything. He couldn't even have a soap and water wank. All he wanted was company.

He was very eccentric, and he used to like a laugh. He'd bring four or five girls out for dinner with him to a restaurant called the Belvedere, where all the waiters used to bow and scrape to him. He'd order really expensive wine, and after a few drinks he'd joke, 'I'm going to get you back tonight, and I'm going to fuck you all.'

In time, I became his favourite, and he fell in love with me. He asked me to marry him. He said he'd give me £120,000 and make me the main beneficiary of his will if I'd say yes. I didn't want to get married. I was fond of him; he was a nice old man, but he'd be up all night long yakking, and he'd only have two or three hours' sleep. He used to take prescribed pills to get any sleep at all, and I was always telling him, 'Be careful with the pills and all the drink.'

When I stayed at his estate, I'd always have my separate room in the Blue Suite. I'd go to bed early and leave him nattering with the other girls. When he stayed at my home in London, he'd have his own room. He used to take me to all the race-meetings, and became so devoted to me that he decided to pay for my keep, even though I wasn't going to marry him. I didn't want for anything.

At the same time, I was becoming very friendly with a titled man I'd met at the Don Juan Casanova. He had a resident suite at Claridge's. He was a charming man, very gentlemanly, with dark hair and beautiful pin-stripe suits. He used to come in with his secretary, Barbara, and his son, and he was responsible for bringing Venezuelan diplomats over to London, sometimes twenty or thirty at a time. Some would bring their wives and a lot of them wouldn't, of course.

Occasionally, this Sir would ring me and he'd say, 'Attend my car!' His car would pick me up and I'd be given a list of items to buy from Harrods. These would be for the diplomats' wives, because they couldn't speak English. In return for doing this, he'd pay me for my time and often present me with a gift, maybe jewellery or perfume. At other times and on the same financial basis, he'd say, 'We want about ten or fifteen ladies for a party at the Inn on the Park hotel.'

If I couldn't find enough classy women in the clubs or out-of-work actresses, I'd go to escort agencies to find the girls. They'd go along to the parties, and they'd be paid an escort fee by the Sir. Some of the girls would go along as hostesses only. Others might get there and decide they wanted to drop their drawers. If they did, it was a private arrangement between themselves and the diplomats, and they were paid their extra money directly by the men. I knew what was going on, of course – the girls used to brag about what happened – but it was nothing to do with me.

Later, I met other titled men who would also need hostesses from time to time. And there were girls in the clubs who would say to me, 'I've got no rent, I'd like to go along and do some of that.' Others told me they worked for escort agencies.

I'd say, 'Well, I've got some men, titled men, who are looking for escorts,' and if I thought the girls were nice enough, I'd send them along. I'd be searching for women who looked glamorous, polished, modelly and not like whores, women who could carry on an intelligent conversation.

Eventually, I was providing escorts for people who were staying in all of the major London hotels. It was later reported that I had more than one hundred call-girls on my books. It wasn't so much 'on my books'. They were girls I knew, or girls I'd recruited through escort agencies. And if I were running a call-girl ring, then so was every escort agency in the West End.

I never expected or received any percentages. It wasn't run on that basis. I'd be given a single cheque for finding the girls or for running errands to Harrods, and I'd accept the odd present, as a friend. The girls would keep the escort fee they were given, plus any extras, which did not involve me at all. Besides, I didn't need the cash. The Colonel was keeping me, he was giving me money, and everything was fine. Just fine.

Through the Looking-glass

Janice came into my life at the time I worked the double-act with my sister Valerie. I gave a birthday party, and Janice turned up with a drama-teacher friend of the club dancer Zelda Plum. She was a tiny little thing, Janice, with waist-length hair. She thoroughly enjoyed the party, we had a good laugh together, and we became friends, but from then on she clung to me like a leech. She wanted to be with me all the time, and when I'd go on tour with Valerie, I'd return to loads of letters from Janice. She couldn't wait for me to come back.

At the time, Janice was suffering from nerves and taking prescribed tranquillizers. She was a very intellectual person, but she had a lot of hang-ups. One boyfriend, going way back, had been killed in a car accident, and she had never got over that. She was haunted, too, by some mysterious family crises in her childhood, but it was never clear exactly what had happened.

I was fanatically opposed to drugs of any kind. I was also worried about the company Janice was keeping. She'd got in with a film-industry crowd who took her on Communist marches and suchlike, and I believed she was coming under the wrong influences. I was extremely fond of her, so I agreed to take her on as a sort of secretary. I hoped the stability of regular work might help her.

By now, it was clear that she was only sexually interested in girls and especially in me. She became obsessive about me. I thought the world of her, purely in a sisterly way, but in the end we did have an affair because it meant such a lot to her. It was no big deal to me, and it was to be my one and only physical relationship with another woman. I liked men, I never stopped going out with men, and Janice knew that. She threw jealous, sometimes suicidal tantrums over my various boyfriends, but while I was in her presence, making her laugh, she reluctantly accepted the situation for what it was, and we stayed together for a lot of years.

By 1967, when the Swinging Sixties had grown into the Summer of Love, peace, hippies and flower power, Janice was living in my home at Campden Hill Road, Notting Hill. We shared a bedroom, although she had a room of her own as an alternative. Janice was revelling in the couldn't-care-less atmosphere of the times, quite taken with the idea that everybody should love everybody else. That was the year I had flowers painted all over my Jaguar car, and I dressed in the height of fashion, with big bell-bottomed trousers and boots with funny, thick heels. We were out every night at clubs and parties, drinking champagne, which I loved, and snowballs, too, a mixture of advocaat and lemonade. I got as high as a kite, absolutely flying, on two or three glasses, so I never needed to be a big drinker.

It was during these intoxicating days of laughter, fun and free love that my own legendary parties began, almost by accident. By now, Janice and I had been joined by my timid friend from Southport. Eric had moved into his own room in the basement of the Georgian house where he and I still live to this day. He'd decided to come to London, particularly because of its history and museums. He began work as a clerk of court, and he used to come home talking about different trials and divorce hearings.

One day he was quite upset: 'Ee, isn't it terrible? This wicked woman was in court for a divorce, and she said that every time her husband wanted to have any intimate relations with her, she charged him money.'

I replied, 'Well, that's just right.'

'Ee, no, you don't understand. They were married. That was all wrong, it was disgusting.'

'Don't be ridiculous, Eric. She was in the right.'

I used to wind him up all the time. I had to shout and scream at him too, but only because he was used to it from his mother. He had to have someone telling him, 'Eric, do this, Eric, do that,' otherwise he couldn't have functioned. There was a standing joke of mine: 'Eric – a complete slave, and paid for the privilege.' But he was never a slave to me. He was my friend, and I'm the only person who has ever understood him.

When he came to London, he was still as introverted as ever. He wouldn't take off his jacket in the house for the first five years in case I would see his shirt-sleeves. Even now, if I knock on the door of his room, he'll pull his dressing gown as tightly round him as it will go, and he'll say, 'What do you want? What are you after?' He's a total innocent. He's never been with a woman – or a man – in his life.

For an avid reader and a very deep thinker, he's never had any common sense. He's learned to cook a little bit over the years, but he certainly couldn't when he moved in with me. He'd bring me a cup of tea and put it down on the opposite side of the room. He'd never been in a restaurant. When I first took him out for dinner, he was so shy he bent his head right down to the plate to take his food off the fork. I kept saying, 'No, bring the fork up to your mouth, Eric,' and he was going, 'Ee, what's the difference?' It was ridiculous. We were two dead opposites, but I loved him dearly, and I still do.

The parties started from the Revolution club, formerly Le Prince, which was in Bruton Place, Mayfair – right in the heart of clubland. It was a very in-place, and I was one of the regular crowd there on Friday or Saturday nights, usually in a non-working capacity. We'd all have a drink, go to the club, and from time to time a gang of us would end up back at my house. Quite a few of the guests would be stars I had got to know through working in shows.

Among them were Tom Jones and his manager Gordon Mills. I'd met them much earlier, before they had so much as a pot to piss in, when

Tom was involved in backing singing, and Gordon was appearing at the London Palladium with a group called the Viscounts. Some of the celebrities who came to the parties included Englebert Humperdinck, Esther and Abi Ofarim, Paul and Barry Ryan, Leapy Lee, Long John Baldry and Cat Stevens, all pop stars. Then there were DJs and television presenters like Johnnie Walker, Harry Cog and Simon Dee, and Zelda Plum would come along to perform her exotic dances. In fact, I'm still in touch with Zelda, but she's very eccentric these days.

Jim Webb, the songwriter, used to turn up too. He wrote 'McArthur Park', 'Up, Up and Away' and 'By the Time I Get to Phoenix' among other sixties chart hits. I met him through Richard Harris, the actor who sang 'McArthur Park', and his brother Dermot Harris. More regulars included Oliver Tobias, another actor, the entertainer Kenny Lynch, Mike Mansfield, who was a top television producer, and Chris and Richard Stamp, younger brothers of the actor Terence. These gatherings would happen spontaneously at first, maybe once every four or five weeks. Then people started saying, 'Oh, Janie's parties are brilliant,' and Tom Jones and Gordon Mills in particular would want them every couple of weeks. Gradually it became automatic: 'Let's all go to Janie's!'

Many of the girls from the Revolution started rowing themselves back to my house with everyone else, just so they could see the stars. I got pally with quite a few of these girls and went on to use them as escorts. However, I kept the escort clients, including aristocrats, away from my parties. These were restricted to show-business friends, and they became hugely popular. As they did, I started having what seemed like a hundred people bowling along to my house, and they'd stay the whole weekend. It got ridiculous in the end. There would be bodies all over the place, and I'd have to make huge pots of stew to feed them all.

We used to have good fun, though. Richard Stamp was a favourite with everyone, and he ended up moving into my front room for a few months. During one of his brother Chris's extended visits to America, Richard had found himself living alone with the late Kit Lambert and his boyfriends. This understandably made Richard a little nervous, which is why he moved into Campden Hill Road. We used to have some screams with him. The girls were all mad about him, but he didn't want to know.

His brother Chris co-ran the Who's record label, Track, with Kit, which is how I came to meet various members of what was described at the time as 'the most exciting rock band in the world'.

By this time, I'd got rid of my Jag. It was taken in part-exchange for a beautiful, old, regal-red Rolls-Royce. One day it disappeared. I said, 'Oh, my God, somebody's nicked the Rolls, and I've got to go to the recording-studio. I'll have to get a taxi.' I was jumping up and down, just about to phone the police, when the Rolls suddenly appeared outside the door. Richard had driven it to the dole, to sign on!

He loved to play the chauffeur, put a cap on and drive us to Harrods. We used to go to the Revolution, too, with as many girls as possible squashed into the car. I'd tell the doorman to take the baggage out of the boot, and when he opened it, another couple of girls would fall out. Richard was up for anything and everything. I used him in the promotional campaign for my single, 'Charlie Smith the Lighthouse Keeper'. There were posters of Richard's face all over London with the slogan: WANTED. CHARLIE SMITH LAST SEEN ON A LIGHTHOUSE.

Really, it was a wonderful time, what with all the personalities and the parties, and how they would swing. Especially mine. They were ordinary enough events for those people who were happy to stay downstairs, drinking and talking and joking, but a few would go upstairs to the bedrooms and screw. And I must emphasize one thing there: no money ever changed hands under my roof for any of the sexual activities that took place at the parties. I'd see the funny side of the sex and the big orgies, and I'd think, Let them get on with it. Personally, I was a bit of a puritan. I'd enjoy the giggles, but I'd rather have had a good cup of tea, myself.

The star attraction upstairs was a two-way mirror, placed between adjoining bedrooms. I acquired that by happy accident, after calling in a builder to install central heating. This builder knew about the parties and asked if he could come along to one of them. I said, 'No, they're showbiz only.'

He offered me a deal. He said, 'I'll put in a two-way mirror for free, and nobody will even know about it unless you want them to.' I thought,

Well, great, I'll get my jollies out of that! So I made an arrangement that the builder would sort out the mirror, and, in return, he could come to the parties as a waiter, serving drinks. I wanted to see what was going on in the bedrooms, specifically so that I could find out what a certain television pop-show host was doing up there. He was always disappearing upstairs with different girls, claiming he was 'interviewing secretaries'.

I used to catch him on his way up and say, 'You're going to give her one, aren't you?'

'No, I'm not,' he'd retort. 'That's just your dirty mind – it's awful. I'm genuinely interviewing a secretary.'

Then I'd want to know, 'Why can't you interview at your office? You are giving her one!'

'Well,' he'd shrug, 'if you want to think that, then you can, but you're wrong.' It went on and on the same way, every time he came to a party – and then I got the two-way mirror. There were fifteen or twenty of us watching through it, keeping as silent as we could, trying not to laugh, when the TV host went into the other bedroom with a 'secretary'. Suddenly it was all happening. She put on this rubberwear, and she started belting into him, really whacking him. He was yelling, 'Watch my face, don't touch my face, I've got a programme to do.' It was incredible.

When it was all over, we all crept downstairs quietly, and I was nearly sick laughing. Only minutes later the TV host casually strolled back down. 'What were you doing?' I demanded. 'Interviewing a secretary,' he answered, as usual.

I kicked him and I said, 'That's one from me, for her.'

'What are you doing?' he yelled.

I took him upstairs to the two-way mirror, and I said 'Look in *there*.' On the other side, we could see Tom Jones and Gordon Mills at it with two girls, all of them in a big, seven-foot bed.

'My God, that's disgusting,' he said.

'I know,' I smirked. 'And so were you when we watched you through the same mirror just now.' Fair play to him. When he realized he'd been caught, he thought it was hilarious and laughed with the rest of us. After that, of course, everyone who came to the parties knew about the two-way mirror, and they had a choice: they could put a cover over it, turn the light off and have their privacy, or they could be exhibitionists who didn't care. It was a free-for-all.

A lot of uninhibited people found their way to those bedrooms. While some stars like Kenny Lynch would come along to the parties but never join in the orgies, others like the singing twin brothers Paul and Barry Ryan were insatiable. They used to go into the bedroom together with two birds and change over at half-time. All the time, I'd get phone calls from Barry's girlfriend, a foreign princess called Marion, and have to tell her that he wasn't there. He later married her. Paul Ryan who was a lovely person, sadly died in November 1992 from cancer at the age of only 44.

One girl, Maggie, who worked as a secretary at the BBC, was in on all that with Paul and Barry. She used to come to all the parties because she loved the sex. She was a real nymphomaniac. Yet she'd keep telling me how she'd tried everything, how she'd been with loads of men, but she'd never had an orgasm. She was always harping on about it. She once locked herself away with a vibrator, and she had it on for what seemed like hours. None of us could sleep for the buzzing. I yelled, 'For God's sake, can you turn that off? Haven't you come yet?' She was going, 'Oh, I'm nearly there, only a few more minutes.' All of a sudden, the bloody thing blew up – I suppose it just overheated.

She was a stunning-looking woman, Maggie, like a young Jane Fonda. She had a big thing about the DJ Tony Blackburn, but Tony would never go with her. He'd only ever ask her to do the oral bit for him. Then she decided she wanted a singer who had a number one hit at the time. She was always saying, 'Oh, I must have him, I know I could have an orgasm with him.' I told him this and introduced them. She made the big play for him, and he invited her back to the Mayfair hotel where he was staying. I don't know where his wife was at the time, but he went to bed with Maggie, and he did – he gave her the first orgasm she ever had.

Maggie swung both ways, with girls and guys. I've seen her with three or four different men in a night. Once, Dermot Harris, Richard's brother, said to me: 'I've just given her a good plating' – meaning oral sex.

I replied, 'Well, then you've plated four other guys because she was with four before you, and she never bothered washing.' He was physically sick.

I remember that at one party, which was attended by a popular DJ and his manager, someone came down and said, 'Cor, Maggie's up there with two girls on the bed.' The DJ had a plaster cast on his leg at the time, but you couldn't see his arse for dust getting up those stairs, with the manager running up after him. He watched through the two-way mirror and then went into the bedroom for an orgy with the three girls. Afterwards, he came out having a good laugh about it. And he ended up marrying Maggie.

Tom Jones and Gordon Mills were another couple of real regulars. I couldn't get rid of them! They used to be fascinated by Eric, especially by the way he would offer them a drink with his head bowed down, then immediately turn his back and walk off to get what they wanted. They used to say to me, 'Tell Eric to come over and ask us what we'd like to drink.'

A lot of the girls used to torment Eric. Knowing how shy he was, they'd pull their tops up and say, 'Look at these tits.' They got their jollies out of seeing how upset and embarrassed he became. He'd go all red and mumble, 'Don't be so ruddy disgusting,' and I'd have to step in and tell them to leave him alone. I've seen girls walk into the room stark naked, just to tease him.

One night, Jim Webb and his manager Phil asked if they could bring a girl called Frankie to one of the parties. I knew she hit the drugs, so I said, 'Well, I don't want any of that in my house. If she is taking any drugs, she'll have to take them outside.' When she arrived, she turned out to be a bit of a nympho too. She tried to get off with a couple of the stars who were there, putting her arms around them, and she went up to a bedroom on at least one occasion. Later that night, she was watching Tom and Gordon going through the routine of what they wanted to drink.

'Who's he?' she asked me, meaning Eric.

'Leave him alone,' I said. 'Have you heard of "The Naked Civil Servant"? Well, Eric's the virgin civil servant. Even the most beautiful women in the world wouldn't interest him.' I kept my eye on her after that. Sure enough, I soon saw her creeping downstairs after Eric, who was on his way to the bar in the basement. I followed and caught her trying to pull down his zip. The veins in his neck were bulging, and he was stuttering, 'Get off, don't be so bloody filthy, you dirty swine.' I'd never heard him come out with the word 'swine' before. That was extreme for him. It was really something.

I dragged her off him. I said, 'I told you to leave him alone. He's not interested. Go and find yourself a celebrity.'

'Oh, I'd love a virgin.'

'You're not gonna get one here,' I told her. 'For the crown jewels you wouldn't get Eric.' I'd had enough of her. She'd had too much to drink, and she was obviously on something else as well, so I ordered her to leave my house. Later the next day, I had a phone call from Richard Harris's brother, Dermot. This girl had gone home and found that she'd forgotten her key. She'd walked along a ledge to get in through a window, fallen off the ledge and landed on a pedestrian. Now she was in hospital.

Phil, who'd lived with the girl in America, went back to the States with Jim Webb, and Dermot Harris, who only vaguely knew her, took flowers to her in hospital until the day she died. This incident would later be brought up in evidence against me during my trial, with the prosecution implying that I'd had Frankie bumped off because she'd tried to interfere with Eric. It was absolutely incredible. But it was merely one of many outrageous accusations that would be flung at me in the dark days ahead.

A certain West End photographer called Nigel used to come to the parties. He was a fantastic-looking guy with a personality to match, and the girls used to fancy him something rotten. He took wonderful pictures, mainly fashion and nude work, and he charged between £50 and £100 a session. But in certain circumstances he'd do it for free. I knew some beautiful models who wanted glamour photographs for their portfolios, so I used to tell them, 'You can go to this friend of mine, Nigel, and you can pay for the session, or if you fancy him, you can screw him, and you'll get the pictures for nothing.' Most preferred to screw him.

One who did was a woman we knew as Peg the Plater. I first came into contact with her through Paul and Barry Ryan. This girl would ring persistently to ask me, 'Can I come to one of your parties?'

I'd say, 'Well, no, they're just for my show-business friends.' Eventually, I asked Paul and Barry, 'Who is this Peg who's always trying to invite herself to my parties?'

They said, 'Oh, that's Peg the Plater. She's plated everybody we know. She just loves it.'

The next time I spoke to her on the phone, I said, 'Is that Peg the Plater?'

She replied, 'Oh, they *are* wicked. Fancy telling you that.'

I ended up inviting her to the next party, just to see what Paul and Barry's reaction would be. Well, they got the shock of their lives – 'What's Peg the Plater doing here?'

She was a strange-looking girl with big eyes and a shy manner. We started chatting because she also had a northern accent, and I found I quite liked her. I said, 'You should stop all this plating business. Look at the name you've got for yourself. It's ridiculous. If you go on like this, you'll have to get your tongue a retread!'

She told me, 'A lot of it's exaggerated. I do like it at times, depending on who I'm with. I love them up-and-coming!' After the party, she continued ringing me up, and she came over to the house a few times. On one of those occasions, I was chatting with some of the girls who were going to a party for the Venezuelan diplomats. My titled friend had asked me to find him twelve or fifteen women. I was saying I was going to have to go to an escort agency because I needed a few more. Peg the Plater asked, 'Why can't I go along, just to be an escort? I'd like the money.'

I said, 'Well, OK.'

So she went along with the others, and the next thing I knew, this Sir was on the phone from his suite at Claridge's telling me that his gold lighter had vanished. He said, 'The young ladies are still here. They have to go through my bedroom to get to the toilet, and I think one of them may have taken the lighter. It has a very sentimental value to me.'

All of the girls – except for Peg the Plater – had been on escort jobs before, and nothing had ever gone missing. So I raced straight over to the hotel, cleared one of the rooms in the suite, and said, 'Right. I want every girl, one at a time, to come in here with me. I'm going to go through your handbags, and I'm going to ask you to strip naked.'

I put three of four of them in before Peg so that it wouldn't look as though I was picking on her. When her turn came, I went through her bag and I found the lighter at the bottom. I said, 'I'll never, ever, send you anywhere again because you're a thief. This man is paying you £50 just to sit with someone as an escort, and here you are stealing from him.' Well, there were tears and apologies, and she promised she'd never do it again. I gave her the benefit of the doubt, and I sent her on another couple of jobs, but then I stopped bothering. She wasn't worth it.

The parties went on for more than a year. The Colonel was keeping me all the way through, and I had a few romances, one with Jim Webb who was very fond of me. I went out with Long John Baldry too, and also Chris Stamp for a good while. Chris was nice, very gentle and shy and so easy to talk to. I'd stay out with him until the early hours, and when I arrived home the door would be locked, and I'd have Janice throwing buckets of water out of the window at me.

I used to get nervous about my female lover's feelings. I'd tell people, 'I've found a man I really like but how am I ever going to get out of the grass with Janice?' I knew it would upset her so much. It was very distressing. I'd tell Janice she should find herself a lovely man and get married, but she wasn't interested.

When I announced my own marriage, there were murders. She got into the bath and threatened to cut her wrists and take an overdose. My husband-to-be was typically sympathetic. He said, 'Let's hope she makes a good job of it.' After that, she started going round with an actress friend of mine, and drinking like mad. She was traumatized. But, it didn't take me long to realize I'd made the wrong choice. I should have kept Janice as my friend, because I was quite happy that way. I realized on my wedding night that I'd just made the biggest mistake of my life.

John Christian Dee conned me into marriage within six weeks of meeting me. It was Long John Baldry who introduced us. Dee, a man I now refer to only as the Crank, was addicted to heroin at the time, and he was very sick. Long John Baldry asked me, 'Could you put him up, just for a couple of days? He's been through all his money, and he's got nowhere to live.'

The Crank was a talented songwriter, with a career that was especially successful in Germany. There, he'd had a Mercedes and a house, but by the time I met him, those had long gone because he'd spent everything on drugs. He was very good-looking, with tattoos on his hands and body, and a charm that could fascinate the birds off the trees. I thought his songs were brilliant. One, 'Don't Bring Me Down', was a UK hit single for the Pretty Things, a sixties R & B band from Kent who were regarded at the time as a wilder version of the Rolling Stones. He wrote that on the back of a cigarette packet and sold it to the Morrison agency for only £60, for drugs.

I said to him, 'You could make a lot of money from your songs. Why don't you pull yourself off the drugs?' And that set the scene for his big proposition, when he confessed he'd fallen madly in love with me. 'I'm not in love with you, and I never will be, but I'm in love with your songwriting,' I answered.

He suggested, 'If we get married, you could manage me and share the money from the songs, and I'd have the motivation to come off the drugs. If you won't marry me, I'll have nothing to live for, and I'll end up staying on drugs.'

I was talked into it. It was a cool business deal as much as anything else, and I'd grown jaundiced with the idea of romantic love and marriage. Why not give it a go? We both might get something out of it. We were married at a London register office on 7 November 1968. Perhaps subconsciously anticipating our disastrous future together, I wore a black dress decorated with spider's web patterns and ostrich feathers. That night at the wedding party at our home, the Crank became wildly jealous of the pop singer P.J. Proby, who I'd always got on with well. Proby used to say he'd married the wrong woman and, to wind us up at the party, he joked, 'You've married the wrong man, too. You should've married me.' The Crank reacted by trying to sling me down the stairs. I had to grab hold of the rail to stop myself hurtling to the floor below.

At the time, I thought his behaviour was something to do with his drug withdrawal. But it wasn't long before I realized that the guy was strange. He was the original Jekyll and Hyde, two different people. At times, he thought the rest of the world was plotting and planning against him, and I was in league with them. He could quote the Bible back to front, and he was a gifted writer, but he had a heart so evil it was unbelievable. He was very violent and vicious. Yet he was shrewd with it. He could put on Oscar-winning performances to gain sympathy from others who didn't know about his instability.

After we got married, he stopped me from driving my own Rolls-Royce. He said a woman behind the wheel of a big car didn't look good, and it also made him appear inferior. So he insisted on driving it all the time. That Christmas, we had to go out to pick up a tape-recorder from a shop in central London. The Crank was driving, I was in the passenger seat, and my friend Gloria from Yorkshire was in the back. We reached Tottenham Court Road, and the Crank said, 'Gloria can sit in the car to look after it while we're in the store.'

We went inside, and while he wandered around the shop for ages, I was watching the street outside. I spotted a traffic warden, so I went back out to the car, just to move it round the corner. He came racing out after me: 'Trying to get away from me!' He hit my face with the back of his hand, his ring struck my lip and the blood just squirted. Gloria had to give me one of the new men's silk handkerchiefs she'd bought for little under-the-Christmas-tree presents, and I soaked it through. I had to have five or six stitches in my mouth.

I told the doctor, 'My husband did this, and I want you to put it on record but without calling the police.'

I went home, and the Crank was crying hysterically, saying, 'I'm sorry, I'd never have meant to do that.'

As a direct result of the incident, I sold the Rolls. If I wasn't going to drive it, neither was he. I tried to get him to a psychiatrist. The doctor asked him, 'Do you mind allowing me a few minutes alone with your wife?'

He replied, 'You don't think I'm going to leave my wife on her own with any man, do you?' By now I was scared stiff of my own husband. I had seen him knock a girl flat out on the floor on one horrific occasion, and I was there when he tried to put his brother-in-law's eye out, at a function with some of his relatives. The brother-in-law had asked the Crank, 'Can I have a dance with Janie?'

He'd replied, 'No, this is a slow dance, you can have a fast one.'

Later, when a fast song was playing, the brother-in-law had asked me, 'Can I have this dance?' The Crank just sat there watching for a while. All of a sudden, he lifted a glass and smashed it into his brother-in-law's face. After some time, though, I learned how to play clever and get round the Crank, drawing on my experiences at the hospital in Bedfordshire. I was lucky enough to be a very strong character. I'd fended for myself from the age of sixteen, and there was no way I was going to let the Crank get the better of me. I'd rather have died. It would have been him or me.

He was absolutely obsessive. Sometimes I'd go shopping with Eric, and when I'd come back half an hour later with loads of groceries, the Crank would insist I hadn't been to the shops at all. He'd say I'd been visiting a boyfriend. Then he'd make Eric stay downstairs, while he'd send me upstairs and then cross-examine us separately about which shops we'd been to. Of course, this would make Eric more nervous and confused than usual, and he wouldn't think straight.

The Crank was insanely jealous of Eric and wanted him out of the house. Every time we had an argument, he'd say, 'I'll get rid of Eric,' because he knew I thought the world of Eric.

I'd retort, 'Oh, no. You'll go before Eric will.' He used to wake Eric at three and four o'clock in the morning and send him out for cigarettes. He was always getting at him. He knew it was guaranteed to upset me. In fact, he was jealous of everybody around me, the Crank. He was jealous of Janice, and he was jealous of the Colonel. He knew all about the Colonel, that he'd been keeping me for three years and that I'd have to dash off to see him when he was in one of his occasional suicidal depressions. However, for all his complaints, the Crank was quite happy to drive other girls out to see the Colonel and then claim back fictitious taxi fares from the escort agencies that employed the girls.

There was no end to the things the Crank would accuse me of. He was adamant that there was something going on between me and an old friend Bob, who was deranged over me – always had been. But it wasn't mutual. Nothing whatsoever was going on. I had first met Bob when I was working in the Georgian club. He was an antiques dealer in the West End and he'd often buy me dinner and drinks. He was very good-looking, and I could hardly believe it when the girls in the club told me that he liked to be tied up and beaten but also loved to punish them. I never got involved in anything physical with him, but I did abuse him verbally, and I told him I'd never fall in love with him.

Even though he was married himself, and I'd met his wife on many occasions, he went up the wall when I announced that I was going to marry the Crank. In the end, he said, 'It's going to give me my kicks to pay for the wedding, the wedding rings and the reception.' He knew that the Crank was penniless, and Bob did indeed foot the bill for the whole wedding. Yet my husband remained madly suspicious of him – and me.

It was typical of the Crank's obsessiveness. He used to say that he needed me like he'd once needed heroin. He hadn't taken that since the day I agreed to marry him. I'd promised to bring him off it and he'd promised to resist any future temptation from drugs. He'd previously been to two addiction centres, which hadn't been able to cure him. But I said it, and meant it: 'No more heroin.' He was crawling around on the floor during his withdrawal, but I gave him drinks, and I guarded him day and night, with a little help from my friends, to make sure he had no opportunity to get or take any more.

He'd been completely impotent. But once he cleaned up his drug habit, his body started working properly again, and he wanted his marital rights. Even though the other girls fancied him like mad, including the BBC nympho Maggie, I really wasn't interested. I'd realized what sort of person he was. I couldn't even stand his tattoos, and the sex, for me, was horrible.

When I discovered I was pregnant, I wanted to fall through the floor. It was bad enough that we were married, because he knew that I wouldn't be able to get him out of the house without a great deal of trouble. But if I'd had his child, I'd never have been able to get rid of him. If I'd been pregnant by a man I was in love with, it would have been the greatest thrill of my life. As it was, I was married to a violent swine. So I went to Harley Street, and I paid to have an abortion, which was a hell of a traumatic experience, and one I never repeated. It was really and truly the end of the world for me.

CHAPTER FIVE

My Lords, Ladies and Gentlemen

I f the devil I knew were my husband, the devils I didn't know were some of the people in my closest circle – people who would eventually lead me to disaster with their lies and betrayals, which they swore by purely to hide the truth about themselves. One such person was a lord I first met in the Don Juan Casanova Club. He had a flat near the back of the Hilton hotel in Mayfair and was the brother-in-law of a famous duke. Tall and in his fifties, he'd been a very handsome man when he was younger and was still charming. He'd been out with some of the most beautiful women in the world, and he became besotted with me.

We'd got to know each other over quite a period of time in the club. He'd always sit and chat with me, and he'd tell me, 'Oh, you make me laugh, you're very funny. I can talk to you about anything.' Sometimes he'd come to me depressed and pour out his problems. He'd say, 'I'd rather be sitting here with you than in the Dorchester having a fifteen-course meal. You're my very best friend.' I believed him, too. Eventually, I realized what a big thing he had about me. He repeatedly asked me to come and live on his estate as the housekeeper, which I declined to do, and he was always putting his arm around me, declaring, 'Oh, I'd like to give you one.'

I'd joke kindly, 'That'll be the day!' I never intended to have anything to do with him in that way.

He wanted to come to my parties more than anything, and I always refused on the grounds that they were showbiz only. But he wouldn't take no for an answer. He began turning up at the door when he knew the parties were in full swing, but I still wouldn't allow him in. 'Can't I even come in for a coffee?' he'd plead. I'd stand my ground. 'Oh, my God,' he'd complain. 'You really are a bitch. You treat me like dirt.'

I did. Where other people would bow and scrape to him because he was a lord, I was the only one who would dare to tell him what I thought of him. The more he tried to take advantage of our friendship, the more I shouted and screamed, and the more he seemed set on me. However, he wasn't to be deterred from impromptu visits. He'd often materialize on the doorstep when I was sitting indoors with the Colonel. Then there were eruptions. The Colonel, who was very jealous of the Lord, insisted, 'He's not coming in, so you can tell him to run away to hell.' And the Lord would be huffing and puffing back, 'Well, if I'm not good enough . . . .' When I went to the race-meetings with the Colonel, we'd usually see the Lord there, hob-nobbing with the royal set in the champagne bar. The Lord would nod his head and acknowledge me, and the Colonel would be absolutely livid, although he'd do anything but admit it. He'd always pretend he hadn't noticed and crow that the Lord was ignoring me.

At this point, I hadn't yet met the Crank, so I was spending most of my time in the clubs, and occasionally used to enjoy a laugh and a joke at down-market joints like the Robin Hood in Westbourne Grove. The Lord was always pleading with me to take him to these places, but I wasn't happy about the idea. There were a lot of seedy people there, and he was ideal blackmail material. He was so full of his own self-importance he couldn't have passed himself off as a John Brown or a Joe Bloggs. It would have been, 'I'm a lord.'

One night I relented after he promised me faithfully that he would come out with me as plain George. We went to the Robin Hood, which was crowded. He got chatting to various people, and I spent the whole time with a couple of friends. Eventually, he disappeared. I was convinced I'd warned him strongly enough that he'd be mixing with the dregs of society, so I went home and thought no more about it. Five or six weeks later, though, I woke up to a loud banging on my door at seven o'clock in the morning. It was the Lord.

He was going, 'Please, please, please, open the door!' So, I let him in, and he told me that he'd met a girl that night at the Robin Hood. She was only fourteen, he said, but he'd arranged to meet her again and had then gone home with her. Now her brother had phoned to say she was pregnant. The Lord had to hand over several thousand pounds, otherwise the police would be informed.

I knew that there were no fourteen-year-old girls at the Robin Hood so I told him, 'Leave it with me. Give me her description and her brother's phone number.' The same night, I went to the club to check the girl out. She turned out to be in her twenties, and she didn't have a brother. Obviously, it was a set-up. When I dialled the contact telephone number, which had been given to the Lord, a man growled, in response to my questioning, 'Your friend made my sister pregnant, and if he doesn't cough up, I'm going to the Old Bill, and he'll be in trouble.'

I reported all this back to the Lord. He kept wailing, 'Oh, my God, this is going to ruin me. I'm going to pay them the money.'

I said, 'No, you're not. Blackmail is murder of the mind. The blackmailer will keep coming back to you. We're going to the police.' So I made him sit in my car, while I drove to Savile Row police station in the West End. I did all the talking. Eventually, the officers agreed to keep the Lords's name out of things, and in the end the blackmail couple were nobbled and charged, although I believe they later skipped the country. Yet, this wasn't the last time I'd have to cover up for the Lord. He had one big weakness that kept getting him into trouble: women dressed as schoolgirls, complete with teddy bears.

He'd started confiding in me in the early days of the Don Juan Casanova. First he'd asked, 'What would you think of a man who likes young girls of thirteen or fourteen?'

I said, 'There's something very sick about it.'

He retorted, 'Well, the thing is they look seventeen or eighteen.' I'd never come across anything like this before, and I was horrified.

Some time later, on another night when he'd had a few drinks, he started to go further back into his past. I soon gathered that he'd spent the rest of his life re-enacting an under-age love affair from his youth. However, when he told me, 'I've got a woman who arranges young girls for me,' I didn't believe him. He persisted, 'Yes, yes, yes, it's quite true, I'll take you along to see her if you like.'

I accepted his offer but added, 'If it's true, I'm going to have her put away. Every little girl of yours could be my sister.'

We duly went along to an address off the Bayswater Road in west London. The woman who opened the door of the house must have been about seventy-five, and she had a talking mina bird, which fascinated me so much I later got one of my own. She knew the Lord of old and as he disappeared upstairs, she motioned me to follow her. I found myself in a room with a two-way mirror. 'Try not to laugh at what you see,' she said.

In view on the other side of the mirror was a 'naughty little girl' in a school uniform. She was twenty-five if she were a day. With her was another woman who was supposed to be her mother. She looked younger than the so-called kid. When the mother left the room, a man – the dreadful step-father figure – came storming in, tearing off the daughter's uniform and yelling, 'You bad girl!' Obviously, it was all play-acting. At this point, the Lord burst into the room screaming, 'Leave the child alone!' The step-father scarpered, and the Lord had his way with the school-girl who was, of course, a prostitute.

I laughed until I cried, probably out of surprise, but I had mixed feelings about the whole thing. I felt a lot of sympathy for the Lord; I thought he was pitiful and in need of psychiatric treatment, but more than anything I was relieved to know he wasn't picking up genuinely young girls. Given his fetish, it was only common sense that a whoring service like this should exist to cater for it. I said to him, 'Don't you ever indulge this fantasy for real. Stick with these girls.'

Thankfully, he never did venture outside the world of prostitutes. But, in all of his dealings with them, he would always manage to convince himself that these women of twenty-something were really in their early teens. In time, I started sending my personal contacts, club hostesses and out-of-work actresses to visit the Lord as 'school-girls'. He'd phone me up afterwards, and he'd want to know, 'Oh, my God, where did you meet that pretty little thirteen-year-old?'

I'd say, 'I was at the television studios, and I met some children with their parents at auditions for Smarties and Silvikrin adverts.' I'd have to make up all these stories just to feed his delusions, and I'd obviously tell the women to back them up.

If he saw the same girl for a second time, he'd say, 'Now, don't you tell your mummy or your Auntie Janie that you've been along to see me again. I'll give you lots of sweeties and lollipops and ice-creams.'

Of course they told me: they had to come to me for 'mummies' to take them to visit the Lord. The 'mummies' would then negotiate a fee from them. He certainly wouldn't discuss finances with a 'school-girl'.

I finally allowed him to attend my parties because he'd become such a well-known and intriguing character in our circles. And that strange family scene I first boggled at through the looking-glass near Bayswater Road would be played out many times, for fun and curiosity but not for cash, on the other side of my very own two-way mirror.

In the summer of 1969, the Crank, Eric and I had two girls living full-time in our home in Campden Hill Road. One girl was a very beautiful, elegant model called Carol Kendall, who was out of this world. She looked like a cross between the actresses Liz Taylor and Kay Kendall, whose name she'd adopted. When I'd first met her, in a West End club, she was based in or around Liverpool but wanted to live in London. I later invited her to come down and move into our spare bedroom. She was trying to find a career in television and commercials, and she did escort work, although she never went to bed with any of the men. And she turned out to be one of the few women in my world then who would not later try to crucify me. She eventually went on to become a top model in Paris.

Carol was sharing her room with Heather, a small Scottish girl who was fated to become my own 'Poison Dwarf'. We'd met her through a Decca Records act, which the Crank had become involved with – a Welsh singer called Roger who recorded under the name of R. J. Hightower. My husband was managing, promoting and writing songs for him. Heather was a groupie. She'd been with various members of the chart-topping band Marmalade, but she was madly in love with Roger Hightower, even though he wouldn't touch her with a barge-pole. It had originally been his idea that she should move in with us.

One night I was sitting indoors with Carol, the Crank and Roger. There was a bit of an argument going on because the Crank wanted me at the studios with him all the time. I said, 'I can't be in two places at once. The house is in a state, and I need to be here to sort it out.' It was then that Roger suggested bringing in Heather as an au pair. As he was speaking, I happened to notice, in one of the mirrors opposite, that the Crank shot a warning look at Roger. The psychic in me realized this girl must know something my husband didn't want me to find out about.

Shortly after, Carol and I went down to the basement kitchen to make tea and sandwiches, but by the time we had come back upstairs, the Crank was suddenly all for the idea of Heather. He must have sorted out with Roger that she would be told to keep her mouth shut. He said, 'Heather does all the housework and laundry for Marmalade. She's a bit of a slag at times, and she's a bit rough, but she's a hell of a good worker. She's just gotta be watched. I was thinking that maybe Roger could go and pick her up now and bring her round here. You can decide if you'd like to have her live in the house and trust her to do the work.'

I agreed, and Roger went off to collect her. I heard later that as he drove Heather to the house, he told her that I wasn't happy in my marriage, and that I wanted a divorce. Much as he respected my husband musically, Roger knew the Crank was unpredictable. He really like me, Roger, and he was there when the Crank nearly put out his brother-in-law's eye, so all in all he had a lot of sympathy for my predicament.

When they arrived at the house, Heather was directed to the basement where I was sitting with Carol. Almost immediately she asked, 'Can John Christian Dee hear me from upstairs?' From above, I could hear him playing music with Roger. I shook my head, and she carried on, 'I'd do anything to live in this house and do the work for you because I'm in love with Roger, and I would be able to see more of him. If you'll take me on, I'll give you the evidence you need for a divorce. John Christian Dee brought a girl back to my place not long after you were married, and he had sex with her there. He didn't give her one, but he made her plate him. I can take you to meet this girl, and I can get a statement from her.'

I said, 'Oh, yeah, I'd like a statement of all of that.' And Heather did eventually give me this account of the Crank's infidelity, but not until after she had moved in. I kept it to myself for a while, but when the Crank found out it added to the trouble he was already giving me, and I had to run away to a hotel for two or three weeks with Heather and Carol, leaving him seething at home.

During this time, the Crank tried to commit suicide by taking an overdose of sleeping tablets. I went to visit him in St Mary's Hospital, Paddington, and he said, 'I love you. Just give me one more chance. I'll change. I'll do this, and I'll do that.' At the same time, he was promising, 'Just let me get my break in show-business, and I'll do what you want and leave.' Then again, he was issuing threats: 'If I can't have you, nobody will. I'll kill you.' And the things he was going to do to Eric were nobody's business.

However, it was still in my interests to keep him as stable as I could. I was biding my time, just waiting for my opportunity to escape for good. A bit earlier on I had started to find out more about my husband's background, not for any vindictive reasons but because I needed to know. He was one of twins. The other had died, and I'm convinced this had something to do with him being two people in one. His mother had gone through hell with his father. She didn't dare look left or right.

Ours was the Crank's third marriage. Coincidentally, his first wife had worked at the Windmill as well. On their wedding night, he knocked off another woman, and his wife got rid of him as soon after that as she could. His second wife was a hairdresser, a young girl, and they had two kids. He was always accusing her, quite wrongly, of having affairs. He went off to Germany and left her with no money, one child and the other one about to be born. Her mother had to look after them.

He made no contact while he was away. In Germany, he had a fancy house with an ornamental tree growing through the middle of it; he drove a Mercedes at all times. Apparently, he was trading in propaganda from the east to the west. He met a Czechoslovakian girl who ended up crossing the border, which was very dangerous, just to get away from him. He was heavily on drugs at the time and went through all his money. When he returned to England to his wife, he accused her of having another man, took a knife to her and threatened to shave off her hair. He said, 'If he loves you as much as I do, he'll love you with no hair.' Of course there was no other man.

After learning all this, I wanted more than ever to get clean away from the violent swine, but I knew he wouldn't let me go, not only because of his obsessiveness but also because he was dependent on me for money. Every penny he ever made he blew. I'd been going along with the sham of a marriage for quite some time, and there were OK spells, such as the days I spent in the studio with him. We recorded a few tracks together, and we released one duet, 'Bwana', under the name of Adam and Eve at the end of 1968 on Decca. But these periods of tranquillity were few and far between. By the time of the Crank's suicide attempt, I had already decided to be patient and wait for the right time to leave the marriage. For the moment I decided to put things on hold. I returned home with Carol and Heather, and of course the Crank didn't change for the better, despite his promises.

One night Eric was in the downstairs kitchen making coffee while the Crank was getting his things ready to go fishing. I had a cold and a splitting headache, caused by the pressures of the marriage, and I went down for a couple of Beecham's Powders – which gave me an idea.

I was always winding up Eric and playing the fool. So I took a pinch of fine sugar, put it into a squashed-up powder sachet and asked him which cup was the Crank's. He pointed it out, and I emptied the sugar in. I told Eric, 'That is a very strong potion. When the Crank is driving his car tonight, he might just crash into something or he might last until he gets to the fishing, and then he'll go into the water. That'll be the end of him. It'll do the world a favour.'

'Ee,' said Eric. 'You can't do that.'

'Don't you worry about it, Eric,' I smiled. And I pretended to go back up the stairs, but instead I hid in the little alcove, which looked into the kitchen. I saw Eric empty out the Cranks's cup, complete with the 'potion', wash it and then refill it with coffee. I had to stuff my jumper in my mouth to stop myself laughing out loud.

We all finished our drinks, and the Crank drove off to fish. I kept saying to Eric, 'Oh, that'll do the trick, he'll not be coming back.' The next day, of course, he did come back. I turned to Eric, and I said, 'Funny that potion didn't work. Are you sure you didn't take it out?'

'No, no,' he squeaked. 'No, I didn't.'

So I got out my big family Bible, and I asked him, 'Do you swear on this holy Bible that you didn't take it out?'

'Ee, I swear I never took it out.'

I looked at him. I said, 'Eric, are you an atheist?'

'I suppose so.'

'That's all right then,' I said. 'OK, that answers my question.'

As time went by, I became quite fond of Heather, and I felt sorry for her too. She was really tiny, only up to my shoulder. She wore great big, thick glasses, had a short, awful hairstyle and spoke in the broadest Scottish accent I'd ever heard. She used to wonder why men didn't like her – particularly Roger Hightower. I advised her to get a pair of contact lenses and a wig and dress to make the most of her ample bustline.

She often used to complain that she was never invited to join the escort girls who visited the titled men. I hated to tell her that she didn't have what it took. Then she'd ask, 'What about George [the Lord]? I'd love to go and see him.' I agreed to that in the end, mainly because she was so small. She dressed up as a schoolgirl with a teddy bear for him – and then she went back again pretending to be her own twin and got another £50 out of him! That's how dumb the Lord was.

During all the time she spent with me, Heather never fell out of love with Roger, but she did develop a crush on Kenny Lynch. Sadly for her, Kenny wouldn't look at her twice. The closest she ever came to getting him was during another mock-rape scene we set up for a giggle with the Lord and the two-way mirror. Heather was the 'schoolgirl' and

Kenny – who never seriously took part in any of the upstairs activities – wanted to be the 'wicked stepfather' for a laugh. The Lord was looking through the mirror, watching Heather on the bed clutching a teddy bear and wearing a wig. Kenny marched in, and he started to rip off her little suit. She jumped up, and he chased her round the room, grabbing her and yelling, 'I'm going to give it to you.'

She squealed, 'I'm going to tell my mummy.'

He replied, 'Your mummy? I spunked up her arse half an hour ago.'

The Crank and I were on the floor laughing, and the Lord was huffing and puffing, 'Oh, my God, I can't believe it, what a beast, what an animal!' All of sudden, he got so excited he rushed into the room, and of course Kenny walked straight out, leaving Heather pretending to be crying on the bed. It wasn't long after that, that Kenny got the OBE. The Crank said, 'It must have been for art in the bedroom, Kenny!'

Our days, though, were rarely so much fun, especially after the suicide bid. For the time being, we were all back to square one, and we remained at square one together for quite some time – until Carol left to pursue her modelling career, and Heather ultimately earned the nick-name I gave her of the Poison Dwarf.

But, Carol and Heather were not the only women in our immediate company around this time. We had several regular visitors to the house, some out-and-out scrubbers who would do anything if the money were right. One girl, though, should never have gone into whoring and that was Jane. She was good and genuinely nice but very lonely and really only looking for someone to marry. She worked in a shop, behind the make-up counter. She lived close to me in Notting Hill, and I got to know her through a mutual friend.

One day she asked me: 'How can I meet somebody nice? I'd like somebody with money. I'm fed up with working in a shop for ridiculous wages.' I told her about the titled men who were always looking for escorts. She said, 'I could do that! It would be great! Marvellous!'

I replied, 'Well, it's up to you. If that's what you want, that's fine.'

So she went to Claridge's and a few other hotels, and the guys loved her. They gave her money and perfume and beautiful silk clothes, and she'd tell me, 'I earn more in one hour that I do for a full week's work at the shop.'

Perhaps she should have been satisfied with the opportunity to make money as a mere escort, but she wasn't. She started going to bed with the men, and she enjoyed it. She bragged that these clients were great, gorgeous, so sexy, and, of course, she was after marrying a rich guy, so she kept it up. She claimed to have taken part in sex parties at the hotels, and she visited the Venezuelan diplomats more than once. In fact, she went out with one of them for a while. But, in the end she moved to Brighton, and I didn't see her again for a long while – until the trouble started.

Another girl I used to see a lot of was Ann. By day, she worked for an insurance company. By night, she'd go with anyone for money. She was married but separated from her husband. She had possession of their two kids, but she used to cry and tell me how her husband kept trying to take them off her. He always had lots of women, and occasionally he'd turn up at Ann's door with a used contraceptive, which he'd then put on to have sex with her. That's God's honest truth.

She worked as an escort and slept with the men, and she lived with a homosexual who'd been head waiter at the Georgian club when I had worked there. He used to take men back home, and he and Ann would both have sex with them for money. She played the 'schoolgirl', and probably the 'mother' as well, for the Lord. And she used to say to me: 'Any men you can get for cash, I'll go with them. I love sex.' When she felt like it, she'd do it for free. She was a raver, Ann. She loved going to parties, just to see who she could screw. Definitely a bit of a nympho.

So was Penny, a blonde from Harlow – the original Essex girl! She worked in some factory or other, and by the time she left, she'd had sex not only with the boss but with his son too. When I met her, she was going through Faith, Hope and Charity, a Decca group managed by the Crank, like a dose of salts. It wasn't long before she said to me, 'I'm pretty. Can't you find me any escort work?' She couldn't wait to go out to the hotels, and when she did, of course, she loved the sex side of it. At the beginning, she used to send the money to her mother and father. Later she started earning for herself.

She wanted to go into show business, wanted to do adverts, wanted to go into modelling – anything 'glamorous'. She reckoned she could do better than the girls she saw on television and in magazines, and she was quite prepared for nude work. She had sex with my West End photographer friend Nigel in return for a free set of pictures for her portfolio.

Penny was mad about the Crank, and he took advantage of the fact. He used to hold parties to promote the acts he was working with, people like Faith, Hope and Charity and a singer called Brian Parrish. He would invite influential music-business people and American contacts, in the hope that they would return some help for the artistes. It was later claimed that my showbiz parties were set up for the benefit of my recording career. They weren't. That was the Crank's way of working, not mine. My parties were purely for fun, and I never received any favours from my guests.

The Crank, however, would get Penny and others, like Ann and Jane, to act as waitresses and make a big fuss of the important men at his parties. He encouraged the girls into sexual transactions, although obviously on these occasions they weren't for money. There was one huge party in honour of a proposed deal between Brian Parrish and the record company, United Artists (UA). The Crank also worked on promotions for Brian and UA, and he often asked Penny to take part.

But even the Crank reached the end of the road with Penny when we came back from a two-week trip to Spain in December 1969. She'd been staying at our house while we were away, and Eric told us that she'd been picking up men in the clubs and bringing them back for sex. I absolutely hit the ceiling. They weren't men for money, they were for her own pleasure, but, nevertheless, how dare she bring strange men to my home to stay all night long! The Crank was equally furious. So I slung her out, and I wouldn't have her in the house after that. She never did get the 'glamorous' job she wanted so desperately. She carried on whoring, picking up a load of guys and taking them back to a flat with a girl I knew very well indeed: my friend Gloria from Yorkshire.

Gloria had first started going off the rails as a teenager and had a very unsettled family background. When she was fifteen, she told her parents she'd got a job at Woolworths. When they discovered she hadn't, to their horror, they also found out that she was going around with a jazz group and getting money from the men she was meeting through them. She ran away to London twice and I met her on her third visit, in 1965, at the age of seventeen. I felt sorry for her in a lot of ways, so I put her up and got her a job in a shop. At the time, I was living in Kensington Park Gardens and trying to sell my place in Holland Park.

I thought a lot of Gloria because she was very good-natured in many ways, and I felt sorry for her too – although I soon realized there was nothing more I could do for her. Eventually she left my home to make her own way, ventured into cannabis heavily and developed a fascination for sex with coloured fellows. She fell pregnant to a boy in a pop group who was too young to want to get married, and she went out picking up men for money in hotels.

She was a whore. Nothing was going to change that, and she'd grown up into a tall and extremely attractive young woman, so I sent her out on escort work to protect her from the sleazier side of prostitution. She was also eager to act out the 'schoolgirl' for the Lord. But, as time went on, she began making her own arrangements with men and became involved in serious sado-masochistic scenes, which appalled me.

Still, I loved Gloria, and I always will. I held back a great deal of information about her during my trial. For her part, she made a damning statement about me, but then so did most of the women who were prominent in that part of my life. Along with the Crank, the Lord and various socially respected men, she feared only for herself when the going got tough, and the accusing fingers were pointed unanimously at me. The outcome of all this would be to condemn me to a future with even more unscrupulous characters – the murderesses of this world and their devil queen, Myra Hindley.

CHAPTER SIX

The Road to Ruin

The Crank said to me, 'I want you to make me bigger than Elvis Presley. Make me famous, and I'll give you the divorce you want so much.' This was when I decided to try to launch his career in America. After all I had an incentive, and with this in mind I enlisted the help of a Japanese multi-millionaire who was a friend of mine. He offered to pay for us to open our own artistes' agency over in California and to fund the Crank's writing, recording and promotion of songs. There was always the chance he'd eventually make quite a bit of money out of the Crank. For the time being, though, my part of the bargain was to introduce the rich man to certain international stars. That's all he wanted in return for his investment money.

My plan was to go to America with the Crank, stay for as long as it took to get the agency and my husband's musical career off the ground and then come home. But, before we left, I had to get rid of Scottish Heather. Eric would have never stayed in the house on his own with her, and, naturally, whatever made Eric happy was what I had to do. I gave her four weeks' notice to move out.

Heather was incensed, not only because I was throwing her out but also because the Crank was talking about taking her beloved Roger Hightower to America with us, although, in the event, he didn't come. She stormed off in a huff and went to live in Paddington with an old colonel she was getting money from. And that was the last I heard of her – until she sold her so-called story about me to a Sunday paper.

Over in Hollywood, we moved into a house, which used to belong to the Supremes, in Nicholls Canyon Drive, and we opened our agency, the 777 Organization, in Ronald Reagan's old offices. The Crank was still convinced he would be bigger than Elvis, so he insisted that our agency would not need to put any other artistes on its books. In effect, we'd set up a whole business for one man. The offices, the secretary, the Crank's recording-studio time, and even the suits he insisted were necessary for his image were paid for by the Japanese man. I kept my side of the deal and took this multi-millionaire to meet Tom Jones in Las Vegas and Englebert Humperdinck in Los Angeles. I've never seen anyone so excited.

In the meantime, the Crank was frightened to go to certain places in Los Angeles because of the Mafia who were after him for their money back over a songwriting deal that had backfired. He bought a gun and took it with him wherever he went. I became paranoid. I thought, Something's going to happen out here, and I'll get caught in the crossfire. I told the Japanese guy, 'I cannot relax with all this going on. The Mafia are after my husband, he keeps on pulling this gun out, and it's making me a pack of nerves.' In the end, he paid all the Mafia money back for the Crank, probably hoping to protect his investment.

We were still in Hollywood in February 1971 when the *News of the World* ran a huge article with the headline: SEX AND CASH PAYOLA FOR TV PRODUCER. This was the start of a long-running investigation, which would eventually lead me to the Old Bailey. To begin with, I wasn't unduly worried. None of the DJs or producers who came to my parties had ever, ever had girls in return for playing my records, and there was never any question of money changing hands under my roof.

The newspaper's information had come from one of the top men at President Records. He'd met two chaps who were claiming to be in the music business, but in fact were reporters from the *News of the World*. He had told them that it was possible to bribe DJs to play records, and that he had them all in his pocket. He also said, 'Janie Jones gives the most fantastic parties ever,' in a reference to two I had held for the record company while the Crank was in America on an earlier occasion.

The *News of the World* enquiries were taken up by the police, and I ended up being accused of offering prostitutes' services for free to BBC agents as a reward for playing records – one of the many charges made against me during my 'vice' trial. Needless to say, I was eventually found not guilty of any payola offences. But, because of these initial allegations, the *News of the World* began a full-scale examination of my life in London: the whores, the hotels, the parties and the people who came to them.

I was alerted to this fact in the late spring of 1971 when I received a frantic phone call in Hollywood from the Lord. He was yelling, 'Oh, my God, my God, you've got to get back on the next plane! *News of the World* are on to me. If you come back, I'll give you £10,000 to fight them. You've got to stop them printing anything about me. You know how I like the schoolgirls. If it comes out, it'll kill me.'

I returned to England, and I had a fit when I saw the state of my house. Eric couldn't bear to touch anything that was dirty, including the little cat's litter tray, and the place was like the biggest tip you've ever seen. When I recovered from the shock, Eric delivered another one. He sat me down and gave me a newspaper clipping with the sad news that the Colonel had died, only weeks after marrying a Swedish girl. He'd taken an accidental drug overdose. I was very upset. The Colonel had kept me right up until I married the Crank, and I carried on visiting him after that. He was a lovable old man.

For his part, the Lord was in hospital recovering from a heart attack. I went to visit him and despite his ill health, despite his problems, he kept saying, 'Come on, give me a hand job under the blanket.' I was really annoyed and sickened by this. I said, 'I will not. You've had a heart attack, you dirty, filthy swine.' Finally, though, I agreed I would take what action I could against the *News of the World*, but first I had to go back to Hollywood to tidy things up there.

By now, the Japanese gentleman was getting fed up with the Crank. He realized he wasn't the full ticket, he wasn't generating much money, and we simply couldn't make a go of the agency while my husband kept refusing to take in other artistes. This man told me bluntly, 'If you go back to England, I can't work with John Christian Dee on his own because he's absolutely impossible. It's you who's got the pull and the respect.' It was obvious that, much as I would have loved to leave the Crank in Hollywood, he was going to end up coming back to England with me.

In June 1971, the *News of the World* published a sensational article about 'Janie Jones's involvement in a call-girl ring and the scandal at the BBC.' The information was sold to the paper by two unidentified girls 'ensnared in the ring', and the story was accompanied by a photograph of me, 'recently returned from America'.

I knew that one of the two girls was Heather, the Poison Dwarf from Scotland, who was still furious that I'd gone to California, still furious that she couldn't get Roger Hightower. Now, she was getting her pound of flesh. The other was blonde Penny from Harlow, who had never forgiven me for dropping her when I came back from Spain and found she'd had fellows spending nights in my house. Between them, they made all sorts of wild allegations and twisted the truth when they weren't ignoring it completely. I was the villain of the piece, and they were the innocents I'd corrupted. Some innocents!

I was particularly outraged by the accusations of payola, and the implication that I was running some sort of 'call-girl system for the stars'. I'd always kept my showbiz parties entirely separate from the escort service. Any girls who were involved in both were perfectly well aware that they would not be paid for any sexual favours they bestowed on celebrities at the parties, which were for amusement only. And they were under no pressure from me or anybody else to have sex with the rich and aristocratic men they visited as escorts. If they did, it was by their own private agreement.

By this time, I'd received the promised £10,000 from the Lord. He said, 'No one must ever know I've given you this money because then it would be obvious I'm trying to cover something up. I'll hand it over to you in cash in three batches.' Eric and I had gone to meet him three times, near Harrods in Knightsbridge, to pick up the money, and I put it all in a deed box. The box had previously contained £12,000 in cash which the Colonel had given me before I married the Crank. I took out £10,000 of the Colonel's money, which was all in old notes, and replaced it with the Lord's because these were all new, crispy ones with his bank wrappers still around them. The Lord's notes remained in the deed box until they were found by the police – which would lead me into a great deal of unnecessary trouble.

In the meantime, however, the huge amount of money I was about to spend on solicitors would come from the Colonel's bundle. My first priority was to seek an injunction to stop the *News of the World* publishing any more stories, and I consulted my solicitors who sent an urgent letter by hand to the newspaper on 10 June. Part of the letter stated that:

> *The allegations against her [me] are completely untrue. Our client has never received one single penny from any man or record company or others, in connection with the procuring of girls for men or the organizing of parties of any sort.*
>
> *Our client is a singer and she has received monies from record companies in respect of records made by her, but that is a normal incident of her profession, and we do not imagine for a moment that you would wish to dispute it.*
>
> *The position is now intolerable. Our client and her husband are plagued constantly by anonymous telephone calls and visitors to the house. By your publication of the picture of the front of the house, together with mention of the street in which it is situated, you must have realized that our client would be subjected to such a campaign.*
>
> *Her professional position has been attacked viciously, and her earning capacity has been seriously impaired. She has incurred vast expenses, and, in all, this seems to us to be a classic case of defamation where the plaintiff has suffered grievously in financial and emotional terms.*

The *News of the World* was not prepared to withhold the next proposed article in the series, and the matter went to court, where the judge pronounced that, 'At this stage, Miss Jones, I can not give you an injunction to stop it.' At the same time, he told the newspaper, 'If you print and Miss Jones proves libel, the sum you pay her will be astronomical.'

This was enough to put a temporary hold on the stories, but it also fuelled the paper's enthusiasm for investigating me. To this end, the reporters doubled their efforts to track down and interview other girls who'd been around me before I went to America. They told women they got hold of: 'If you give us information against Janie Jones, we'll refer to you only as Miss A, B or C. If you refuse, we'll put you all over the paper.' Any statements they got, they handed over to the police, the police used them for their own enquiries, and that's how the whole thing snowballed.

In the meantime, I was receiving phone calls myself from some of the girls, including Heather. She'd seen the article and suddenly panicked because of what she'd done. She rang up pretending to be on the continent, asking, 'Oh, who's put this wicked thing in the paper?' I'd known straight away that it was her and Penny, so I said nothing of any significance. I was later informed she made the phone call to me from the *News of the World* offices.

In a rare moment of agreement, the Crank and I decided we should immediately try to make with contact with characters like Peg the Plater, Ann, the insurance-company raver, and the lovely Jane, who'd been merely looking for a husband. Our idea was to ask them for statements to confirm the truth: that they knew no stars had ever paid for sex at my showbiz parties. The celebrities, after all, were innocent and deserved whatever protection we could give them.

Despite the fact that we'd been away in America for some time, we found Peg, Ann and Jane within a couple of weeks. They were all scared stiff by the threat of exposure as prostitutes. Ann had phoned me first of all, on 23 June, crying and telling me that the police were trying to get a statement from her. The coppers' tactics were the same as the newspaper's. Ann said the police had shown her a statement made by the Poison Dwarf and advised her to go along with it.

If she were prepared to give court evidence against me, she could do so without being identified. If she confessed to her own actions and decisions and was honest about my role in things, she could find herself on vice charges in a major trial, which would spread her name across the country. As a result, she might lose the two kids her estranged husband was always trying to take away from her. She'd therefore given the police the statement they wanted. One of the most enthusiastic nymphos I'd ever met was a 'good girl really', led astray by me! I suggested, 'Why don't you tell my solicitors exactly what you've told me? They can help you find a decent way out of this without threats and pressure.'

She said, 'Oh, yes, that would be great, come over to my place.' In Kensington High Street on my way to Ann's, I bumped into another girl I knew. She'd been at one of the parties, and she wanted to make a truthful statement about them on my behalf. By the time we'd finished chatting, I was late getting along to see Ann and no one was in when I arrived. I went home again and phoned her at the insurance company where she worked. She asked me to come to see her there and told me to park in the square.

Eric and I drove to the square, and as we parked a police officer jumped out of a car behind us. 'Ann doesn't want to see you. You're bothering her, so go away,' he said.

'That's a load of crap,' I retorted. 'You're the ones who are bothering and threatening her. She's invited me here.' At that moment, I knew that there were going to be a lot of problems, that something was being set up. I later told my solicitors, 'She's playing into their hands and doing a deal with the police.'

I started to suspect that my phone was tapped, and this appeared to be confirmed by my experiences with Peg the Plater only a couple of days later. Peg had gone up north to live with a couple of girls she'd been to Turkey with, doing marijuana and all that. She phoned me sobbing her heart out. She'd also told the police what they'd hoped to hear about me. She sniffled, 'They came here and interrogated me for three hours. By the time they'd finished, I would've said my own mother was a whore to get away from them.'

I invited Peg down to talk to my solicitors. She said, 'No, I'll give you my address to come and see me. I'm scared to go to London on my own in case the police are watching me.' Eric and I went up there, and Peg agreed she would sign a statement saying that she never screwed any celebrities at my parties for money. I said, 'Why don't you come back to London with me? The cops wouldn't dare touch you.'

She laughed and joked with Eric and me all the way down on the train, and I was trying to give her confidence. I told her I was only interested in proving that nobody went with any stars for cash. Back in Campden Hill Road on 27 June, I phoned my solicitors and told them Peg was at my house. Next thing, two police officers were at my door. 'Have you got Peg here against her will?' they wanted to know.

'No,' I said, 'you bastards had her against her will up north. She is here, though. She's upstairs. I've got nothing to hide, but I think you have and I think it's something very dicey.'

I went up to get Peg, and she started to shake like a leaf. She'd always been a nervous wreck, on prescribed pills and tranquillizers. She came down to the front door and the coppers said, 'Would you like to come outside with us, Peg?' 'No, I wouldn't,' she said. So they went off, and she then collapsed on the floor, hysterical, saying she wanted to commit suicide. She was going, 'Now they know I'm here, what am I going to do? They'll cause havoc. They told me not to get in touch with you.'

My solicitor arrived, took her statement and went. I was worried sick that something might happen to her in the night, because even though she'd calmed down a little bit she was still very jittery. So I called in a doctor, and he admitted her to hospital. Two days later, she was discharged and promptly disappeared. The police had been at her again.

At the beginning of July, the Crank and I went to visit Jane in Brighton. She was absolutely paranoid, frightened out of her wits about the prospect of ending up in the newspapers, because the police had been down to see her too. She had also co-operated with them, but in her case I understood it because she was different from the others. She wasn't a whore by nature, she was a likeable, lonely woman who'd wanted to find a husband. She gave us a statement – for what it was worth – about the parties and how she'd never accepted money for sex with a celebrity. Later, faced with the usual police reprisals, she claimed she'd made the statement only because she was scared of my husband and me.

I never held it against her, although I felt betrayed by the other girls, the real tarts, including my friend Gloria. She was worried about losing her child, Martin, should the truth about her activities in the alleged vice ring be publicized in court and therefore the newspapers.

She was also protecting her boyfriend. The police already knew a lot about him. So, she later gave the police their statement.

It took a lot of persuasion, but somehow I managed to convince the Crank that it was time for us to separate. I had to agree to pay for him to move into a flat in Heber Road, Cricklewood. I also pointed out that with all the scandal going on around me, he was never going to be able to revive his career. I told him straight. 'This marriage was a foolish mistake. It's not working out. There's no way I'm happy with your violence and possessiveness. I can't move without you.' He reluctantly agreed to go as long as we could remain in touch, and I spoke to a record-industry contact who gave him a deal on a couple of songs he'd written, including one called 'Shooby Dooby Doo'.

The divorce proceedings began before the end of 1971 on the grounds of his adultery with Rita Wick. Again, I was using the Colonel's bundle of old notes to pay for the solicitors. The Crank had been worried about the divorce action and had asked me not to use the statement I'd been given by Heather, which involved the girl who'd given him a plating. He said it would be too humiliating because she was a 'right old slag'. Instead he offered me a deal. He told me he'd been with another girl, Rita, a few times, and he offered to go round to her place so that I could send a private detective over to catch them together, which I did.

Much later, after the divorce came through, the Crank told the police that I'd fixed the scene with Rita. So that was added to the long list of charges at my trial: plotting to deceive the Queen's Proctor, an officer of the High Court responsible for ensuring that there's no collusion in divorce. In fact, the set-up was the Crank's all along, and his attempts to incriminate me didn't wash in court.

In the early days of my separation from the Crank, our relationship was almost amicable. I was paying for his flat in Heber Road, he had a nice sum of money from his record deal, and he thought we were friends. But the uneasy truce didn't last long. When he got through his savings, he wanted to come back, and I wouldn't let him into the house – which is when he really started harassing me. He was ringing, ringing, ringing – at all times of the day and night. He was coming round in his car and sitting outside my home, watching. I became very fearful for my own safety. I believed that Eric and I needed someone else in the house, not just for the moral support but to bear witness to whatever the Crank might do next.

I used to tell all my problems to my hairdresser Chris when I went to his salon, Michèlle's, in Notting Hill Gate. One day I said I needed a lodger, somebody who wasn't scared of anybody or anything, to witness any threatening phone calls or violence. At the time, a girl called Claire was in there washing hair. She was about eighteen or nineteen. 'I'll come in,' she said. 'I'm not frightened. I'd attack him.'

I replied, 'No, you're too young, He's a violent man.'

'Huh!' she said, 'You don't know the violence I've put up with for years from my mother.' I told her I'd think about it. Meanwhile, Chris confirmed that she actually had had a lot of trouble with her mum.

I saw Claire several times after that. She was a lovely-looking girl, with waist-length hair. One night I went out with her to a local club called Hers and Mine, which was mainly populated by gay boys. She had a good few drinks and then confided her family problems. She said that her father had started interfering with her at the age of four. When she was fourteen, her mother caught him having sex with her. She split the father's head open so badly he had to have stitches. She then demanded he move out and took the Mercedes and the house in return for an agreement not to go to the police.

Now, the mother was jealous of Claire and repeatedly accusing her of making eyes at her boyfriend. She'd often fly into violent tantrums over this. Claire nevertheless loved her mother, who had done nude modelling in her younger days and who didn't seem to mind that Claire was frequenting dodgy clubs. I decided after hearing all this that she was obviously a very hard-bitten person, and potentially a staunch ally who would be able to stand up to the Crank. So I invited her to move in with Eric and me.

At around the same time, the Crank intensified his terror campaign. He told me I wasn't to leave the house or he would get me. He'd sit outside watching me for hours on end, and I didn't dare move. I was a prisoner. It was intolerable, yes, but I couldn't do anything about it. I changed the locks, and I had bolts and bars put everywhere around the house.

I used to have to get Chris, my hairdresser, to come and do my hair at home because I couldn't go out. Chris would have to dress as a woman, with a wig on, because if the Crank had seen a man coming in, he'd have killed him. Even when he saw the 'woman' visiting, he'd be on the phone yelling, 'I've seen the whores going in, get them out of the house!'

Then he started lying in wait for Eric further down the road. Eric was so petrified of him he'd just hand his keys over, so I had to take Eric's keys away from him and devise a way of letting him in. If Eric rang the doorbell rather than rapping the knocker when he came to the door, then I knew the coast was clear for me to open all the locks. Also , I had to warn Eric not to leave the door ajar when he went to water the plants outside the front basement. It was sickening. And the police weren't going to interfere, because it was a husband-and-wife thing.

This continued throughout 1972. In October of that year, I had an injunction served upon the Crank, forbidding him to come within two hundred yards of the house. If he did, he could be sent to prison for contempt of court. But, in my heart, I knew that the man was reckless enough to ignore any number of injunctions.

Claire was sticking with me through it all, as strong as the Rock of Gibraltar. But, on the other hand, it had taken her no time to show her true colours. She was another nympho. She'd go to clubs and pick up two or three gay boys to have it off with at the same time. Next day, she'd be back home telling me, 'Ooh, I had some fantastic cock last night, a lovely orgy, a laugh and a joke.'

It made me feel sick, and I told her so. I said, 'One of these days, you'll get in so much trouble, dear. It's nothing to do with me, and I'm not by any means narrow-minded, but this is not right. It's disgusting. You're only young, and you'll end up getting diseases.'

'Oh, I love the cock, the bigger the better,' she'd shrug. She was always on about it, and if she could get it, she was happy. Yet, when it came to my trial, she became another 'poor little innocent' whom I corrupted.

By the end of the year, Claire was out whoring regularly with my friend Gloria, who had just moved into a flat around the corner from my house with her boyfriend and their little boy, aged six or seven. Gloria had asked me for the initial down payment of £400 as well as my agreement to be a guarantor for the rent. I refused both requests and told her to ask her boyfriend. Apparently he didn't have £400. So Gloria made a private arrangement to earn it from Bob, the man who was so devoted to me he paid for my wedding. She took Claire with her.

Bob, sexually, liked to give and take punishment. So, on the appointed night, they set up a special card game. If, say, a king came up followed by a ten, he'd be tied up and lashed ten times. If it were a queen and then, maybe, a five, he'd tie the girls up and whip them five times. Gloria came round to visit me not long after this, and as she sat down, she groaned. I asked if she had piles. She then pulled down her knickers and showed me lash marks like I've never seen in my entire life. I said, 'Get into a bloody hot bath with salt in it. Whoever did that wants to be put away behind bars. It's disgraceful.'

She told me, 'I went round to Bob with Claire and got £400.'

I replied, 'I wouldn't have taken £4000 for that.' Well, I rang him up, and I screamed at him. He said it was none of my business and slammed down the phone.

I was getting very worried about Gloria's son Martin. I flipped my lid when I found out that she was leaving him alone in the bedroom while she was smoking pot and playing cards with her boyfriend and their mates in an adjoining room. At other times she'd go out whoring all night and not come back until eight o'clock the next morning. I stormed, 'If this carries on, I'll report you to the welfare. This little boy never sees the light of day.'

The Crank, meanwhile, had no intention of observing any court injunction. I knew he wouldn't anyway, just from his terrifying behaviour the evening Eric went out to water his plants and absentmindedly forgot to close the front door. Next thing, the Crank was in. I pushed Claire towards the door, yelling, 'Get out,' to protect her. And then he had me by the throat on the floor with a knife against my neck. He told me, 'If the police come, you shout to them that everything's all right.'

He forced me down to the bedroom in the basement. He was back on drugs, and his eyes were wild. He kept intoning, 'You're going to die,' so I had to comply when he forced me to have sex with him at knife-point. Afterwards, he held me there for two and a half hours, with the knife at my throat, until he fell asleep. I escaped then and sent for the police. When they arrived, the Crank stared at me and insisted, 'I've never seen her before in my life.' Out of his brains. The police got rid of him.

I felt sick and humiliated. I was on the bidet, crying my eyes out for hours after that. I didn't know where it was all going to end with him. But I did know that he'd be back. I didn't have to wait long. Within a month of my High Court injunction against him, he tried to break into my house. I was in the kitchen early in the morning of 14 November. I said to Eric, 'You know, I've got this eerie feeling the Crank's around.' Next minute, there was a smashing of glass. He was trying to force his way in through the back, but he hadn't realized I'd had all the bolts and bars put in, and he couldn't get through.

Immediately, I rang the police, because he was breaking the injunction. Detective-Sergeant James Hopwood came straight over with another officer, and within minutes the Crank was on the phone threatening me. He didn't realize the cops were there, and I asked them to listen to what he was saying. 'You can't prove I came over the back,' he stormed. 'You can tell the police, but you've got no evidence.'

Det.-Sgt. Hopwood took the phone. He said, 'We're police officers, and we'd like to see you now.'

'Yes, you cunt,' boomed the Crank. 'You'll see me in three minutes.' He was as high as a kite on drugs. Sure enough, he appeared three minutes later, tried to burst in through the lounge window and was grabbed by the police. He was like a madman, brandishing a penknife, and they had to retaliate with their truncheons. Finally, they arrested him and took him away.

He appeared in the local magistrates' court the next day, to the great interest of the press. Det.-Sgt. Hopwood opposed his bail application, and he was quoted in the *Sun* of 16 November as saying, 'Dee was like a wild animal, and if he were released, he would be liable to repeat the performance.' According to the same article, the detective-sergeant also said in court that Dee had 'a long history of violence to his wife'. Another newspaper reported that my husband allegedly told a detective, 'I would rather kill her than let someone else have her.'

The bail application was refused, and the Crank was remanded in custody at Brixton Prison, pending his Old Bailey trial some three months later. He was charged with entering my home with intent to do me grievous bodily harm, attempting to wound Det.-Sgt. James Hopwood, assaulting him and possessing a knife.

This was one of the best times of my life. I'd been under the Crank's thumb for four years, and now I could relax and go out to enjoy myself. But he was determined to hound me, even from behind bars. He sent me a stream of letters, which changed in tone from day to day and often from paragraph to paragraph. They were littered with dramatic underlinings and frantic exclamation marks. Some of the writing was sickly sweet, with kisses surrounding his passionate and sentimental declarations. This was probably for the benefit of the prison censor and any other authorities who might obtain access to the letters.

I never replied to any of this correspondence, but one recurring feature intrigued me: the Crank was adamant that something was about to befall me, and, at the same time, he was equally certain that, against all the odds, his own court case would end in his favour. It did, too.

In February 1973, the detectives, Eric, Claire and I gave evidence in the Old Bailey, which seemed to prove beyond any reasonable doubt that the Crank had come to my house to do me harm after being served with an injunction, had attacked Det.-Sgt. Hopwood and was in possession of a knife. The jury was told that he was 'hysterically violent' and had to be hit three times with a truncheon when he lunged at the detectives. Yet, he was cleared of all charges.

I was very suspicious. I was sure he'd been getting inside information and help from a certain police sergeant friend of his, even though he'd given an Oscar-winning performance on the stand. His tears fell as he related how much he loved his wife Janie. He said, 'She brought me off heroin, and I needed her like I needed a fix of that. One of the policemen was in love with her too, and he was trying to take my wife away from me.'

The Crank was such a good liar he could make anybody believe him. But he didn't enjoy his freedom for very long. Just a week after his release, he made another attempt to get into my house and succeeded. This time he came over the neighbouring rooftops and entered through a skylight. I called the police, and he was arrested.

This was all big news in the national newspapers of 9 March 1973, after I'd described the incident to the London Divorce Court and produced the tapes I'd made of his threatening phone calls on that night. On 14 March, the Crank was ordered to be arrested and sent to prison for a flagrant breach of the court order restraining him from molesting or annoying me. And so he was back in jail three weeks later when I was granted a decree nisi on the grounds that our marriage had broken down after his adultery with Rita Wick. I was quoted in the press as saying, 'I'm so relieved. I'll never, ever marry again.' And I never have.

Unfortunately, the Crank hadn't finished with me yet. I discovered this through another of the Lord's hysterical phone calls. He spluttered, 'Oh, my God, that damned husband of yours! He's gone and told the police that I gave you £10,000 cash, and it's all because you wouldn't take him back. Never, ever say I've given you a penny. The police have been questioning my housekeepers, and they've been questioning me, and I swore an oath. I said, "No, no, no, I never gave her anything." You must say the same, because if you don't, they'll know you're covering.'

The Crank knew all about the money the Lord had given me to come back from Hollywood and fight the *News of the World*. And once my husband was in prison, aware that the divorce had come through, he leaked that information, without explaining the background, to get back at me, and it would eventually result in my being charged with blackmail.

Certainly, some sort of net was closing in on me, although I didn't know what to expect, or when – until the evening of 16 May 1973. I was sitting indoors and suddenly I said, 'I don't know what it is, Eric, but I feel we're both going to be arrested tomorrow.'

'Ee, don't be daft. What are we going to be arrested for?' Eric soothed.

I answered, 'I don't know. But my psychic's on, and I can tell you we'll have policemen calling on us.' Bright and early the next morning, we heard it: bang, bang, bang on the front door.

CHAPTER SEVEN

Remand Me to Cancel the Milk

'We've come to arrest you,' they said, and they read out the charges. They marched into the house. My niece's young daughter, Melanie, was with me at the time. She was bewildered. 'You leave my Auntie Janie's things alone!' she kept wailing at the policemen. 'What are you doing at my auntie's desk?' What they were doing at my desk was removing my tape recordings of phone calls from girls who wanted me to meet them so they could make statements on my behalf about the celebrity parties. I could have gone on to use these tapes to establish the truth of what I'd been involved in. Now, the potential evidence was being taken away, never to be returned. It was going to be my word against everybody else's at the trial.

Obviously, my first priority was to arrange for Melanie to be taken back to her mother. Then I was rushed away by the police to Bow Street station. The first charges were connected to the alleged BBC payola scandal (of which I was later found not guilty). Among others arrested at the same time were a leading radio producer, a high-ranking man from President Records and the singer Dorothy Squires who recorded for President.

At Bow Street, I was put into a cell with Dorothy. It was an horrific and disgusting experience. There was excrement all over the floor and walls. To make matters worse, Dorothy suffered from claustrophobia – she'd never even been able to ride in the lift at the record company offices – so she started banging on the cell door with a shoe. 'Let us out!' she shrieked. 'We're stars, we're not criminals, you bastards!' She was effing and blinding like mad.

'You silly old bag,' the coppers shouted back, 'you're not stars in here, you're prisoners.' They were definitely getting their jollies out of it all, seeing Dorothy under pressure and cracking jokes about her age.

I just couldn't believe what was happening. Three whole years had elapsed since the parties I'd innocently held for President Records, and in all that time, I'd never tried to reinstate the separate escort service I'd once provided for rich and titled clients. Since 1970, I'd been busy trying to help the Crank start a new career in America. So I sat calmly in the cell and tried to comfort Dorothy, confident that I'd be granted bail and would soon be home for a cup of tea.

Unfortunately, I wouldn't see my kettle again for a very long time. My application for bail was vigorously opposed. I was charged, I was kept in Bow Street overnight, and the next day I was on my way to Holloway Prison, just north of central London. On 19 May 1973, the *Daily Mail* trumpeted the news: JANIE GOES TO JAIL blared the headline, and I was pictured doing just that.

When I was taken into Her Majesty's reception, the prison staff took away all my possessions and made a list of my clothing. Then they put me into a cage, like a tiny horse-box with a wire-mesh top. I had to sit there waiting for what seemed like hours, reading the graffiti on the walls: cheerful messages like I WANT TO KILL MYSELF. All around me were the sounds of other women shouting and screaming. Finally, a screw returned and handed me a big plastic mug of tea. It was vile. I was then taken to see the doctors, who gave me a full examination and looked through my hair for lice. Needless to say, they didn't find any.

Next, a whole bundle of stuff was thrown on to the floor. I had to pick it all up and carry it upstairs to my cell. It contained a blanket, sheets and a face-cloth. The cell door shut with a great big clanging, and I could hear the echoes of the screws going along the corridors, away from me, jangling their keys. The next thing that struck me, with a sudden dreadful fear, was the mayhem all around. Girls were yelling at the screws and at each other.

'I can't sleep!'

'I'm gonna commit suicide!'

'Shut up, you bastard, or I'll fucking kill you!'

Chaos and violence. I'd never known anything like it in my life. I wanted more than anything to go to sleep, to blot it all out, but I couldn't. I lay there thinking, What have I done? What am I here for?

Still, I was convinced that I'd be able to sort out the bail problem very quickly and be out in no time. But as days turned to weeks and weeks into months, it became clear that there was no way the authorities were going to set me free. They intended to throw the book at me. Every week there were more charges – and more charges and more charges. They kept opposing my bail applications. One of the people most interested in keeping me inside was the senior police officer I suspected of being in league with the Crank.

My thirteenth application was successful, and I was asked to guarantee an astronomical sum – my own recognizance of £20,000 and two other sureties of £10,000 each. Against all the odds, I managed to arrange this, only to have more obstacles put in my way. It was deemed that my brother-in-law was not eligible to stand bail for me because he wasn't a resident of the United Kingdom, living as he did in America. Another friend, who owned a West End club, was also ruled unaccept-able, because of a drinks' charge he 'wasn't of pure character'. I believed there was a conspiracy to keep me inside. I knew I was banging my head up against a brick wall. And so, sadly, was Eric. He was being held on remand, on various charges of being my accomplice.

I was more worried about Eric's predicament as a prisoner than my own. I can manage to get along with people in any circumstances, but I knew that Eric, being shy and introverted, would be going through hell. His bail applications were opposed as strongly as mine, even though he wouldn't hurt a fly and had never been in trouble. You couldn't find anybody more honest than Eric. I was once walking out of a shop with him when he found he'd been given change of a £20 note instead of a fiver. He went straight back in saying, 'Ee, no, no, you've given me too much change.'

Now he was in the nick through no fault of his own. I advised him to make a little statement against me, painting some picture of me as a domineering woman, because I knew that if he did, he would get bail. He might even get out of the trial altogether. So Eric made his 'little statement'. And they got him singing like a dicky-bird. They scared the daylights out of him. They told him that if he gave them enough information, he would be all right. If he didn't, he'd get eight years.

He was so frightened, poor Eric didn't know if he was coming or going, and his statement ended up about five miles long. I could understand all this. I'd never have fallen out with him over it because I knew how timid he was – I knew the pressure he was under. I knew he'd say his old mother was a whore, just to get out of there, but they had him saying some of the most diabolical things about me. They asked him 'Wasn't there a time she tried to murder John Christian Dee?'

Eric replied, 'Ee, well, she once put a sleeping powder in his coffee just before he drove off on a fishing trip.'

I nearly fainted. I'd never admitted to Eric that the incident had been one of my wind-ups, but here it was now, set to be brought up in court. I just couldn't believe it. I said to the police, 'You'll probably find out next that I robbed a bank. There must be more things you can accuse me of.'

Every week, there would be something else. I was charged with the ridiculous payola allegations, exercising control over prostitutes, attempting to pervert the course of justice by intimidating witnesses, blackmail, demanding money with menaces, obtaining money by deception, making false statements to get a divorce, attempting to drug the Crank, corruption and forgery. I was found not guilty of some of these charges, while others were dropped or amended during the trial, or finally adjourned *sine die*.

Eric was charged with plotting to pervert justice, sending forged postcards, intimidating witnesses, making false statements to help me get a divorce by claiming that the Crank had committed adultery, and aiding and abetting me to control prostitutes. He was acquitted of some of these; the rest were dropped or adjourned *sine die*. The Crank was also up on two charges of attempting to pervert the course of justice by intimidating witnesses. He was eventually found not guilty.

But the verdicts were still a long way off. I was on remand waiting for the trial to begin, Eric had been granted bail after making his statement, and the Crank was out on bail too – despite his recent imprisonment for breaking my injunction and despite his history of violence. My bail applications were being reported with increasing interest by the press. *The Times* of 20 July 1973, quoted the magistrate as saying: 'If she were on bail, she would leave no stone unturned to try and get witnesses to water down their evidence or to disappear.' It was extremely depressing. I couldn't recognize myself in this monster that was being created in the papers. I was doomed to stay in prison for ever, it seemed. The cell was coming in on me. I felt closed in on all sides.

This was two months after being arrested, with the trial still not even on the horizon. I went on a hunger strike to protest. It went on for several weeks, into August. I was kept under supervision by the prison hospital staff while I refused everything except hot water. The first week I felt ill, desperate to eat a little bit of something, but I was determined to make my point. The second week, I actually was ill. The third week, I felt like I was floating on air and hallucinating, as high as a kite, although my brain was alert. After that, I just didn't want to eat at all. I didn't care about it.

Eventually, I went back on to milk and soft foods because I was told that if I didn't, I would be force-fed through a tube, which I was assured was a very, very painful thing. Then, in September, I was granted bail for the first time, but my joy was short-lived. The obstacles placed in my way by police regarding my guarantors made my freedom impossible. I wrote a poem in my diary:

> *If tears could build a staircase*
> *And memories, a lane,*

I'd climb the walls of Holloway
And soon be home again.

My health deteriorated in the months leading up to the beginning of the trial in early December. I started to get horrific migraines. I'd never had a migraine in my life before.

I'd been warned that something was going to happen by no less than the governor of the prison. I'd consistently refused to take any tranquillizers or tablets, and despite all my inner build-up of tremendous tension and worry, I was outwardly smiling and cracking jokes. I would've died rather than let anybody see how much I was suffering.

'I know what you're doing,' the governor said to me. 'You're laughing on the outside and crying on the inside. You can't pull the wool over my eyes. How you haven't had a nervous breakdown by now, I don't know. What I do know is that this will all come out in some way later on.'

And it did. I started to vomit. I would bring up green bile, and my head would absolutely throb. I'd have to take a hot-water bottle to put on my head, get underneath the bed, pull a cover down to block out the light and stay there for three days. There was nothing they could give me in there, maybe just a couple of paracetamols, which didn't do a thing.

I still suffer from migraines to this day, and a lot of food and drinks I used to enjoy I can't have any more because they trigger them off. I can't have chocolate, I can't have cheese, I can't have eggs, I can't have oranges, and I can't have anything to do with booze. I used to love a couple of glasses of bubbly, but now even tiny drops of alcohol used as an ingredient in recipes will set off a migraine attack.

I kept grinning, though. When the trial started at the Old Bailey, it was more important to me than ever that I kept up appearances. The police, the court officials, the judge, certain prison officers – they all would have loved to think they'd got me on the bottom. The police officers wound me up all the time. They'd say, 'Cor, you should see the evidence we've got against you from Johnny Dee,' and 'Wait till you hear what Eric's had to say.' But I was determined not to let the bastards grind me down. I was fighting the system.

I'd get up really early before each daily journey – I'd do my nails, I'd fix my hair into a fantastic style, and I'd be immaculate in that court. Some of the press reports said that I looked a million dollars. I used to pray all the time. I'd think of Jesus on the cross, and I'd say to myself, 'They crucified Christ, and what did he ever do?' That would give me strength, and I'd go into court and keep on laughing and joking, even though the evidence I was hearing made me feel physically sick.

It was an exhausting routine. I'd get up at about 5.30 a.m. to start getting myself dressed and ready. The cell door would open, and I'd be taken down to reception for a complete strip-search. I'd have to wait in one of the dreaded horse-boxes with the mesh on top, flanked by ten or fifteen other women, also going to court. When the van arrived, we'd be driven off. As we passed through the streets, I'd see the newspapers' daily hoardings. Often, I was their major selling-point. TWENTY-FOUR PEOPLE IN ORGY IN TOP HOTEL! one screamed. The allegations got bigger and more sensational as the trial carried on, and the screws in the van were telling me they couldn't believe it.

I'd be delivered to the back of the Old Bailey, and by the time I went into court the public gallery would be jam-packed with people. They were my audience – I was on stage, I was playing to them – I was coming out with the gags, they were laughing, and the whole thing, as far as I was concerned, was a load of bollocks. Literally! I tried not to take any of it too seriously. 'Married to John Christian Dee,' I agreed. 'Bi-sexual. Tri-sexual. Try anything once.'

One day, during some evidence about the parties at my home, it was suggested to me that if anything sexual had ever occurred on the seven-foot bed, I would have been aware of it. I said, 'I'd know about it if it were something unusual.'

'What do you mean "unusual", Miss Jones?'

'Well, sex swinging from the chandelier I'd find out about,' I replied.

'Wouldn't that worry you?'

I said, 'I wouldn't be worried about the sex, but, by Christ, I'd be worried about the chandelier!'

Out of court, at weekends and in the days leading up to the trial, the prison routine would be fairly humdrum. We'd be wakened at 7.30 a.m. and allowed out of the cell for breakfast. There was a second break for lunch and another for tea-time. Sometimes when the prison was short-staffed, you'd be locked in the cell for twenty-three hours out of the twenty-four, because no one was available to supervise exercise or any other free activities. There used to be ructions then. The women would all be yelling and smashing their tiny little cell windows open to get some air. A lot of them were mentally disturbed. They shouldn't have been there.

On better days, you could get out for some fresh air or go to the workroom. I remember making clothes and fiddly little toys in there. You could choose to stay in your cell and read, or work on details of your court case. I was always writing things out and having visits from my solicitors.

Remand prisoners could have food sent in if we wanted. We could wear our own clothes, and we were allowed to have three changes. It was a big, draughty place, Holloway. Towards the end of my sentence, the prison moved to more modern premises, but in those early days on remand, I was fascinated by the eerie atmosphere of the old building. It was like a castle – it had a million ghosts.

Ruth Ellis's was one of them. She was the last woman to be hanged in Britain – in Holloway in July 1955 – for murdering her lover, David Blakely. It always upset me when the screws talked about walking over the spot where her body was buried. One officer told me that the whole prison observed a ten-minute silence as a mark of respect when it was known that she was going to be hanged. I had a lot of sympathy for Ruth Ellis. It was very, very sad, because the murder was a crime of passion. But it wasn't just the ghosts that kept me from sleeping when I first went to Holloway. It was something a lot more human – and a lot more disturbing – than them.

There was shouting and screaming going on all night, and then the screws would come round threatening, 'If you don't stop that yelling . . .' Then the abuse of the screws would start – 'Oh, shut up, you fucking bastard,' and 'Fucking screws!' I'd just be managing to doze off when it was time for the doors to open in the morning. I didn't sleep properly for a hell of a long time.

It was all very frightening, especially when the fights started during the day. Some of the coloured girls would use their steel combs as weapons, and there would be people throwing tea over each other and then getting chucked into their cells and threatened with punishments. It was absolute bedlam. The fact that the prison was so jam-packed, and I was having different cell-mates coming and going all the time, added to my sleeping problems. There were alcoholics, a lot of strange ones. It was awful.

Some of the screws there had the wrong idea about me from the start. They'd sneer, 'Janie Jones, the star, coming to Holloway. You're not a star in here.' They'd take great pleasure in giving me the worst job, which was scrubbing out the toilets.

I'd say, 'I never act like a star. I wouldn't really call myself ordinary, in fact, I'm quite extraordinary, but nevertheless, I don't mind scrubbing toilets. No big deal.' It didn't upset me. I came from a coal-mining background, and I'd scrubbed floors before. I scrubbed those toilets out harder and better than anybody else, singing at the top of my voice, sounding all happy, just to let them see that there was nothing I'd refuse to do. As a result, I gained respect from the officers and women alike.

Some of the younger prisoners used to say, 'Cor, I'd love to have gone out with men for money. I'd never have told tales on you, Janie, not even if they'd pulled my fingernails and toenails out.'

I'd say, 'It's not a question of telling tales. You've got the wrong end of the stick, my love. Don't believe what you read in the newspapers. These girls were whores who were doing it already.'

Quite often the young prisoners would insist, 'I used to go to bed with my boyfriends, and I enjoyed it, so why not go out with men for money?'

I'd tell them, 'Well, if that's your thing, then that's up to you but it's not an easy life. I've known hostesses who hated it, having to hold the same conversations with different men every night, pretending to be a parent with a poor young kid to keep. It's just like serving in a shop, but the money's better.'

In time, everybody knew me. They'd be shouting, 'Hello, Janie,' out of their cell windows. It was hilarious. Gradually, I began to cope with my situation inwardly as well as outwardly. I was there, there was nothing I could do about it, and I had to make the best of it.

I knew I had to be strong or I would end up like some of the women around me who cracked up completely. They'd get pieces of glass and cut their wrists. One very young girl tried to put some silver paper into the light bulb to electrocute herself. Another one, I'll never forget, used to try and pull her womb out, put one hand up inside herself and tear with her fingers. It was horrific. They put her in the hospital in a padded cell.

Then there were the zombies, who'd been there a good while on remand taking tranquillizers. They'd trade tobacco and money for even more medication, and they were all in a dreadful state. So were the other junkies on illicit drugs. They'd always find ways to get them in and push them around. They carried substances inside themselves, they left them behind the toilet seats for each other, and all of this served to compound my hatred for the whole drug scene.

I continued to refuse medication of any kind in prison, even when I developed a bad cold and cough two-thirds the way through the court case, at the beginning of February 1974. There was a flu epidemic going round, and when one of the jurors caught it, the trial was brought to a halt and the other eleven jurors offered an anti-flu jab. Notably, I wasn't asked if I wanted one.

The fact that I was locked away in Holloway did not deter the Crank from persecuting me in his usual hysterical manner. Nor did the fact that he was on charges connected with mine. Nor did the fact that he'd started up a 'romance' with Claire, the gorgeous girl who'd befriended me in the first place to protect me against him, who'd enjoyed as much hospitality in my home as I could give her, and who ended up going out on the game with my friend Gloria.

Soon, the Crank, one of the defendants in the trial, was living with Claire, one of the witnesses, in her mother's house, and he had persuaded Claire to make a statement implicating me deeply in many of my charges. He'd got around the mother first, going to visit her at home, making a big fuss of her, being all pallsy. Then he'd started confiding in Claire: 'Oh, you don't know what I went through with Janie . . . .' In the end, she fell madly in love with him.

The Crank was using her as a dish-rag, really. When Claire was my live-in ally he had hated her. Now he thought he could get himself off in the trial by using this beautiful girl to give false evidence. Throughout the case, they said they had a 'father and daughter' relationship. By the end of the year, they were singing a different tune, claiming to be madly in love. But their happiness was short-lived. He started locking her into the flat. He attacked her, he lacerated her legs, he brought girls back and had sex with them. She remembered then how frightening he was, all right. She tried to escape three times, but he got her back by threats.

Later, he went to Germany. I was still in prison, two years after our Old Bailey trial, when I heard that he was up on an attempted murder charge, accused of stabbing and attempting to kill his 25-year-old mistress, Angela Fronek. He was jailed for six years. He would still have been doing his time when he sent me a Christmas and New Year card from Altstadt, West Germany, in January 1977. And that was the last I ever heard of him, apart from a rumour that he came out of prison, went to the South of France and got married.

Claire, for her part, could never live with her conscience over what she'd done to me. She sent letters, visited and phoned me over a period of years, apologizing and trying to be friendly. She showed me the scars on her legs. She said she'd been so young and foolish when she fell in love with the Crank that she'd have done anything for him, including the statement against me. She'd been sure that he'd mended his violent ways, and because he was so persuasive, he could make her believe anything. When the violence started, she became terrified of him and thought she'd never be free of him.

I said, 'You deserved all that, Claire, I'm sorry. You knew what he was like and you still went off with him.'

She replied, 'I found out the hard way, and I'm very sorry because you're the best friend I ever had. I'll never, ever forget what I went through.'

On 4 February 1982, we had a long conversation on the phone. By now she had married and settled down in the home counties where she and her husband were running their own courier business. I taped the call, and among other things Claire told me this:

He [the Crank] terrified me . . . . He said it would take one second to put acid in my face, and I'd be scarred for life . . . . I was so scared I got alopecia and went bald, just through nerves . . . . It took me two years before I could socialize with anybody . . . . He said, 'I'm going to murder your cat, I'm going to cut it up into pieces and deliver it to you . . . .' My mum wanted to kill him with a butcher's knife, and in the end she kicked me out . . . .

He said he was going to get me, 'I'm gonna kill you . . . I'm gonna haunt you for the rest of my life and you'll die . . . .' He nicked everything I had, a few pieces of jewellery. He conned all my family, he conned me . . . . He nearly killed my brother . . . .

My family took it all out on me, I lost a lot of my friends, so he ruined my whole life . . . . I was turned into a gibbering idiot . . . . I thought, I'm gonna kill that bloke if I can. If you said to me, 'John Dee's at the hotel,' give me a gun, I'll go in and I'll kill him . . . . I nearly committed suicide . . . I'm lucky just to say that I got out of it alive.

CHAPTER EIGHT

Trials and Tribulations

O n 10 July 1973, *The Times*, no less, announced: COUNSEL IN
BBC 'PAYOLA' CASE TELLS OF A TWO-WAY MIRROR IN SINGER'S
HOME. And so the onslaught began. At the time, my charges
were incomplete, and they were still being built around a so-called payola scandal. The courts went on to handle the payola aspect
separately and to find me not guilty. But, in the meantime, I had to suffer
the slings and arrows of accusation from every direction.

The evidence of each witness was seized upon and quoted at length
throughout the committal proceedings held over ten days in July at the
Mayor's and City of London Court. Anecdotes from former friends and
colleagues were coming so thick and fast they seemed to be tripping
over each other to be printed: the sex parties; the celebrities; the
prostitutes; the Lord and the 'schoolgirls'; the lesbians; the whips; the
vibrators; the hotel clients; the hotel orgies; my bid to silence witnesses; my attempt to drug the Crank; my blackmail schemes. It was
endless.

A good 75 per cent of all this was untrue because it was based on
false premises: that I controlled all of the people involved, that they

themselves had no freedom of choice, that I lied to, manipulated and threatened certain individuals, and that I resorted to attempted murder. In short, I was responsible for everything that happened to everybody, and if it hadn't happened, damned if they wouldn't make it up. I was shocked to discover for the first time the extent of the case against me, but then again I was comforted by my own belief that whatever you do to someone else, be that good or bad, you get back three-or four-fold.

On 19 July 1973 I was sent for trial at the Old Bailey Central Criminal Court. My trial judge was Alan King-Hamilton QC, the same man who'd presided over the Crank's court case of February 1973 – the time he was astonishingly cleared of all charges after coming to my house to harm me, attacking Det.-Sgt. Hopwood and being in possession of a knife. The trial began not much more than three weeks before Christmas the same year. It was conducted in two separate parts: the vice and alleged intimidation charges, which involved Eric and the Crank; and the blackmail charges, which did not. All three of us pleaded not guilty to everything.

The vice trial stretched over 51 days. The girls who gave evidence against me were Heather (the Poison Dwarf), Peg (the Plater), Ann (the raver), Penny (the nympho who brought men back to our house while we were away), Gloria (the tearaway), Jane (the lovely girl who should never have been a prostitute) and Claire (the Crank's new girlfriend). Rita Wick was also brought up as a witness to say that her sex scene with the Crank was set up to provide false evidence for my divorce. As I have said before, the whole thing was the Crank's idea, and I was not convicted of it.

Together, these women came up with such ridiculous stories that, at times, I could only laugh. I thought, Well, if I don't see the funny side of it, I'll commit hara-kiri. Only a couple of days into the trial, I was told off for making faces at the jury. One after another, the girls claimed to have been innocents lured into prostitution by me. I'd done this, they said, by falsely promising them that if they had sex with certain men, they would open up for themselves the prospect of stardom with jobs in modelling and show business.

Did I hell! They were out-and-out whores, and they were doing it for the money. They knew who the men were, and if they dropped their drawers it was because they themselves decided to. I sent them out merely as escorts. What they did after that was their own private arrangement and for cash.

Jane, for instance, giving evidence under the alias of Miss H, said I told her she'd lost the contract for television advertising with the Venezuelan titled man (Mr X) because she hadn't gone to bed with one of his diplomats. What a load of crap. Mr X had nothing to do with television, and she knew it. She'd got lots of presents from the diplomats, she'd visited them at hotels more than once, and she went out with one of them for a time. She was looking for a husband. In fact, the Venezuelan gentleman gave some good evidence at the trial on my behalf.

Heather (Miss A) stated she'd been sent to see a man described by me as a television producer for Smarties and Silvikrin adverts. I'd allegedly promised her she could get some television work if she slept with this man. This was an appalling twist of the truth. What actually happened was that girls who went to do the 'schoolgirl' for the Lord (Mr Y) had to pretend to be children working on Smarties and Silvikrin adverts, because this is where I told the Lord I'd found them – in a television studio with their mummies. The Poison Dwarf also told the court about the mock-rape scene she'd been involved in with the Lord, Kenny Lynch and the two-way mirror. What she didn't explain was that we set it up purely as a giggle.

Another variation on the 'schoolgirl' scenario was described in court by Peg the Plater (Miss B). She said I told her to behave like a twelve-year-old girl and put on a baby voice to meet a man to perform sexual acts with another girl who was supposed to be her mother. She agreed that this act took place.

A recurring allegation by the whores was that I took money from them or received money from the clients and then paid the girls. This was never the case. I received direct payments, or sometimes gifts, from the clients in return for services, which ranged from doing their shopping to sending them escorts. Any cash the girls made was their own. Can you imagine them taking money and bringing it back to somebody else? Madness! However, the accusation or implication that I was bleeding these girls dry underlay all of the stories they told in court.

Peg went on at great length about a two-and-a-half-hour sex party, with six girls and two men performing lesbian and heterosexual acts, at the Inn on the Park Hotel. Claire (Miss G) talked about King Faisal and the princes he used to bring over to the Carlton Towers Hotel, and she told of the night she and Gloria (Miss L) whipped, and were whipped by, Bob (Mr Z).

The events of that night were confirmed by Gloria, and I was accused of organizing it all. As I said earlier, I didn't even know about it until Gloria came round and showed me her dreadful lash marks. They arranged it themselves because they needed money, Gloria for a down payment on her flat. Gloria also testified that she had become a prostitute at seventeen, at my suggestion. On the contrary, there was nothing she didn't know, and there was nothing she wouldn't do. She was already a whore when I met her.

At the same time, Gloria was coming to see me on remand, telling me she had to give evidence, had to get herself out of trouble, for fear of having her son, Martin, taken away from her. She was also worried about antagonizing the police in case they turned their attention to her boyfriend. As it happens, he was later jailed for six years for offences connected with forged money.

Back in court, my West End photographer friend Nigel was among those giving evidence. He confirmed that girls I knew had given him sex in return for free pictures. The Crank, for his part, staged another of his brilliantly convincing performances. He insisted that he had detested any of my activities involving prostitutes, and that he had shouted and yelled at them. It was a load of bollocks. He loved it. He used to drive the whores down to visit the Colonel on his estate near Bicester in Oxfordshire. He said what he had to say to get himself out of shit street and to get me further into it. Behind the scenes, he was also influencing everything Claire said in evidence, and to a lesser extent what the other girls said too. They were all quite afraid of him.

All in all, the papers were having a field day. The headlines continued:

MISS A'S KINKY SEX ON A KING-SIZED BED *Daily Express*
MY THREE ORGIES IN ONE NIGHT FOR £15 BY MISS A *Daily Mail*
LOVE SLAVES OBEYED JANIE JONES *Telegraph*

JANIE JONES SENT ME TO PRINCES FOR SEX, GIRL CLAIMS *Telegraph*
THE KING AND I – BY JANIE JONES *News of the World*.

The Times reported an alleged orgy with 'nine slaves' at Claridge's.
The celebrity parties at my home also cropped up quite a bit in evidence,
but few witnesses made the point: the sexual activities that happened
were for fun only and not for anybody's financial gain. One person who
did point this out was a well-known DJ. He admitted that he and two
other men were on the bed with three naked girls, and that he had
looked through the two-way mirror.

But while admitting that there was 'never any question of payment', he also said that he was under pressure from me to join in, that I
whipped his arse, and that he only screwed two of the girls, not all three.
He needed no persuasion. Did I force his cock to get hard? Did I force
him to screw them? He fancied them as a man, and he went in there and
screwed them as a man. I might have whipped his arse for a joke, but I
didn't do it on that occasion. And as for his argument that he screwed
two and not three of the girls – well, what's the difference? What did it
matter?

There was an incident in January 1974, a month into the hearings, that
almost brought the trial to a halt and which, I feel, put me at a major
disadvantage with the jury. A document relating to two charges I'd been
acquitted of several years earlier was found in the jury's bundle of
exhibits. It shouldn't have been there. And despite a legal argument
about it, despite the fact that this could well have been prejudicial, Judge
King-Hamilton refused to stop the trial. Instead, he ordered the jury to
'disregard that matter. Shut it out of your minds.'

I could imagine the jurors thinking, Oh, well, she's been up on all
this brothel thing before, she must be guilty. I was furious, but the trial
carried on, and the evidence progressed through the alleged intimidation of witnesses. Peg and Jane had retracted the statements they
originally gave the police. They told the Old Bailey that they did this
after intimidation by me. Jane stated that the Crank and I had traced her
to a south-coast town and entered the shop where she was working. We
were said to have persuaded her to come outside with us, and we then,

allegedly, threatened her with publicity and violence. She would be branded a prostitute if she didn't withdraw her statement.

She claimed I told her that a lot of people could find themselves in serious trouble, and that certain persons were going to 'get' Heather for giving her story to the *News of the World* in 1971 – the one about being ensnared in the 'call-girl ring'. Jane then said that the Crank and I drove her to her home so she could make a statement for us.

'I was very frightened,' she told the court. 'I didn't want to make the statement because I knew it would not be the truth.' She said that the Crank wrote out a statement and 'said I would get a copy of it when I had written it in my own writing'. She said she signed it. Well, yes, she did give us a statement. But, no, we didn't threaten her. We merely asked her for written confirmation that she had never slept with a celebrity for money.

Peg said more or less the same: that I had tracked her down to the north of England and threatened her with publicity and violence. As a result, she agreed to return to London. In reality it had been Peg who had given us her address on the phone. She was referring to the occasion when she travelled back with Eric and me and ended up in hospital after a hysterical collapse brought on by police harassment. As described earlier, we were merely doing our best to protect and help her, while securing a statement to say that she did not accept money for sex with any stars. This was confirmed by my solicitor, Michael Simmons, when he was brought up to explain the reason for his visit the night of Peg's breakdown.

Some similar tales of threats and fear were forthcoming from other girls, including Ann who conveniently forgot that she'd been perfectly happy to see me until the police intervened. But the most upsetting claims of intimidation were those concerning my relationship with Eric. He himself had been responsible for some of this nonsense in the five-mile statement he gave the police and subsequently repeated in court. I was said to have 'browbeaten, knocked about and dominated' him to the extent that he was afraid to leave my home and was forced to become my 'accomplice'. The jury was informed that Eric's feeling for me was 'friendship . . . turned to love or infatuation, but during the next ten years it turned to fear and terror'.

There were photographs of Eric in the papers, and the headlines chronicled his supposedly sad life:

CLERK TELLS JANIE JONES JURY HE IS CELIBATE *The Times*
CLERK IN JANIE JONES CASE 'NEEDED MOTHERING' *The Times*
ERIC'S LIFE OF MISERY *Telegraph*
MY LIFE AS A 'PRISONER' WITH JANIE ran another heading.

The Old Bailey heard that Eric 'unfortunately for him, was very taken with Miss Jones and came very much under her influence. A good deal of what he did was because he was undoubtedly under her domination.' It was said that I demanded and took money from Eric and insisted he do housework, cleaning and shopping. In fact, if I were waiting for Eric to get to grips with any housework, I'd be waiting a very long time! He did, admittedly, give me money at the beginning. He did help out. He gave me lump sums to help with different things when he first came to live with me, and he gave them voluntarily. I never bullied anything out of him. He was borrowing from the bank because he wanted to impress me, poor old Eric, but I didn't know that at the time.

The court was told that I used Eric as a 'runner' for my 'call-girl ring'. Eric wouldn't have had the foggiest idea how to be a runner. The man was a complete innocent. On three or four occasions, he did pretend to be from an escort agency, and he went to clubs to collect the girls' money for them from their clients. This was to help individual girls who didn't want to sit around with a man until the early hours, just waiting for their money.

The prosecution evidence with regard to Eric was full of errors. It was stated, for instance, that when he came to live at my 'brothel' – which my home never was – he occupied a bedroom with a two-way mirror. The court heard:

> If one stood in his bedroom, one could see into another bedroom, which had a double bed in it. At some time, girls would perform acts of indecency on other men in that bedroom while other clients would go into Eric's bedroom to watch what was going on.

Eric himself had told the police, 'On many occasions, I used to sit in the kitchen until three or four in the morning because men and girls were using my bedroom.' It was bollocks. The two-way mirror was between two of the upstairs bedrooms. Eric had the bedroom downstairs in the basement. He didn't move upstairs until after I married the Crank, shortly after which the parties ground to a halt. He did come out with some things, Eric.

And when the verdicts were brought in, at the beginning of March 1974, he was acquitted of the charges against him: trying to pervert justice by threatening violence, with me, to one of the girls, and two counts of counselling and procuring with me, plus aiding and abetting me to control two prostitutes. He was discharged. So was the Crank, who was found not guilty on two charges of attempting to pervert the course of justice. I was found guilty on seven charges of controlling the operations of six prostitutes and guilty on three charges of trying to pervert the course of justice by threatening girls to stop them giving evidence.

I was acquitted of one charge of trying to pervert the course of justice by threatening another girl, and of exercising control over a seventh prostitute (Claire). I was found not guilty on three charges of controlling prostitutes for gain. Six other charges survived the trial and were adjourned *sine die* after the crown said it did not intend to go ahead with them. Four were against me. These were: soliciting a man to murder the Crank; perverting justice; giving a radio producer a prostitute for a record plug; and plotting to issue forged postcards. Two were against Eric. They were: plotting to pervert justice and sending forged postcards.

The business about the postcards was to do with some trumped-up allegation that I'd been trying to fix the result of the viewers' votes for *Opportunity Knocks* to the advantage of a pop group called New World. The story was that a lot of the club girls had written out hundreds of postcards voting for this particular group. I was supposed to have given Eric a big bundle and sent him off to Manchester as a starting-point. From there, he had to travel to various British cities and post the cards – and I had allegedly expected him to do all this in a day and be back in London for tea-time! That was hilarious, that one.

A lot of entertainers appearing on *Opportunity Knocks* got cards done out for themselves and posted, and many of the club girls were happy to help. They were always at it. But it was a nothing charge –

farcical, really. It was introduced at the time they were trying to pin anything and everything on me.

The £12,000 blackmail trial began almost immediately afterwards, again in the Old Bailey. I was accused of blackmailing two men – the Lord and Bob – and of getting money by false pretences. The prosecution said that after publication of the first *News of the World* article, I hit upon the idea of blackmailing a couple of my clients.

One charge accused me of blackmailing Bob (Mr Z) for the trifling sum of £40. £40! This was the man, remember, who insisted on paying for my wedding. He even offered to put the money up for my divorce. Now, he was telling the court I'd been pressuring him for money. He said, 'The overall position was that I was being badgered continually. She was pushing, pushing, pushing. . . the phone was ringing every five minutes.' He said that he'd had sexual intercourse with me more than once, which was untrue, and he admitted receiving girls who took part in sexual beatings.

On 2 April, he burst into tears on the stand. Crying his eyes out. It blew my mind. He was getting his jollies out of it all. I couldn't help laughing. I thought, Oh, he's wonderful, marvellous, the way he's putting that act on. It was worthy of the Crank. I felt like shouting at times, but I knew I had to be quiet. I really had to restrain myself, biting my tongue time and time again. Even Judge King-Hamilton later commented that, for different reasons, Bob was 'not an impressive witness'.

Quite a few years later, maybe ten years after I came out of prison, I had to go to the small-claims court after an accident in which another driver smashed into my car. Someone came over and spoke to me in the courthouse, and I nearly exploded. It was Bob. He said 'Oh, Janie, I'm sorry.'

I replied, 'Don't ever speak to me again, because if you do, I won't be capable of controlling my anger. You are the scum of the scum, a big fat slob.'

However, Bob was pretty small fry in my blackmail hearings. Far more serious was the accusation that I'd blackmailed the Lord (Mr Y) to the tune of £12,000. This had all stemmed from the panic-stricken phone call he'd made to me in Hollywood, asking me to come back straight away because he was convinced the *News of the World* was about to identify him, having already written about an unnamed aristocrat who liked schoolgirls and teddy bears.

As I have already related, he offered and gave me £10,000 to fight the newspaper and stop the articles. I spent this sum on legal action and advice regarding the immediate scandal and also my divorce from the Crank. But the money I was physically handing over was the Colonel's. Of his original £12,000 in old notes, which was in my deed box, I'd taken out £10,000 and replaced it with exactly the same amount given to me by the Lord in new, crispy bundles. So when the police officers broke open the deed box taken from my bank, they found all of the Lord's money, untouched, in neat packages, each one bound with a wrapper from his bank. This proved that the Lord had given me the money. But because he continued to swear blind that he'd never given me a penny, the police assumed he had a very big reason for denying the obvious: blackmail.

To begin with, I did cover for him. I'd known him for years. He'd always told me, 'I think the world of you, I love you, you're my very best friend, and with friends, my word is my bond. You can trust me now and for ever.' But when it became obvious that he was going to tell lie after lie to save himself at my expense on a blackmail charge, I had to tell the truth. I thought, The gutless wonder is not getting up there and leaving me in all this shit. I've been as loyal as the Rock of Gibraltar to him – I even came back from Hollywood at the drop of a hat when he phoned – but I'm really going to go to town now.

I was broken up inside, it *burned*, that it had to come to this, but I had to tell the truth. Yes, he did like little girls dressed as schoolgirls, which was why he paid me the money in the first place – to fight the *News of the World*. If I were blackmailing him, I wouldn't have been so stupid as to leave his bank wrappers on the notes in my deed box. I would have taken them off before I'd put them anywhere.

Nevertheless, the Old Bailey was told that after the 'call-girl ring' article that Heather and Penny had had published in the *News of the World*, a man who had 'a lot to fear socially by reason of publicity' was approached by me.

She said that if he wanted to keep his name out of it, he would have to pay her in order that she might fight the News of the World. . . . She was suggesting to him, according to his evidence, that she should receive from him a loan, the money to be paid back if her action was successful. It was made plain by Miss Jones that unless she got the money, his name would be flashed over the headlines.

The Lord, throughout his evidence, denied 'schoolgirl' and 'rape' scenarios, while confessing that his association with me, particularly, could have been damaging and, for that reason, I knew I could blackmail him and did. He made reference, too, to his heart condition. This was all reported in the press. He told the court: 'I don't like making excuses for stupidity. But I had hit trouble and was almost dead. I suppose in a position like this, one is inclined to take the easy way out. But I was extremely low and very depressed.'

He was asked if he had a fear of publicity. He replied: 'Yes, I could not afford it.' The next question was, would he be adversely affected?

'Very much so.' The Lord stated that I first asked him for money in 1971 when he was in a medical establishment, very ill. In reality, the first discussion I had with him about money was during the phone call to me in America, when he offered it.

To his credit, the Lord did disclose the truth about the time I saved him from a blackmailer by taking him to Savile Row police station after the incident with the 'fourteen-year-old' at the Robin Hood in Westbourne Grove. I always did say that blackmail was murder of the mind. This view was so close to my heart that at the end of a three-week hearing that branded *me* a blackmailer, I couldn't help myself. One day in mid-April, the one before the verdicts were announced, I was led to the cells after an outburst at Judge King-Hamilton.

'I'm not a blackmailer!' I sobbed. 'I'm not! I'm fed up with listening to this! This is not a court of law! This is a joke!' I was cleared of all the blackmail charges. At the same time, the judge announced my sentence on the vice charges. He gave me seven years in prison, ordered me to pay £4000 towards the prosecution costs of the 'vice' trial and also said I had to fork out the whole of my defence costs or £12,000, whichever was less. My total debt was £16,000.

I must observe that Judge King-Hamilton didn't seem to like me.

While passing sentence, he said:

You knew the risks you were running in operating a call-girl service, but such was your greed for money that you were prepared to take that risk. You lured these girls into your web of vice by false promises to get them work in television or films. Once they realized what they had let themselves in for, you prevented their escape by a form of blackmail by threatening to expose them either to their parents or employers.

He referred to 'your loathsome trade, which over the years must have made you many, many thousands of pounds'. So many thousands of pounds that I had to try and sell my house from inside prison just to raise the £16,000 I owed the court! He added:

In spite of the verdict of this jury, to which I will be completely loyal, I am bound to say that I regard you as using blackmail in one form or another as one of the tools of your trade.

In my time, I have come across many men whom it would be right to describe as evil, but, in all my time at the Bar and on the Bench, I have only come across one woman, so far as I can recall, who merited such a comparison. You are the second, and, beside you, she was comparatively harmless.

The press picked up on the 'spider's web' analogy and called me 'an evil spider'. By this time, it was water off a duck's back. That wasn't me they were talking about. I knew what I was, and I rose above it. The papers were calling me 'Vice Queen Janie'. I was wondering why it wasn't 'Nice Queen Janie'.

I believed I was this country's answer to Bette Midler. Nowadays, I feel more like an Oprah Winfry. I could do her job as well as she can, getting people to open up and bring everything out. I wouldn't be afraid to ask anything. I wouldn't be afraid, either, to ask Judge King-Hamilton about the things he wrote about me in the book he published in 1982. It was entitled *And Nothing but the Truth*, a title tinged with irony for me.

He devoted a whole chapter to me, and near the beginning of it he mentioned the whores who ganged up against me and sent me to prison. He said that 'not one of them was a prostitute before working for Jones'. He was talking about girls who'd seen more cock-ends than I'd seen weekends. He reiterated the prosecution evidence about the whores and my alleged intimidation of them, incorporating a lengthy passage about the night Peg collapsed at my home. I was there when it happened. He wasn't. I know what went on, and I have already detailed this, as I have everything leading up to my arrest, to the best of my ability. These were the facts as I lived them. The judge merely trotted them out as other people told them, in order to save their own bacon.

King-Hamilton also described his reactions to Eric:

He was friendless, timid, shy and very weak-willed; almost the last person one would expect to become associated with Janie Jones. But once he was drawn into her web [Spider Woman strikes again!], *he was caught, trapped like a fly and quite unable to break free.*

Throughout the six or seven days during which he was giving evidence I was, by turns, filled with pity and contempt, nausea and anger that he should have been treated as he was and put up with it as he did.

The judge went to on to reveal that even if Eric had been convicted on his charges, 'I would not have sent him to prison.'

In a frenzy of elaboration, the QC made a huge song and dance about the 'evidence' that Eric had made repeated and desperate – but ineffectual – attempts to escape from me and my home, because he felt scared and trapped. Had Eric been that desperate, I'm sure he could have disappeared quietly while I was in prison. Instead, he came to find me when I was released and moved back into Campden Hill Road, as my very best friend. He's still there now, and I'm sure Judge King-Hamilton will be happy to hear it.

I wore my mink coat when I was driven off to prison to start serving my sentence. As usual, I was keeping up appearances, but it became a lifeline to me in Holloway because the prison was so cold in winter. I slept in it. As we approached my new home, I couldn't help thinking, ironically, of a verse in a song the Crank had written way back:

I stood accused of having two people slain,
My only witness lied to save his own son's name,
Lady Justice on that day was raped,
She stands pregnant today,
And it's me that's gonna pay.

The words kept going round and round in my head, and I remember thinking, 'This is the finish. I'll never trust anybody again, ever in my life.' I wish I'd taken my own advice.

CHAPTER NINE

A Forbidden Love

Someone else who could have done with following my advice was Patricia – Trish – Cairns. She was one of the screws. One day during my months on remand when she was opening up the cells, I got my psychic on and I said to her, 'I've just had a premonition about you. I don't know what it is, but you're doing something you shouldn't. You're going to be on the other side of a cell door before long.' She went white. And only a few weeks later, she was arrested for trying to organize the escape of Myra Hindley from Holloway.

On 1 February 1974, at the age of twenty-nine, she was sent for trial, and she ended up sitting in the cells below the Old Bailey with the rest of us. We met again in Styal Prison in Wilmslow, Cheshire, after being sentenced. Trish had got six years. I liked her very much, and we've stayed friends right up to date. Which is more that I can say for myself and Myra Hindley.

Trish was a lovely, lovely woman. Before joining the prison service, she'd spent time as a nun, and it was probably this training that made her such a nice officer. She was very pretty, with big brown eyes, black hair and a sweet little face. Her manner was shy and I knew from my own experience of her while I was on remand that she did what she could to make life more bearable for the women. Sometimes, at the end of the day, there'd be a lot of milk left over. While the other screws would take it home or put it down the sink rather than give it to the prisoners, Trish would open the cell doors and hand the milk in to the women. That's how good she was.

Trish had a special friend in prison. Her name was Jan, and she was also a warder. Jan was a wonderful officer, a sweetheart. She was very well-liked, and she thought the world of Trish. They were always together. She'd never been married, Jan. In fact she'd never had a boyfriend. Jan could hardly believe it, couldn't understand it at all, when Trish took up with Hindley. She realized Trish was being manipulated, but there was nothing she could do about it. When the whole thing finally came to a head, with Trish being arrested for trying to help Myra escape, Jan nearly had a nervous breakdown.

At first, Trish had treated Myra just like any other prisoner. But, gradually, she started feeling sorry for her because it looked as though she'd never get out. When Myra noticed this sympathy, she played up to it, turned on her pious act, and began to take advantage of Trish. Everyone else was aware that Myra was using Trish for her own ends. We used to say, 'It's a shame. Patricia Cairns is such a good officer, and Hindley has hypnotized her with the goody-goody routine.' We all knew Myra was pulling the wool over her eyes, although at this point, Myra wasn't on our wing, and nobody had any inkling of the impending escape bid.

I confronted Trish one day. I asked, 'How can you be friends with the scum of the scum, the real dregs at the bottom?' I told her she was a popular officer and wanted to know how she could let somebody like Hindley mesmerize her.

She turned to me and said, 'All prisoners are prisoners to me, all just numbers'. She told me that when she was a Carmelite nun she never read any newspapers, never heard about the Moors Murders and simply took Hindley as she found her when she met her in prison, craving forgiveness.

I said, 'Forgiveness? Crap!'

Trish replied, 'Everybody deserves forgiving. Anyway, I don't discuss other prisoners. I wouldn't discuss *you* with anybody else.'

Trish and Hindley used to make regular visits to the prison church where, apparently, they would talk to each other through a partition. There were a lot of rumours that they used to have sex there, but they both later denied it to me.

The escape plan itself had been an elaborate affair involving another prisoner. Maxine Croft was originally taken into the confidence of Trish and Myra because of her status as a trusted prisoner and her relative freedom to move around within the jail. She became a go-between, smuggling letters and presents to and fro between Trish and Myra. This was possible because of Maxine's cleaning duties in the officers' lounge, where there was a clock used by Trish as a hiding-place for items, which would later be collected by Maxine and given to Myra. Similarly, Maxine would store Myra's communications in the clock for subsequent pick-up by Trish.

Later, there were rumours all over the prison that an item connected to the escape was found in the clock by a screw. We never discovered exactly what it was. It certainly wasn't the camera, which Maxine had found previously hidden in the clock. She was persuaded to take a series of secret photographs in Myra's cell, one of which would be used for a fake passport – the intention being that Trish and Myra would run away together after the escape to become missionaries in South America. That's how infatuated Trish was: she was prepared to give up her job, her home, her friends, her family, everything, to become an exile abroad with Hindley.

In the next step towards the escape, Trish and Maxine collaborated in making plaster moulds of certain useful keys. Maxine was shortly to be released and entitled to go out of the prison every now and again on home visits. On one such home leave, she met up with Trish in central London. Together, they set off for one of the big railway stations where they planned to deposit the key moulds in a luggage locker. They arrived, however, to find the left-luggage service closed. And that's when it all went drastically wrong. Maxine suggested sending the moulds to a friend for safe keeping. But this friend became suspicious of the parcel, because of a recent spate of terrorist letter bombs and handed it over to a policeman. On discovering the makeshift keys and a letter from Maxine, he notified the Home Office straight away.

Maxine ended up breaking down and blabbing everything, insisting that she'd been too scared of Trish and Hindley to refuse to go along with them, or to report the plot. When it all came out in the Old Bailey, Maxine was sentenced to eighteen months but was later released on appeal. Hindley was given an extra year on her sentence.

In evidence for Trish, the court was told that her relationship with Myra was purely platonic, based on friendship and a shared Roman Catholic conviction. It was claimed that she organized the escape as an act of Christian duty, due to her belief that Myra Hindley had suffered enough and would never be fairly considered for release because of her notoriety. Trish was sent down for six years, and she would be serving part of that sentence in Styal Prison, Cheshire, when I next met her.

It was during her time in Styal that Trish had the next bit of trouble from Myra Hindley. Hindley had taken to sending her illicit love letters, using prisoners travelling from Holloway to Styal as carriers. Trish was furious. If these girls had been searched and found with the notes, they would have lost their remission, and Trish didn't want to see that happening to anybody. She sent a verbal message back to Myra with a girl who was going from Styal to Holloway. She said that if Myra sent so much as one more letter, she, Trish, would tell the governor, because people were at risk of losing even more of their liberty.

Myra responded by sending another letter, and Trish was as good as her word. She handed it in. The letter was subsequently slammed down in front of Hindley, who was outraged at what she saw as a betrayal by her disciple. She ranted and raved like a lunatic and insisted for quite some time afterwards that she wanted nothing more to do with Trish.

Trish, meanwhile, was in between the devil and the deep blue sea. In one sense, she'd already been with the devil, which is why she ended up in prison. But her particular dilemma in Styal was that she had no allies. The screws detested her because of her relationship with Myra Hindley. The prisoners detested her for the same reason but also because she had been a screw. She really did suffer. The screws used to put her down in the punishment block for the least little thing, anything they could get her on. She was sent there time and time again. But, in the end, I think it was a relief for her to go into isolation because it got her out of the way of the other women. She used to get diabolical abuse when she walked around on exercise. People would be yelling, 'Myra Hindley, murdering bastard!'

However, by the time I moved from Holloway to Styal, I'd developed quite a strong sympathy for Trish, not only because she was such a lovely person to begin with but also because I believed her good intentions in the escape plan. I'd also met and befriended Myra Hindley, and I understood her tremendous magnetism. I'd never have become besotted with Hindley in the way that Trish did, but I had succumbed to her charm and fallen for all of her tearful accounts of herself as a victim. (It wasn't until much later that I discovered the extent of her deception.) And so we became firm friends, Trish and I, and now that we were of equal status, a pair of numbers, she was able to talk to me about her feelings for Hindley. She told me over and over; I can still hear her voice in my head:

> *When I first met Myra I knew she was one of the lifers, I knew she was a convicted murderess, but I knew nothing about the Moors case at all. I'd been in the convent, as you know, and I got to know her before I knew anything about what she was involved in, so there was a difference there.*
>
> *I never asked her about the case, and she never volunteered any information. We never discussed anything like that. It was never of any interest to me, in part due to my training as an officer. Because when you're on the wing, it doesn't enter your mind what they're in for. They're just individuals. You wouldn't be able to do your work if you thought, Oh, that one's murdered her kid, That one's a dirty old prostitute and That one's a sodding thief. You don't think like that as a member of staff. I saw her as I saw her, just as an individual. I'd never associated her with what she was accused of, so that's why I still see her differently to most people, I suppose.*

Trish would often think about the escape plan. She'd say:

> *It was just sheer madness, really. Sheer, stupid madness. It couldn't have come off. Even if it had succeeded, what would we have done? You need plenty of money. Still, it's all in the past, and I won't be trying to spring her out again.*

I'd occasionally remind Trish about the day I had the premonition that she'd be behind bars herself soon, and she'd laugh and tell me, 'I think you're psychic. You should have stopped me. Then again, I wouldn't have taken any notice.'

I could never get Trish to explain why she'd been so determined to go ahead with a scheme that was obviously going to end in disaster. She agreed with me that it was a terrible thing to try to do on behalf of a convicted murderer, but she would never admit that she'd fallen so deeply under Myra Hindley's spell that she would have done absolutely anything for her. She'd reply, 'I wasn't coerced into it, Janie. I have a mind of my own. I knew what I was doing. Myra didn't force me into anything.'

Privately, Trish believed Myra's talk and writings about the 'pure love' between them. I didn't. Words are only words. The thing with Myra is that she's got to possess somebody, body, mind and soul, and that's exactly what she was trying to do with Trish. She did like Trish very much – that was clear enough from the writings I saw – but, at the same time, she knew she could mould her and use her. This was how a lot of prisoners thought. If they could pick and choose their friends from people who could help and fight for their freedom, if they could manipulate a screw who was a lesbian, then they would.

If Myra had really thought the world of Trish, if it was genuine, she wouldn't have talked her into helping her escape, she wouldn't have got her six years inside, and she wouldn't have ignored Trish's plea about the letters she was sending into Styal. There was no love there. Even though I was friendly with Hindley at the time and prepared to support any call for her release, I was upset by her treatment of Patricia Cairns. I told Trish that I believed Hindley could be very ruthless. She just replied, 'You have to be, to an extent, to survive. It depends upon your point of view, doesn't it?'

I'd already spoken to Hindley about all this in Holloway. I asked her 'How could you ruin such a good officer?'

She didn't seem too bothered and answered, 'As soon as I saw Trish Cairns walk on to the wing, I knew she'd be putty in my hands.' When she realized what she'd just said, she started back-pedalling, and quickly added, 'I became extremely fond of Trish. She was a grown woman and what she did, she did because she wanted to, not because I pushed her into it.' There was another reason, though, for me to doubt the value of her 'pure love' for Trish. And that was the fact that Myra had fallen in love with me during our months together in Holloway.

I thought it was important for Trish to see the light of day about Myra Hindley, so I showed her some poems Hindley had written for me. These declared that she idolized me above all others she'd ever met, that I was her whole world, the very breath in her body, and so on in her typical, flowery fashion. Again, they were only words, as I told Trish, and I didn't necessarily believe them. Trish was upset, but not to the extent that she'd hear a word against Myra. She remained under her hypnotic spell for many years to come – and it would lead her into another major scandal, long after we'd both been released from prison.

If I could have foreseen my own dramatic involvement with Myra Hindley, I would have fainted. When I was starting out on my sentence at Holloway, I rarely thought of her, and if I did it was only to hope that our paths would never cross. My main concerns were for my own sanity, for finding some way of keeping my head above water through the coming years of imprisonment.

Some of the women around me were absolutely hysterical. They'd be shouting and screaming and threatening to commit suicide. Even when they only had six months to do, they'd be plotting and planning ways to kill themselves. I used to get mad and tell them, 'You're only in for bed and breakfast. I got seven years, and I haven't even done anything to deserve it. I just made people happy.'

They wouldn't believe me. They'd say, 'You couldn't be in for seven years. Impossible. I'd be looking for a way to die if I were you. I'd hang myself.'

At times, I did plunge to that level of desperation. I'd think, God is this worth it? Maybe I could just do something quick. Then I'd think of my poor little mother, what a state she'd be in if anything happened to me, and my wonderful sister Beatrice, I'd say to myself, If it wasn't for them, I would definitely do something, there's no doubt about it. I cannot put up with all of this. And I'd just start singing, singing at the top of my voice, drowning out the prisoners who were weeping and wailing. The other women would be bellowing, 'Hey, shut up, shut up, Janie's singing,' and they would all quieten down, and then they'd start clapping and shouting out requests. I'd be singing anything, to keep them quiet and to forget my own troubles. At other times, I'd do a bit of mind over matter. I'd say to myself, Right, I've just got to calm down, and I'd put myself in a trance using yoga.

I'd try to keep my spirits up by thinking of my appeal and banking on it being successful. When it wasn't, I couldn't believe it . At first I was in despair. I'd be crying, Oh, my God, I can not do all this time. And then I forced myself to face reality: I'm just going to have to put up with it. I'd carry on as best I could and assure myself I'd be released when it came to my first application for parole. I wasn't. The second parole went down, too. I realized then that that was it. I'd just have to sit it out.

It was tremendously frustrating. I was seeing murderers getting out on their first parole, and there I was, still inside. Some of the most violent, violent girls you could ever imagine were being released – I think because they were too much trouble for the system to cope with. Yet the placid ones never seemed to win their parole. I used to study it all, and I could never accept the obvious injustices. In the end, I served four years out of the seven – which gave me plenty of time to sit and think about everything. My mind often dwelled on the people who'd put me in this predicament. I'd go back to how I'd met them and to the great times we'd enjoyed, and then I'd remember the trial and how, one by one, they stood up on that stand to put me behind bars so they could save themselves.

I thought of the Lord who liked the 'schoolgirls' and the teddy bears with particular contempt. I'd remember him going on and on about 'loyalty' and 'my word is my bond', and I'd stew over the fact that he finally didn't have the guts to stand up there and tell the truth about the money he gave me to fight the *News of the World*. You know, I'll come before him the day he dies. I will haunt him for ever for what he did to me. I was a fool, though. I never learned my lesson. I still hadn't learned it inside, as my experiences with Myra Hindley would later prove. I listened to all sorts of people in the nick, and I always lent a sympathetic ear, even when they were giving me bullshit.

One thing I never lost, though, was my sense of humour. That, coupled with a natural defiance, probably helped me more than anything as I came to terms with the truth: I would have to serve the lion's share of my sentence. I was only a little 'un in there. I'd never been heavier than eight stone in my life, and I went down to six-and-a-half in prison. But I got a strength from somewhere else, because I vowed to fight and fight that system inside, and I did, throughout my whole sentence. I fought for my rights, I did my best not to let the authorities get me down, and they didn't like that.

But at the same time, I did everything I had to do. I'd never refuse to do anything within the rules and regulations, in keeping with the regard I had for my northern background and the work ethic. My mother's visits were a constant reminder of this. She was a sweetheart and a tower of strength to me. Yet despite my attempts to fit in, people still made up stories about me because of my celebrity. At the beginning of my sentence, I met a woman called Maureen Bingham, who was arrested after telling journalists about her spying activities with her husband, David. Shortly afterwards, she was released from Holloway, and I was in the headlines again. The papers reported her as saying 'It's not like Janie Jones, you know. Nobody scrubbed my cell floor. I did it myself.' That was such crap. I used to scrub the floors all the time. Now and again girls would come up and say, 'I'll polish your floor if you get me some dog-ends.' Well, naturally you'd say yes. It was an honour for them to gaze upon my beauty! But most of the time, I did the floors myself.

There was all sorts of stuff in the papers. They said that in Holloway I had silk sheets and bubble baths. They said that the screws were my slaves and that I used to get them to leave my tea on a silver tray outside my cell every morning. They said I had a record player in my cell. Well, the 'bubble bath' was shampoo I used to swish up in the water. As for the silk sheets, the slaves and the silver tray – I wish! And I never had a record player in my cell. Ever. It was infuriating, because I didn't have the opportunity to defend myself against these allegations of favouritism. But, in the end, as usual, I just laughed it all off.

I spent quite a lot of time in prison just lying in my cell reminiscing, learning and drawing strength from childhood memories. I'd always had a resilience, a knack of conquering problems through an ability to see the funny side of things and a stubborn determination that whatever the situation, I wasn't going to let it beat me.

The day I first spoke to Myra Hindley in Anna Mendleson's cell was the day I decided to dabble in psychology, to analyse exactly how her mind really worked. I started watching and listening to Hindley from a discreet distance, only speaking when it was absolutely necessary in case she mistook my interest for an offer of friendship. However, after weeks of observation, my reactions to her slowly changed. Half of me still felt sick at the sight of her, but the other half was beginning to feel sorry. I felt sympathy because she was going to be in there, I believed, until the day she died.

She had a lot to put up with. The screws were coming out with the most terrible jibes at her, all the time, and she was constantly under the threat of attack from other prisoners. Yet, I'd noticed two sides to her. One was temperamental: if she couldn't get away with what she wanted, if something went wrong, she would throw a tantrum, she'd shout and perform, and they'd just lock her in her cell where she'd sit and sulk. The other side was very gentle and kind, and this was what made it so difficult to come to any real conclusions about the woman.

She loved children, really loved them. She'd always be cooing about her sister's little girl, and how she wished she could have gone to the christening. She used to love going to the prison's mother and baby unit, picking up the kiddies and making a big fuss of them with sweets and cuddles. She used to shriek with delight over them and tell the mothers, 'Remember me when you have her christened.' I found it absolutely amazing, given what she was in jail for, that so many women were willing to let her anywhere near their children, let alone kiss them. But, at the same time, I couldn't help thinking that if Hindley hadn't met Ian Brady, she might have been a fairly nice person, someone who could have had a normal family life with a man she was in love with.

She seemed so sweet and church-going, very righteous, and she couldn't stand any kind of violence. She'd been attacked herself of course, but she hated violence of any sort within the prison. She couldn't sleep in the dark. She had to have a night-light on all the time, which made me wonder on and off if she was, as she claimed, an innocent party to the Moors Murders – one who was suffering still from the nightmare of her experience.

Most of the time, she appeared to be shy, introverted and sensitive, sometimes breaking down in tears. She had great charm, too, which explained the number of women she had running round after her. The priest was also impressed by Myra, and she fascinated the education department and the welfare people. She had them all eating out of her hand. She spent years educating herself in prison, reading avidly and studying for degrees. It wouldn't surprise me if she'd also studied hypnosis, because she did have an indefinable power over certain people, something bigger than the sugar-and-spice nature of her own personal appeal.

Her daily routine was nothing out of the ordinary. She worked on her tapestry, she went to the education department, she took courses and she attended church. She occupied the rest of her time by reading, writing and listening to music, all kinds of pop music. She liked watching television, especially comedy programmes – she loved black comedy – but her trouble was that she didn't like going into the television room unless she was accompanied by somebody she felt safe with. She never knew when another prisoner was going to jump on her.

She wasn't a fussy eater, and never spent her prison wages on edible luxuries or picky diet stuff. She blew all her money on tobacco. Smoke, smoke, smoke. She never stopped. Yet, Myra Hindley seemed so normal and so vulnerable for most of the time that I decided, after much soul-searching, to become more friendly with her. The screws would say to me, 'She's a manipulator. We read the notes.' Others, who had particularly liked me and had particularly hated Myra, jeered openly. They said, 'Oh, so she's got you too now. You're bewitched, aren't you? You said you were never, ever going to associate with her.'

I had merely decided to give her the benefit of the doubt for the time being. I was prepared to give her the chance to tell me her side of the story, while remaining on my guard and bearing in mind the crimes she'd been convicted of. I could take my role as psychologist one step further. Then I would be able to make up my own mind about her. And so I started talking to Myra Hindley, telling her all about all the sexy goings-on with the two-way mirror at my celebrity parties. She'd read everything about it in the papers, from A to Z, and she thought it was wonderful to hear the stories first-hand. She'd laugh until she cried, waving her hand and spluttering, 'Oh, you are awful.' I'd go on about the different things that happened – the beautiful girls, the booze, the seven-foot bed and all the change-at-half-time exploits. And, eventually, she started to confide in me, very gradually at first. I suppose she thought that with all the things I'd seen and done, she could chat to me and say things that she couldn't, normally, to anybody else.

I would not pander to her, though. I used to laugh and joke and take the mickey out of her something rotten. I don't think anybody could have got round to the verbal with her like I could. She could be very witty herself, I discovered, although her humour could get quite weird now and again. She once opened a paper, looked through it, and said to me, 'Can you imagine it? They're at it again. "The Moors Murderess." I don't remember ever murdering a moor.'

Sometimes I'd give her back as good as I got. If we ever had any little argument, I'd say, 'You'll have a place on the moors for me next,' and she'd think that was hilarious.

More often, though, she was her familiar, demure self. I'd be winding up the screws, and she'd come on like a Mother Superior and say, 'Oh, you shouldn't be wicked like that. That's terrible.' She couldn't believe how I could be so cheeky to so many of the officers and prisoners, and yet get on so well with them. It was all a laugh and a joke to me. One of the best laughs I had with Myra, though, was when we went to see Spike Milligan, who came into the prison to do a concert. She really liked him – she'd seen him donkey's years ago – but she was afraid to be in the middle of so many prisoners in the audience.

I said, 'If you come with me, you'll feel better about it, especially with all the officers around.' It was a great show. We went to quite a few together, and no one picked a fight with Myra, because I was with her. She returned my help with a great deal of kindness when I had my migraines, a recurring feature of my life in prison and an ailment I had never suffered previously. These were incredibly violent attacks, which often lasted more than one or two days and brought on vomiting as well as unbearable headaches.

Hindley used to bring things in and out of the cell for me. She'd give me her hot-water bottle for my head, and she'd fuss over me like a mother hen. The other women used to say, 'Christ, how can you trust her coming into your cell all the time when you're only half awake?' I did trust her, though, on a practical level. And, by now, she trusted me enough too to regale me with her personal problems. She worried constantly about her age, her looks and her future. She'd fret, 'I look in the mirror, and I see a grey hair, and I go mad. I get premonitions and dreams that I'm an old woman of ninety in a wheelchair, being wheeled out of the front gate of the prison with silver hair.'

In reply, I'd crack my usual joke: 'Don't ever touch them. For every grey hair you pull out, you get sixty in its place.'

She'd laugh a lot, and then she'd become serious again. She'd tell me, 'I'm so distressed and upset. You're the only woman I've ever been able to pour my heart out to, really and truly.' As the friendship progressed, she poured her heart out more – or, at least, what she said was her heart. She talked for hours on end about Ian Brady and about the Moors Murders. My amateur psychology had begun in earnest.

Top: As a glamorous
fledgling, I was about to spread
my wings throughout all the
major West End clubs.
Centre: Here I am with
Christine Keeler, who stayed
in my flat for a while. As
hostesses at the Don Juan
Casanova, we began to mix in
really exclusive circles.
Bottom left: At the Windmill
Theatre, I could be a star.

Right: I wore a funereal black dress for my wedding to John Christian Dee, whom I came to call the Crank. Perhaps I was subconsciously anticipating our disastrous future.

Below: Enjoying the limelight: seen here at a Lionel Bart première with Marc Bolan.

Above: My sister Valerie's *Witch's Brew* cast its spell to become a smash hit for me.

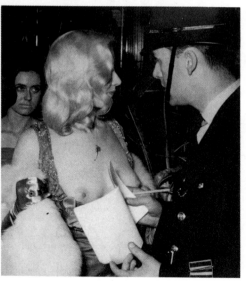

Top: My temptation of Richard Stamp, brother of actor Terence and Chris, who ran the Who's record label, Track. This is how I came to meet 'the most exciting rock band in the world'.

Left: Teasing in the spotlight: after sister Valerie and I appeared topless at the première of Michael Klinger's *London in the Raw*, we were offered money to do our act topless. But we wouldn't.

Above: Posing at home in front of my wardrobe mirror. In earlier days, the notorious two-way mirror, installed in the wall behind the wardrobe, was to make my celebrity parties so much fun.

Left: Englebert Humperdinck was another star attraction at my showbiz parties, along with other sixties pop stars such as Tom Jones and Cat Stevens. Actors, media personalities and DJs all turned up. We'd have a ball.

Top: In my regal old Rolls-Royce, parked in Campden Hill Road, the smart Georgian street in Kensington, where I lived and hosted my brilliant parties.

Centre above: Eric, my friend and virgin civil servant. He moved into my house in the 1960s and still lives with me to this day. At the parties, he kept a low profile: even the most beautiful women in the world wouldn't interest him.

Left: Flamboyant Zelda Plum, entertainer and hostess extraordinaire and a regular at my parties.

Above: Cynthia Payne, the luncheon-voucher madam, Lord Bath and I all pose for the camera at a birthday party at Longleat in the 1980s. I never thought it particularly impressive that she ran all those services for geriatrics in wheelchairs.

Right: In playful mood during the launch of a single which I recorded with the Clash in 1983, *House of the Ju-Ju Queen*. The 'judge' quaking in fear of me is holding *And Nothing But the Truth* by my trial judge, Alan Hamilton-King, QC. – *Anything But the Truth*, I called it.

Top right: The apparent innocence of Myra Hindley's schooldays: Myra, top row, second from the right, appears in a group photo of her netball team, 1956.

Far right: A youthful Myra Hindley on Blackpool Beach, long before I met her in Holloway Prison, and before she met Ian Brady.

Right: Myra Hindley and her lover Ian Brady, whose summer snapshot smiles give no indication of what was to follow. Myra told me: 'I clung to what little Ian offered me, for I could not envisage life without him any more'.

Below left: Myra Hindley, 1965, with pet dog. Once when she rescued a malnourished stray dog she'd said: 'I don't know how people can be so cruel'.

Below right: 16 Wardle Brook Avenue, Manchester, where Myra Hindley and Ian Brady lived. It was demolished after residents complained about macabre sightseers.

DANGER DEMOLITION

Left: Cold-eyed Myra Hindley in an angled snapshot, with her familiar black mascara and bleached blonde hair, enjoying a drink.
Below: The Moors Murderers at home with a pet cat. Animals were more their line: 'You should get a puppy, they're better than babies,' she told her sister.

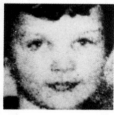

Above: Pauline Reade (top) on 12 July 1963 became the first victim of the Moors Murderers, followed by: John Kilbride, Keith Bennett and Lesley Ann Downey.

Right: After killing 17-year-old Edward Evans, the final murder victim, on 6 October 1965, Myra told me that Brady had commented: 'It's the messiest yet'.

Top left: With Myra's sister, Maureen Smith. Like me, over the years she'd become convinced by Myra's version of events.

Centre: Hindley the hunter, taking aim with Brady's rifle on the moors.

Below: Myra on the moors: They 'have no grisly connections . . . I am one of the people who does not know where the alleged graves are.' Years later, Myra admitted her lie:. she should have been strung up.

Above: Ian Brady after having been found guilty of three murders, 6 May 1966. Myra Hindley had stuck to her story that she was really just a love-struck bystander. My big mistake was to underestimate how very shrewd, cunning and clever Myra Hindley could be.
Right: David and Maureen Smith (Myra Hindley's sister) after giving evidence in the Moors Murder trial. On one of her favourite hobby-horses, Hindley used to bang on and on about David Smith, that he had far more to do with the murder than he ever admitted.

Above: With principal officer, Miss Golding, from Holloway Prison, I attended Bow Street magistrates' court. I had to try and sell my house from inside prison just to raise the money to pay my £16,000 trial costs.

Below: HMP Holloway. I wore my mink coat when I was driven off to prison to serve my sentence. As usual, I was keeping up appearances, but it became a lifeline to me. Because the prison was so cold in winter, I slept in it.

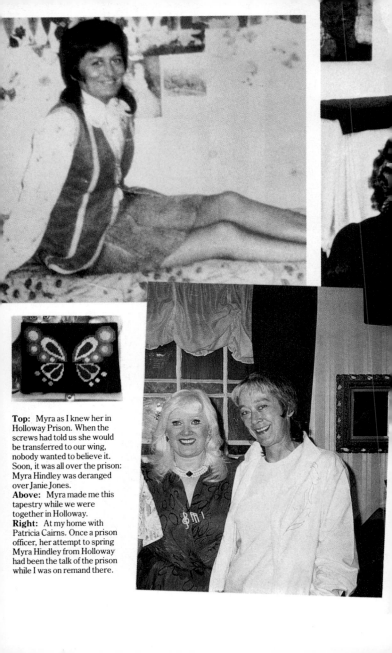

Top: Myra as I knew her in
Holloway Prison. When the
screws had told us she would
be transferred to our wing,
nobody wanted to believe it.
Soon, it was all over the prison:
Myra Hindley was deranged
over Janie Jones.

Above: Myra made me this
tapestry while we were
together in Holloway.

Right: At my home with
Patricia Cairns. Once a prison
officer, her attempt to spring
Myra Hindley from Holloway
had been the talk of the prison
while I was on remand there.

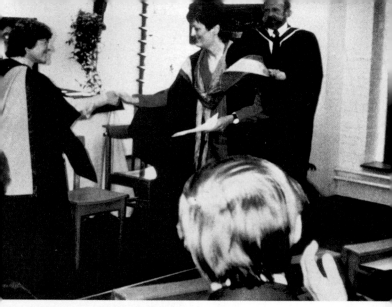

Top: Myra insisted that she had survived her years in prison by using the educational facilities. Here, in 1980, she receives her certificate for a BA degree – in the Humanities.
Above: Dorothy Wing, governor of Holloway prison. Her walk on Hampstead Heath with Myra was a mistake.
Left: A later prison picture with two pet dogs. She was silly about animals.

Top: Following Myra Hindley's confession, Det. Chief Supt. Peter Topping on Saddleworth Moor in July 1987, where police officers continued the search for more bodies following the discovery of Pauline Reade's body in a moorland grave. Myra had told me and the world that she did not know the whereabouts of the murdered children's graves. The change in her story made me realize I had been conned by her all along.

Right: Travelling by train to appear on a TV programme, *Brass Tacks*, July 1977, accompanied by Lord Longford. We and many others had campaigned for her release. Now I know differently: she should never be released.

CHAPTER TEN

Myra on the Moors

Moors Murderers Ian Brady and Myra Hindley have been immortalized as people who 'assaulted and killed children for "kicks"'. They were described by their trial judge, Mr Justice Fenton Atkinson, as 'sadistic killers of the utmost depravity'. In May 1966, at Chester Castle court, they were found jointly guilty of two murders – those of ten-year-old Lesley Ann Downey, of Ancoats, and seventeen-year-old Edward Evans, an engineering apprentice, of Ardwick. Brady was also convicted of the murder of twelve-year-old John Kilbride from Ashton-under-Lyne, with Myra Hindley found guilty of being an accessory after the fact.

More than two decades later, after co-operation from Brady and Hindley, police found the body of sixteen-year-old Pauline Reade from Manchester. She'd been missing since 1963, another victim, it is believed, of the Moors Murderers. Twelve-year-old Keith Bennett vanished from his home in Manchester in 1964. The police are still convinced that his body lies undiscovered, at some spot near to where the murderers buried Lesley Ann Downey, John Kilbride and Pauline Reade, in peat graves on the Pennine Moors.

When Myra Hindley first started talking to me about the Moors Murders, I gave her one simple warning: 'You can tell me as much or as little as you like, but don't ever lie to me, because if I find you out in lies, I'll nail you to the cross.'

The basis of her story, which I will go into in more detail a little later, was that she was not responsible for, or even present at, any of the murders. She blamed the whole lot on her lover Ian Brady and her brother-in-law David Smith, who was married to her sister Maureen. She swore that she could never murder a little child. She admitted only that she helped clean up after the murder of teenager Edward Evans in 1965, in the house that she and Brady shared with her grandmother, and that this was the only body she ever saw. Brady and Smith had killed him, she told me.

'I never entered that room except to go and mop up the blood,' she insisted.

I said, 'I couldn't have done that. I'd have been vomiting my guts up. In fact, I'd have raced out of that door and gone straight to the first policeman I could find.'

She replied, 'Well, I was frightened. I thought I could have been the next one.'

Hindley was emphatic that she had never even heard about the other murders, never mind suspect Ian Brady's involvement. I challenged her: 'You must have seen the newspapers.'

She replied, 'No, I didn't. I think Ian must have kept them away from me if there was anything in them about the murders. It would have been easy enough for him to do that. We only ever looked at the papers for the sports and entertainments pages.'

I carried on, 'Well didn't you see anything on television?' 'No,' she said. 'I rarely watched TV.'

I was sceptical. I told her, 'I find that very hard to believe.'

Sometimes she'd back down a bit and suggest that she could have been suffering from what she called 'overtones of selective amnesia' – blocking out any information that started alarm bells ringing in her head. But she remained adamant that she had no recollection of hearing anything about missing children. Myra also denied she'd ever suspected Brady of the gay inclinations he'd later been accused of or had noticed anything pointing to the reported physical attraction between him and David Smith. Similarly, she refused to admit knowing that Brady's motivation for murder was sexual. It was only much later, she said, that she'd started to think about these possibilities.

She told me, 'I knew nothing about Ian going to homosexual clubs until it came up at the trial. I was absolutely stunned. Looking back, I think it's feasible that there was something going on between him and David. They were always together, the pair of them, plotting and planning things.' What they plotted and planned, usually when Myra had gone to bed, were armed robberies and murders.

I asked, 'You knew they were chatting about murders?'

She answered, 'Yes, but I thought it was only talk, after they'd had a few drinks. I never imagined it would actually happen.'

She also said to me, 'In retrospect, I think it's possible that Ian had it off with Edward Evans.'

I came straight back at her: 'What you're trying to say is that he got his jollies out of murdering.' 'Well,' she said, 'that's how it must have been.'

Maybe she did know all about the gay aspect at the time. Maybe she didn't. I never knew what to believe on that, but I do know that whatever Brady had wanted to do, he'd have done anyway, and Myra had two choices. She could either stand by or go. She'd never have gone. She idolized him: he was the god on the pedestal.

She told me she met Ian Brady when she began work in a typing pool of a Manchester chemical firm. It was 1961, and she was eighteen years old. He was already employed there as a stock clerk, several years her senior. At the time, she was engaged to a policeman, but it was Brady she soon started writing about in her diary every day, what he wore and what he said to her. She'd note down every little disappointment – 'The swine walked straight past without looking at me, again.' She continued to be an avid writer in prison, Myra. She was always composing 'learned' poems and essays and documents based on her own experiences, and many of these she showed or gave to me.

But, I digress. To return to Brady, she thought he was wonderful, and she fell madly in love with him. She dumped the policeman without ever having slept with him, she claimed. But it was a long time before

Brady asked her out. During the months of waiting and hoping, Myra Hindley lurched to and fro on an emotional roller-coaster. She confided, 'My feelings for him ranged from loving him desperately to almost hating him, from the total despair and hopelessness of unrequited love to wild, passionate hopes and prayers that he would somehow begin to share and return my feelings for him.'

When he finally did invite her out on a date, almost a year later, it was like a dream come true. They started going to see films about the Nuremberg rallies. By all accounts, he was a Hitler-lover, Brady, and I gave Hindley hell about it. I told her several times, 'You must have known he was a bit of a crank if he took you to see Nuremberg rally films.' She always just shrugged and replied, 'I was in love with him.'

I wanted to know what had attracted her to him so wildly. She told me that, oh, he was fantastic-looking, he had confidence, there was something about him that was different to other men and, in her own words, her feeling for him 'soon became an obsession'. She said she was enthralled by his 'powers of persuasion and his lofty, convincing means of speech'. She didn't understand a lot of what he was saying at the time, but what she did grasp, she held as gospel truth. She recalled in writing:

He convinced me that my faith, that all religions, were superstitions instilled in us as conventional norms. Religions, he said, were a crutch people used to hobble through life on, the opium of the people. And I believed him because I thought I loved him, and his arguments were so convincing, he demolished my tiny precepts with a single word . . . .

I now look back with incredulity to the teenager that I was, who allowed her whole world to revolve solely around one man who soon became the sole focus of her existence.

Because he wasn't very sociable and was reluctant to get to know either my friends or my family, my world became gradually almost confined to him.

But, in those early days of the relationship, she remained what she always referred to as a Saturday-night-stand – which only fuelled her adoration. She once wrote:

Although I saw him almost every day at work and every Saturday, with just an occasional week-night thrown in at first, for most of my

*free time he just wasn't available. He didn't volunteer much informa-
tion about his private life . . . .*

*Because our relationship was new and very unsure, I was
afraid to do or say anything which might jeopardise it, so I stifled my
curiosity and accepted what little information he volunteered.*

*When our relationship first began, I was stupid and naïve
enough to believe it would eventually lead to marriage. But I soon
learned that marriage was foremost amongst the things that Ian
didn't believe in, and I resigned myself to nothing more than an
affair.*

*Although it was the first and only affair I had ever had, and I
knew that my family were unhappy with the situation, I clung to what
little Ian offered me, for I simply could not envisage life without him
any more, even though I could hardly describe myself as happy or
contented. It was, at best, a tenuous, unsettled relationship, but I
cannot deny that I didn't prefer it to an existence from which he was
absent.'*

It was when Brady bought a motor-bike that they began to see
each other far more regularly, often riding out of town for a drink or two
in a country pub. She stated that although she could not honestly say she
felt particularly secure, 'a pleasant sense of permanency' entered the
relationship, and Brady moved in with Myra and her grandmother.
During this period, the pair started visiting the moors around Manchester, spending warm evenings and weekend afternoons just sitting in the
peace and quiet, soaking up the scenery. Myra kept enthusing about
them, dreamily, as places of 'lovely countryside and peaceful moorland.'
In one of her persuasive pieces of prose, she declared:

*I must make some explicit reference to these moors as people think
about them with reference to me. I want to state that as far as I am
personally concerned, the moors, and Saddleworth Moor in particular, have no such grisly connotations . . . .*

*It is ironic, to say the least, that in spite of the charges found
against me, I am perhaps one of the only people concerned who still
does not know where the alleged graves were.*

Many years later, Myra Hindley herself would dramatically expose
this statement for the lie it was. She should've been strung up: this,

after all, was crucial to her claims of innocence in the murders, and to the argument with which she won over her allies. She proclaimed it so often, so convincingly, so tearfully, and to so many people throughout the time I knew her, that I could recite it backwards in my sleep.

I was, as I said, keeping an open mind about Myra, and I pursued my lines of questioning with the determination of a true psychologist. I was particularly interested in the sexual side of her dealings with Ian Brady, in the light of his known sadistic and gay tendencies and her boast that he was the one and only man she'd ever had.

I asked her straight out, 'Well, how did he have it then?'

She giggled, 'Oh, you are awful . . . .'

I pressed the point: 'Let's be honest. When you had it off with him, was it all lovey-dovey and the normal thing?'

She responded, 'He'd usually come to bed after playing cards with David Smith, who was around most nights, and we always did it in the dark.'

I said, 'What? Couldn't he bear to look at you in the light?'

She shook her head, 'It's not that. It's just that he was shy, and so was I.'

'Did you enjoy it?' I probed.

'Well, it was nothing, really,' she said. 'I'd never known it before so I couldn't compare it to anything else. It didn't mean anything.'

I was amazed, and I kept on interrogating her. 'So here you were with this fantastic, good-looking man you were head-over-heels in love with and he just didn't do anything for you?'

'I just wanted to be with him,' she declared. 'I loved him, but I think he just used me. That's all.'

'So,' I said, 'this man who was so different to all other men came to live with you and your grandmother and turned out to be as strait-laced as anybody else, if not more.' She fidgeted and said nothing, but I wouldn't let her off the hook. 'When Brady used to go to bed with you, did you do it doggy-fashion?' I demanded.

'Oh, you are terrible,' she hedged, with her familiar little-girl laugh and a coy Princess Di look of embarrassment.

It didn't work. I rephrased the question: 'Did he do it like he was with another boy?'

'Oh, no,' she said, realizing I wasn't going to be deterred. 'It was just normal.'

I persevered. 'Did he whip you and tie you up, what with him being into violent things like the Nuremberg rallies?'

'No, nothing like that.'

I wasn't convinced, and I told her my opinion: 'You were mesmerized by the biggest crank there ever was. He was into violence, but you want me to believe he was going to bed with you all sweet and normal. I can't believe that.'

She stuck to her story, but it turned out that I'd hit the nail right on the head. When I came out of prison and read up on her case history, it emerged that photographs existed of Myra, nude and semi-nude, as the submissive partner in a bondage situation with Brady. He did tie her up. He did whip her. He did injure her. It came out in evidence in their trial.

From what she told me of her childhood and teenage years, she wasn't any stranger to aggressive behaviour. Her father was a bit violent, and when her younger sister, Maureen, married David Smith, she saw violence there, too. I think that, maybe, she had grown used to being treated violently, but was too sensitive to other people's opinions to admit it. She might have enjoyed it, or she might have felt, subconsciously, that she deserved to be punished. Certainly, on the one occasion I saw her being viciously attacked in prison, she offered no resistance, just took it like a rag doll.

The contradiction was that she used to shake like a leaf if she heard any trouble starting elsewhere in the wing, which made me wonder if the explanation could be staring me straight in the face: she might have involved herself in sado-masochism purely and simply because she loved Ian Brady. She'd fallen out of love with him in a big way by the time I met her. She wasn't in touch with him. She said she detested him, that he was the worst thing that had ever happened to her. She'd loved him, yes, but she wished she'd never met him because of these terrible things that he'd got her mixed up in.

I once asked her, 'Do you think you would have ended up in prison if you'd married the policeman?'

She said, 'No.'

I believed that. And to be truthful, I still do, even though my opinions of Hindley have changed dramatically since our days together in Holloway. If she'd married the copper, she would probably have gone down a different avenue altogether, one which didn't involve cruelty and lies and manipulation. It was the union of those two people – Myra Hindley and Ian Brady – which ignited the fire of destruction. Whatever he could have asked her to do, she would've done, just to keep his love.

I understood the power of obsessive love and how it changes people – in the same way that I knew the power of fear, through my own experiences with the Crank. I was prepared to accept that Myra Hindley could have been driven to extremes of uncharacteristic behaviour through both of these furious emotions, one coming hard on the heels of the other. Her version of each event, individually, was plausible, if unlikely. Her version of the whole story was, therefore, plausible, if very unlikely. But, as I said to my cell-mate Jenny, there was always that slight chance that Myra was telling the truth. I was sure that at least some of her account was genuine, and I would have felt very disappointed in myself to have disregarded this.

I thought about her central argument, that Brady and Smith were the murderers. Well, Brady was a weirdo, and Smith had a history of violence dating back to his early teens. It wasn't beyond the bounds of possibility that they were the culprits, and that Myra really was just a love-struck bystander. Then I considered her claim that she hadn't seen or heard any press coverage of the murders other than Edward Evans's. I said to Jenny, 'Let's say Brady and Smith had done it all – two cranks who might have had homosexual tendencies, getting their jollies out of murdering youngsters. It's obvious that they wouldn't want Myra Hindley to know, especially since she was living with one and related to the other.'

I had to bear in mind Myra's normally caring personality and her persuasiveness. She was very, very convincing. She'd get distressed and cry real tears in her confessions and talk about her pain, and I did feel sympathy. I ended up feeling really sorry for her. Mind you, I still wasn't ready to believe Myra Hindley's every word, sobbing or no sobbing. I'd memorize every single word she told me, and I'd go back to my cell and sit with Jenny planning trick questions, writing them down in a note-book, to see if I could catch her out. I used to lie awake at nights trying to work out more ways to trap her. I used to get her to tell the same stories over and over again, waiting for her to get a tiny detail different. She never did.

I'd say, 'I'm going to ask you a question, and I don't want you to think about what you say. I want you to speak immediately. If Brady and Smith committed the murders and you had nothing to do with them, then you'll be able to answer me straight away, and you'll tell me exactly the same as you've always told me.' And, my God, she would come shooting back the right answers every time. We never once caught her out on a contradiction. But even then, I didn't want to commit myself to believing the word of Myra Hindley. In confusion, I went to the church to pray for advice.

I said, 'Please, God, I've been in here, and I've got seven years, but what have I really done? I've talked to you about this before and you've said back, "Well, look at me, look what they did to me." I used to think, That's right.

'I've never asked you for anything for myself, and I know it's awful to start asking now, but I don't know what to believe about Myra Hindley. She is starting to convince me. She really is a clever woman. I'm pleading with you to let me know if she's telling me the truth. Could you just give me a sign, so that I know whether or not she's conning me rotten? Is she just a pathological liar?'

I went back to my cell and Jenny was there. So was Myra. I looked at her and I said, 'There's nothing for you to worry about. I just want you to stay where you are and look at me, without turning away for a second.'

She said, 'What for?'

I replied, 'Never mind, "What for?" Has there got to be a "What for?"? Just look at me.'

She looked at me, and she kept looking, and I was looking at her. Then I got the shock of my life. She appeared to be coming off the bed, floating upwards, and she was surrounded by all the most beautiful colours of the rainbow. She was saying, 'What are you doing? I feel like I'm rising.' She saw the colours too.

I squealed, 'Christ! What are *you* doing?'

She said, 'I feel all funny.'

'Just forget it,' I stammered. 'Leave me alone for a minute.' She went out of the cell, and I talked to Jenny about it. Jenny hadn't been aware of what had happened, even though she was in the cell, watching. I confessed, 'I've never seen anything like that before. It's frightened the life out of me, that has. I don't know what it was.'

Jenny said, 'I've never heard of anything like this happening before.'

I assumed I'd been given the sign from God that I'd asked for, assuring me that Myra had been telling the truth – maybe because, by now, I wanted to believe a lot of the things she'd said. Months later, when I went to Styal Prison, I spoke to a psychiatrist about this experience. I told him I thought God had given me a sign. 'No, you just hit some sort of wavelength,' he replied.

'Wavelength? What bloody wavelength?' I demanded.

He tried to explain, but the more he said, the less I understood what he was talking about. As far as I was concerned, the belief I'd had in Myra since the day I'd received the 'sign' would continue, and I would misguidedly go on to become one of her strongest supporters. My big mistake was to underestimate just how very shrewd and cunning and clever Myra Hindley could be.

She told me first about Lesley Ann Downey, the young girl whose murder horrified the nation and has still never been forgotten, not least because of the hair-raising evidence produced in court. This included a tape recording of the terrified child's last minutes of life, begging for mercy, and a series of photographs intended for sale to paedophiles for large amounts of money. Taken in Myra's bedroom, the pictures showed the naked youngster gagged with a scarf and posing 'indecently' in a way no little kid would naturally do – unless she'd been made to.

Lesley Ann went missing after visiting a Christmas fair near her home on Boxing Day 1964 – an event which, according to Myra, 'shattered my life into fragments'. It was alleged that Hindley had tempted the young girl from the fairground to the house where she lived with Ian Brady. Brady counter-claimed that David Smith brought the girl to the house after she agreed to pose for ten shillings (50p). At the house, Lesley was reportedly made to undress, pose for the pictures with the gag in her mouth and submit to sexual abuse. She was then apparently killed for fear of what she would be able to tell people afterwards.

The fifteen-minute-plus tape recording features Hindley's voice saying to the girl, 'Shut up or I'll forget myself and hit you one,' and, 'Put that in your mouth.'

Brady instructs the child, 'Put it in.'

For her part, the little one is begging, 'Don't undress me, will you?' She's screaming. She's yelling, 'Don't – please, God, help me.'

Brady later said in evidence in court, 'After completion, we all got dressed', thus compounding the prosecution's argument that the photo session, terrifying in itself, served a further purpose, a sexual one, for Ian Brady and Myra Hindley – a thrill only surpassed for both of them by the ultimate act of murder. The final, chilling detail was in the background of the tape: a recording of Christmas carols, among them 'The Little Drummer Boy'.

When Myra talked about the case, the versions she gave me matched in every detail the account she later wrote in a mile-long document for the Home Office, supporting her plea to be considered for parole. The only difference was that her verbal style was conversational, while the tone of her writing was very formal and 'educated'. Her statement said:

> At my trial, numerous allegations were made – among them being that I lured her [Lesley Ann Downey] from a fairground back to my house where a tape recording was made of an alleged orgy involving torture and pornographic photographs, and the child being subsequently killed and buried on Saddleworth Moor.
>
> That she was found buried on Saddleworth Moor is beyond dispute. That I lured her to my house, that an orgy or torture of any kind took place, and that she was killed either by me or with my knowledge, let alone my consent or co-operation, is a matter of dispute, matters which I strongly denied at my trial and which I shall continue to deny until my dying day, for it simply isn't true.

She told me that the photographs were taken after the tape

recording was made, and that this had 'reluctantly' been conceded by the prosecution. She kept saying that the photos showed that Lesley Ann had not been touched or marked in any way, and that she appeared to be 'relatively calm and showed no signs of fear or great stress'. According to Myra, David Smith wasn't present when the tape recorder was on. He was, however, present when the photographs were taken. His presence, together with the fact that Lesley Ann finally believed she 'wasn't going to be hurt or physically harmed', accounted for her calm composure in the pictures. Therefore, the tape, recorded previously, was not the 'death document' the public seemed to believe.

Myra acknowledged that 'the general consensus of opinion is that these photographs and the tape recording are the ultimate in torture and obscenity.' She also admitted that 'they were both degrading and grossly insulting to the child, and with regard to the recording, frightening in the extreme.' But she insisted that Lesley Ann left the house with David Smith, 'alive and physically unhurt'. She added in her statement:

That she was emotionally affected I do not attempt to deny, but I stress that for as long as she was in my house and thus in my company, she came to no physical harm. She was not killed in my house or anywhere else within my personal knowledge. My involvement in the whole unsavoury business ended when she left the house, less than an hour after she'd arrived.

At the time of the trial and also for some years afterwards, I was totally convinced of Ian Brady's innocence of the charge of murder. For when David Smith and the child left the house, Ian remained with me . . . .

It was a long time later when going over the whole sequence of events in my mind, searching my memory for everything I could recall, that I recollected although he remained with me on Boxing Night, he spent the following afternoon and night away from home, telling me he was going to pay a belated Christmas visit to his mother . . . .

I have often wondered whether his absence that following evening had anything to do with events of the previous one.

I have heard Myra Hindley tell the story of Lesley Ann Downey many times, but the official, written version is the one that covers everything she told me in the sum total of our conversations. It states:

> *On the evening of 26 December 1964, I had no idea that anything untoward was about to happen. It was my grandmother's eldest son's birthday, and as had been the custom for many years, I took her round to his house sometime during the day to spend the afternoon and evening there, planning to pick her up around 9 p.m.*
>
> *Ian and I were alone in the house after tea, watching TV, when someone knocked at the door. Ian went to answer it. Ten minutes or so passed . . . .*
>
> *Then I was called by Ian into the hall where he and David Smith and a child, a girl, were waiting. Ian told me, without preamble, that he was going to take some photographs of her and wanted me to be there as 'insurance' in case they ever fell into police hands, so I could be a witness that nothing other than the taking of photographs had taken place.*
>
> *I began to remonstrate immediately, shocked at the idea of a child being photographed, and indignant that they proposed to do it at my house.*

Myra said that she then had an argument with Brady. He told her that he and Smith had planned to take photographs of an eighteen-year-old girl, but that Smith had instead turned up with this young child who was known to him (Smith). Brady then, apparently, told Myra that he was reluctant to be involved but didn't want to lose face in front of David Smith.

'I said I wasn't having anything to do with it and didn't want him to do it either,' said Myra. 'But after arguing again for several minutes, he just looked at me and told me to please myself.' Her statement adds:

> *I know now and probably knew then that it was at this point that I could and should have stuck to my refusal, for it was my house and there was no obvious force involved. I should have said no, but I didn't, for I felt that in those words, 'Please yourself,' my whole future with Ian Brady lay in the balance.*

That was the story of Myra. She did what Brady wanted all the time, and that was one of the reasons I believed her version of events: because of the total power and influence he had over her. She admitted in writing:

We had had disagreements before, though not nearly so serious as this one, and I almost always ended up having to acquiesce – even about matters like where we went on holiday . . . .

Before I met him, I had a very strong character, but Ian Brady's character and personality were such that my whole individuality became completely submerged in him, almost to the point of complete submission.

I think it was partly because of his forceful nature and selfish character that I became so fascinated by him, never able to fathom out what it was that had such an effect on me, that caused me to become so submissive and pliable when all the time I deeply resented the situation and was often filled with self-disgust.

Yet I remained fascinated and unable to extricate myself from my tangled emotions. But I knew the decision over the matter of the photographs was one which would affect my whole life and change it completely, whichever way I decided. Even though our relationship had survived over three years by then, I had never felt secure or completely sure of him . . . .

So I felt that if I pleased myself and refused, where the photographs were concerned, there was a strong possibility that he would leave me.

For him to lose face was, I knew, an almost unforgivable thing and if I were the cause, it would be even worse. So even though I knew I would surrender all my self-respect and a great deal of my misplaced respect for him too, and shrinking from contemplating the consequences, I agreed to what was proposed.

I tried to justify it by telling myself that it wouldn't take long, that the child would not be harmed, and all sorts of other excuses.

Myra told me she didn't know which district Lesley Ann came from and had no knowledge of fairgrounds. She also said that when Smith brought the girl to the house, he insisted that Lesley Ann was aware of what was going to happen, had agreed and had received some money.

'I don't even have the excuse that she looked older than she was,' said Myra. 'She looked exactly what she was: a child of ten.' She recalled that she started to follow Brady and Lesley Ann upstairs, by which time Hindley was 'extremely tense and uptight'. On the way, she stopped to have a short argument with Smith, saying she would never forgive him for what he had done, and that if he wasn't married to her sister and friendly with Ian, she'd never have him near her door again. She claimed that at this point, she heard a scream from upstairs, and ran up to the bedroom where 'Ian was remonstrating with the child'. Myra's Home Office statement continued:

> I cannot recall what my first words were, but because I was so frightened that the neighbours would hear and perhaps come and investigate, I must have told her to be quiet or to shut up, and I did this several times during the next ten minutes or so.
>
> For from the moment that Ian had told her to take her coat off, the child had panicked and become very frightened . . . .
>
> I wasn't very far off hysteria. I knew I was brusque to the point of cruelty, for I was so frightened about the noise, and instead of trying to calm her quietly, which I should have done, I probably frightened her even more . . . .
>
> At the time, I was unaware of the true value of fear in that room, fear from the child, from myself and probably from Ian too, for I don't think he had expected what was happening.

Myra said she tried to quieten the situation in the room and then ran out to fetch David Smith who had remained downstairs. She found him out on the front path and told him to come to the bedroom because the child had panicked. Her writings stated:

> When I returned to the bedroom, Ian was trying to put a handkerchief into the child's mouth to prevent her from making a noise. Several times on the tape, the words 'Put it in your mouth' are heard.
>
> This point was strongly taken up by the prosecution who were implying that it was something very different to a handkerchief . . . .
>
> What has continued to be ignored is the fact that my voice is recorded as saying, 'Bite hard on it'. I would hardly have suggested such a thing had it been anything other than a handkerchief.
>
> By making the point that it was a handkerchief and nothing else she had in her mouth does not mean I am glossing over the fact that it was shameful treatment of a young girl anyway. It was, and I have never tried to deny it.
>
> I can only say that I was acting under stress and out of

character, that I behaved disgracefully, but that the whole situation, as bad as it was, was a far cry from what it has been alleged to be.

When Hindley first told me about the gag in the girl's mouth, I felt physically sick. I said, 'Oh, my God, the poor little thing. I don't want to hear any more today. I feel ill, just on that.' We returned to the subject on later occasions, and she kept repeating that she was more frightened than the little girl. She simply wanted to get the photographs taken quick, so that Smith could take the kiddie back to her mother. Myra said that Lesley Ann eventually relaxed, and while Brady prepared to take the photographs, she switched on the radio. Among the songs that filled the room was 'The Little Drummer Boy'. She promised me that this was neither a perverse soundtrack, nor an effort to create 'normal' background noise, as many people had assumed. It was just an incidental detail.

The gospel according to Myra carried on that shortly after Brady unplugged the tape recorder – which she did not know had been switched on in the first place – David Smith came into the bedroom and the photo session began. Myra's Home Office confession stated:

At this point I had had enough and just wanted it all to be over. I had nothing at all to do with the photographs. I was there because Ian had asked me to be.

I was both ashamed and embarrassed and stood with my back to the room, half behind the window curtain. I heard David Smith telling the child to take off her clothes, which she did herself and without objecting. It was obvious that she had some kind of trust in him. For whereas Ian and I frightened her, he didn't . . . .

The radio was still playing and stood on the window ledge, so that whilst I could hear their voices, I couldn't distinguish what was being said. The whole thing lasted only ten minutes, after which the child dressed herself.

I asked her: 'Were they abusing that child?'

She swore on her mother's life that they weren't. Myra said that while there was 'widespread belief that those photographs depicted all kinds of outrages', including pseudo-religious poses, it was not true that they had included torture shots or pictures of the girl's hands tied with rope. She did her utmost to convince me that the child was at no time restrained, while admitting that 'she does appear in the photographs with a scarf tied loosely around the lower part of her face, which Ian said would prevent identification.'

Lesley Ann, she insisted, left with Smith in a dark-coloured van, and Myra never saw her again. Later that evening, she revealed, Brady told her that a tape recording had been made as another piece of 'insurance'. He said he hadn't liked the set-up, especially since a third person, whom he didn't know, was waiting for David outside in the van. According to Myra, Brady then also told her that Smith had contacts who would buy 'blue photographs'. Ian had agreed to take the pictures for his share in the money-making scheme. Said Hindley, 'I told him that I was worried and frightened about the whole thing, and asked him to destroy the photographs as well as the tape. He assured me later that he had.'

She contended that she was present some days afterwards when Brady informed Smith that the photos had not come out because they'd been exposed to the light, and that she now believed this conversation was held purely for her benefit. She was also emphatic that Smith said he'd dropped the girl off home. At the trial, Smith denied that he'd been anywhere near Hindley's house at the time of the abduction. With Myra's sister Maureen as his alibi, he stated that he'd been out with his wife.

Despite the widespread newspaper coverage of the hunt for Lesley Ann, Myra insisted:

I don't ever recall reading about a missing child. I can say in all honesty that I don't ever recollect reading or hearing about Lesley Downey's disappearance. I mixed with very few people apart from Ian and my family and colleagues at work and even had there been anything, 'a child named Downey' would have meant nothing to me, as the child at the house had given her name as Westwood, which can be heard on the tape recording.

As for the recording itself, Myra told me that she was later 'appalled' not only by the fact that it still existed, but by its contents. She added: 'To be involved in such a situation is one thing. To read a transcript of the event in black and white almost a year later – and to know that the child was then dead – is something I can never erase from my memory.' In her statement, she claimed:

> To say that I was filled with shame, disgust and despair is to barely scratch at the surface of emotions . . . .
>
> That the tape was horrific I do not deny. I myself would have described it as such when I first heard it. But it was neither a recording of torture, an orgy or anything along those lines. There was a lot of thoughtless cruelty involved in trying to keep the child quiet, but it was confined solely to verbal cruelty.

Her final comment was this:

> Believing that the things [tape and photos] had been destroyed and that therefore some of the guilt about the event had been somewhat assuaged, I did my utmost to force the memory of that evening out of my mind. It wasn't very difficult to do because my mind and whole being rejected the idea of it all, and it was only by refusing to think about it, consciously, that I could continue to live with myself.

I, personally, was torn in two over all of this. On the one hand, I felt that Myra Hindley should have been boiled in hot fat for her part in the gagging and photographing of Lesley Ann Downey. On the other hand, I was convinced that Myra had had nothing to do with the murder of the kid and that she genuinely believed she had been taken home. All of a sudden, I had more to worry about than my own seven years and more people to think about than myself. I would even dream about them: Myra Hindley, Ian Brady, Lesley Ann Downey – and Edward Evans, whose story she told me next.

CHAPTER ELEVEN

Deadly Persuasions

Myra Hindley met Edward Evans for the first time after Ian Brady picked him up at Manchester Central station, with the intention of later killing him. Evans was an apprentice with a large electrical company, local to Hindley and Brady. He was a good-looking seventeen year old and, allegedly, a homosexual who frequented gay night spots around Manchester. The Moors Murder jury heard and believed that just after pub closing-time on 6 October 1965, Brady (who'd met Evans before) picked him up at the station as his next murder victim. Myra Hindley, waiting nearby in her car, was introduced as Brady's sister, apparently so that Brady's sexual invitations to Edward would seem convincing. She drove Brady and the young lad back to their two-bedroom council house in Wardle Brook Avenue, Hattersley – scene of the photographic session with Lesley Ann Downey. Upstairs, Myra's grandmother was in bed, having taken her sleeping pills.

Brady's plan to murder Edward Evans was motivated by more than sex. It was intended as the ultimate step in their joint corruption of David Smith. Myra went round to her sister's house to fetch Smith, who had spent months reading books about violence and sadism, reportedly plotting robberies and murders with Brady and going on shooting practice on the moors with guns and bullets provided by Hindley. She got Maureen and David Smith out of bed and went into the house with the excuse that she needed to leave a message with them for her mother. She then asked David to see her home because she was frightened to be out on her own in the dark.

When they arrived at Myra's, she tempted Smith indoors with the promise of some booze. He was shown into the kitchen where Brady was fiddling around with bottles of alcohol. Brady then went out to the living room, and a couple of minutes later, Smith heard a blood-curdling scream, the first of many. Then he heard Hindley yelling, 'Dave, help him!' He raced into the living room where he saw Brady flailing a hatchet, hacking at young Edward's head and writhing body, over and over again, like a madman. Brady then finished him off by strangling him with a length of flex.

As Smith surveyed the blood-splattered room in horror, Brady remarked matter-of-factly, 'It's the messiest yet.'

Myra, meanwhile, had returned to the room after running upstairs to reassure her grandmother, who was awakened by the terrible noise. Hindley said she herself had been screaming because she'd dropped something on her toe. With granny dozing off again, Brady, Hindley and Smith set about mopping up all the blood. They trussed Edward up with string, wrapped the body in a big plastic sheet and hid it away in Hindley's bedroom, which was then locked. They planned to bury Edward on the moors the next day. But when Smith returned home, he was sick with revulsion and fear. He confessed the whole thing to his wife, and together they went to the police.

Myra's version of events was, of course, quite different. She used to tell me, 'I still don't know the truth behind the murder of Edward Evans.' She said the evening began with a visit from David Smith, who was riddled with debts and had come round to ask for the loan of some money. When Smith left, Brady and Hindley went for a drive into Manchester. On the way, they saw a dog being hit and slightly injured by the car in front of theirs. Myra claimed she spoke to its owners and offered to drive them to a vet, but they declined. She attached great importance to this incident, because she believed it proved that she had no 'sinister plans' for the night.

As they drove past Manchester Central, Brady asked to stop, saying he fancied a drink before the station buffet closed at 10.30 p.m. Myra waited in the car, which she parked on a double yellow line. While she was there, she said, a policeman strolled up. She told him she was waiting for her boyfriend and would be moving on any minute. The copper said he would walk round the block, but that if she was still there when he got back, he would have to book her. She pointed to this as further proof of her own innocent intentions and said, 'If I had any idea of what was going to happen, I would not have agreed to take Evans anywhere, in case my number had been written down, or the policeman had taken special notice of the car.'

At the same time, Myra wasn't that happy to see Brady walking back to the car with someone else. Ian, she said, introduced Edward as 'a friend of his' who was coming back to the house for a drink. She claimed she was 'surprised and annoyed', because she had to go to work the next morning; she'd been planning on an early night. When they arrived home, Brady told Myra to go for David Smith. She said, 'I complained about this, knowing it would turn into another of their all-night sessions, boozing and playing card games. But I set off to his house on foot, which was only a minute or two away.'

Myra denied that Smith was in bed when she rang the buzzer. Far from it, he was fully dressed and looked as though he'd been expecting her. She went back home with Smith and went into the kitchen to feed her two dogs. What she told me happened next she repeated, in detail, in her Home Office statement. In that she declared:

> *I was standing at a cabinet, about to open a can of dog food, when I suddenly heard the sound of a chair scraping across the floor, as though someone had pushed it suddenly.*
>
> *Startled, I looked in through the serving hatch on the wall and saw, fleetingly, Ian and Edward Evans fighting. They had each other by the collar and were struggling together. I couldn't believe it at first, to see them fighting when they were supposed to be having a drink*

together. I immediately ran out of the kitchen towards the living room to stop them.

I now wish I had done that, for what eventually happened would probably not have done if I'd gone into the room.

However, as I opened the kitchen door and ran into the hall, I saw David Smith standing on the front doorstep, holding the large, nobbled stick he usually carried when out with his dog. I called to him to help Ian . . . .

Smith rushed into the living room and as he did so, a most terrible noise began, shouting and banging and God knows what else. I was terribly frightened and ran back into the kitchen and stood behind the door with my hands over my ears to block out some of the noise.

I don't know how long I stood there like that, but eventually I took my hands away from my ears, and the noise had stopped. I went out of the kitchen into the living room and stopped dead in the doorway.

I will never be able to describe how I felt at the sight which met my eyes. All I could see was blood everywhere, with Edward Evans crumpling on to the floor and David Smith kicking him as he went down. I was completely frozen with shock and rooted to the spot . . . .

When my senses had finally registered what they had seen, my grandmother, who had been sleeping, called down the stairs to ask me what all the noise was, I realized that if she came downstairs, the shock would probably kill her, and I managed to tell her I had dropped something before I ran into the kitchen and was sick.

I was being sick and crying when Ian came into the kitchen. He told me there had been a fight and he had killed Edward Evans. He asked me to try and pull myself together and he would explain things later, but first he had to clear things up in the living room. He went for the mop and bucket and asked me to get some cloths.

I moved about in a trance, automatically, really, without comprehending much about anything.

Although she told me personally that she helped with the cleaning-up operation, she argued in her document that she had not entered the room until it was over. She further alleged that while Brady's clothes were covered with blood, and Smith's were almost as bad, her skirt showed only tiny spots from when she'd 'unknowingly' walked into the living room doorway. Myra's statement continued:

During the initial struggle, Ian had been kicked on the ankle which had begun to swell and was painful to walk on. He and Smith had decided to dispose of Evans' body that same night so as not to be found out, but because of Ian's ankle, they decided to leave it until the following night. I had very little to do with their plans, although I knew I had been nominated to drive the car.

She added that when David Smith left the house at around 3 a.m. she asked Brady what had happened. He refused to answer any of her questions, just barked at her, 'Leave it for now.' Still, she was going to do anything she could to help and protect him. And even after I'd heard and questioned Myra's version of the murder so many times that I believed her, I still could not work out her devotion to a man who had brought such horror to her house.

She'd reply with her usual appeal:

I challenge any woman who loved a man as deeply and as blindly as I loved Ian Brady to look into her heart and say that under similar circumstances, she would have gone to the police and given up her very raison d'etre.

My future was bound up with his. I had always put his comfort and welfare before my own. I was almost fiercely protective towards him with no thought for the danger surrounding the whole thing.

On her other favourite hobby-horse, Hindley used to bang on and on about David Smith, that he had far more to do with the murder than he ever admitted, that it was in his own interests to 'implicate' and 'discredit' her as much as possible, and that he only went to the police to get his story in first and thus appear innocent – because he was worried that Myra would crack and report the crime. She said:

Smith knew how I had reacted over the photograph incident, he saw how much shock I was in over Edward Evans, and he knew that I disliked him intensely. He was frightened I'd spill the beans, and that's the only reason he got in first. He was as cool as a cucumber.

He told my sister that he was sorry I had had to go down, but it was either him or me, and it wasn't going to be him.

Myra made a big song and dance about the fact that Smith was never charged with any offence connected to the Evans murder, in an exchange deal for all the information he could possibly give the police – much of it, she stormed, untrue. She was furious, also, because she believed that Smith had copped a load of money from the *News of the World*. She fumed that he'd been given a lump sum for his story, along with syndicate rights, plus holidays abroad and a five-star hotel room in Chester for the duration of the trial. The murder of Edward Evans, she ranted, had certainly solved Smith's financial problems.

The police arrived at around 8.30 a.m. the morning after the killing, one copper knocking on the back door of the house disguised as a bread delivery man. Myra was up and dressed. Brady was lounging in the living room where they'd had to spend the night. The initial police search of the house turned up the body, the axe (which Myra claimed had originally been in the living room for furniture-repairing purposes) and a box containing two loaded revolvers. Brady was taken away to Hyde police station where he was charged that evening with Evans's murder. Myra would remain free for another five days, while visiting the same station for questioning. She said:

> I was convinced that the whole thing had arisen from a fight between Ian and Edward Evans, and I was both terrified and reluctant to tell the police anything which could have harmed Ian in any way.
>
> I said such stupid things as, 'What Ian has told you, I say the same,' and 'Wherever Ian has been, I've been with him.' My sole concern was to try and save him from what I was convinced he wasn't guilty of. Added to that was the fact that I was completely in the dark about what had happened, so I couldn't tell the police much anyway, even if I'd wanted to.

In the meantime, the police had been carrying out more searches, some of them just routine. Through this, they found some paper, featuring Brady's writing, in the car. It was believed that the words, in code, amounted to written evidence of a murder plot, made out before Edward Evans was picked up. Myra told me:

> Ian said this was a 'disposal plan' which he wrote out after Evans had

been killed, when he and Smith were discussing what to do about the situation.

After Smith had left, Ian told me to go down and lock the car up, for if it was stolen, it would be catastrophic. I refused to go down. It was pitch black outside and I am afraid of the dark, normally.

I knew this to be the case from Myra's insistence on sleeping with the light on. Myra continued:

That night I was even more afraid. So Ian went himself, with me standing by the door waiting for him. He said he had put the piece of paper in his wallet which was in his inside pocket.

As he was fixing up the anti-theft device on the steering wheel, he was leaning over the front seat and his wallet fell out on to the floor. He picked it up and put it on the dashboard while he continued securing the car, and forgot to pick it up afterwards. That's how it came to be there.

This piece of evidence, which I had nothing to do with, was what the police alleged to be conclusive proof that the murder was premeditated, and that I was part of the premeditation.

Yet, the paper contained no reference to myself, nor was my handwriting on it.

The routine police checks also uncovered an exercise book, which contained the name of John Kilbride, among assorted scribblings. But the biggest find of all was a couple of left-luggage tickets, handed to Myra the night before Edward Evans's murder, in return for two suitcases she had deposited at Manchester Central station. Detectives collected the suitcases and found a whole array of damning evidence – weapons, ammunition, masks and wigs, sadistic and perverted books and writings, and lists of information, which would be useful in robberies – not to mention two tapes and a bunch of photos. The tapes included the Lesley Ann Downey recording. The photos included indecent shots of the same, poor little girl. Some showed Brady and Hindley on the moors, and there was one portrait of Myra Hindley kneeling, like a mourner, over the spot where John Kilbride was later found to have been buried.

Myra of course, had a plausible explanation for all of this, and she only ever referred to one suitcase. She said:

Ian asked me to drive to the left-luggage place for the suitcase to be lodged. For once, I refused to be put off with a 'no explanation', and demanded to know why.

When I persisted, I was finally told that it had something to do with a robbery, which didn't concern me. I had suspected that Ian and Smith's friendship involved something criminal, since they had both got police records, but I believed Ian and I were too domestically settled for him to go beyond fantasising with Smith.

They had been friendly for several years now and nothing, barring the interest in blue photographs, had evolved.

I later learned that they had planned to rob an electrical firm as 'practice' for other robberies. That is why the suitcase was taken out of the house when it was. If anything went wrong, everything of an incriminating nature would be out of the way.

As well as routine detective work, the police were also following up what they'd been told by David Smith, and, in their initial questioning of Hindley, they only gradually introduced the idea of bodies on the moors. Said Myra in her Home Office declaration:

Apparently, when the police had contacted my family, they told my mother, aunt and uncle that David Smith had made numerous allegations, including one of bodies buried on the moors. The police had said I was in great trouble, and wouldn't answer their questions.

This terrified my family into thinking I was involved in all kinds of things and endangering myself by refusing to talk about them. They begged me to talk to the police and get everything sorted out before I was in as much trouble as Ian was.

It was obvious the police were using my family to cause me to 'co-operate', for all kinds of things had been mentioned to them which hadn't been put to me.

When 'bodies on the moor' was mentioned to me by the police, I thought it was all a combination of David Smith's wild allegations to ensure both our arrest and his non-arrest, and 'police tactics' of which I knew very little, except what I'd seen on TV and in films, but was naturally very suspicious of, having had no criminal dealings with the police before.

Knowing nothing whatsoever of such an allegation and being totally unaware that there were bodies on the moor, I rejected the whole idea.

On 16 October 1965, the naked body of Lesley Ann Downey was found in a shallow grave on Saddleworth Moor, buried with her clothes, shoes and a string of beads at her feet. On 27 October, an intensive search of the same area led to the discovery of John Kilbride, buried face-down in a grave near Lesley Ann's. He was clothed, although his trousers and underpants had been pulled down. Myra:

I first knew that they'd found the body of Lesley Ann Downey when I arrived at Hyde police station to be remanded to Risley prison for another week. I had seen no newspaper nor heard the radio and was unaware of what the large crowd outside the courtroom signified.

Upon arriving, the solicitor who was acting for me saw me privately and told me that the body of a child had been found buried on the moors. He asked me if I knew anything at all about it.

I was totally shattered and could still hardly believe it even when he showed me a newspaper. All I could think of was that the police were right, that it hadn't just been provocation and the whole thing was a dreadful nightmare.

I had sustained so great a shock from the still-unexplained murder of Edward Evans and its aftermath that I had become almost completely numbed and frozen. Outwardly, I still functioned and responded, but part of my mind seemed not to function at all. I simply could not take in or cope with the enormity of the situation . . . .

I think I had entered into a state of shock, which lasted for well over a year after my conviction. Sometimes I wish it had lasted indefinitely. Things were painful and incomprehensible, but they lacked the worse pain of stark reality.

Instead of going back to Risley, Hindley was taken to an office which had MURDER ROOM in large letters on a piece of cardboard on the door. She was shown various articles, including Lesley Ann's clothes and her string of beads. Myra told the Home Office:

I still find it impossible to convey my feelings when the facts began to sink in, when first of all a bunch of photographs were spilled out on the table in front of me, photographs I hadn't dreamed still existed, which I had never wanted to see again, and as the first spasms of shock and horror hit me, a scream suddenly rent the air, which at first I thought was my own soundless scream, but which came from a tape machine on a table in the room.

The stark horror of the whole situation is beyond description. I was in a room filled with policemen, with my eyes and ears assailed by shameful associations with a child I now knew to be dead, and with whose murder I had been charged.

That my connection with that child had been for less than an hour, that she was alive and well when I last saw her, and that the criminal connection with her had, to my knowledge and belief, been destroyed on the same night as she left, meant nothing to the police, I know.

I was only too aware of the situation I was in. For a short time, I cried from sheer fright and remorse for what I had been involved in, and when the barrage of questions began, I took refuge behind the mist that swam in my mind . . . .

I do know that my instinctive reaction to escape the unbearable reality was construed as arrogance and hard defiance. But I ask you to imagine, even for a moment, how I felt at the time, and how I continued to feel.

I was so terribly ashamed of what I had done that I desperately put up a front to hide behind, a veneer of – I don't know what, but anything which would deflect some of the contempt and loathing directed at me. I sustained this veneer throughout the trial, for how else could I bear the condemnation of those present?

And gradually, the veneer became a kind of second skin which I could rarely afford to doff. Such is how one part of my reputation evolved.

Myra never, ever talked about Pauline Reade and Keith Bennett, the other children who'd gone missing during the Moors Murders era and were now presumed dead. She only ever mentioned schoolboy John Kilbride to deny all knowledge of his death, after which she was convicted of being an accessory. She repeated emphatically: 'I know absolutely nothing about the boy or his disappearance. I hadn't read about him, hadn't even heard his name mentioned, until the police questioned me about him.'

Hindley claimed that the police case against her was based on the fact that she'd hired a car on the day he disappeared. She used to remark, rather flippantly, I thought, 'That I had hired cars from the same firm on other occasions when no one else disappeared was ignored. The Director of Public Prosecutions took nine weeks to decide whether I should be charged with that offence, for there simply wasn't any evidence.'

She refused to admit to anything with regard to the snapshot of her with her dog, standing over John Kilbride's moorland grave. If she told me this once, she told me ten dozen times:

It was one of Ian's many ordinary, insignificant photographs. When that photograph was taken, John Kilbride had not even disappeared. The dog I'm holding in the picture is only a puppy. At the time of my arrest in October 1965, the dog was almost three years old.

This means that the photograph was taken approximately nine months before John Kilbride went missing. There couldn't possibly have been a grave there. So as far as I'm concerned, that 'sinister' photograph is sinister in no way at all.

The popular image people have of me being pictured over the grave of a child alleged to have been murdered by my lover is consistent with the myth, but entirely inconsistent with the truth.

Myra Hindley's campaign for parole occupied a great deal of her time. It was all so carefully thought out and intelligently presented that it won her many supporters, ranging from fellow-convicts and prison officers to such prominent public figures as Lord Longford.

The effectiveness of any case she put forward depended on several things. The first was her version of the various events as I have described it, bringing in every minute detail that could help her to argue her innocence of the worst allegations against her, while admitting guilt in some of the lesser crimes. The second was her contention that she'd been judged in a 'trial-by-newspaper', not in a fair court of law where twelve good men and true were able to make a decision through 'evidence' and 'proof'. Then there was her self-portrait – the lovesick woman, unwittingly led into terrible trouble by the crank she blindly adored and wanted only to keep and, finally, protect.

But to stand any chance of winning her parole, she also had to have a bit of the 'reformed character' about her. Therefore she had to renounce Brady, had to tell the world that she'd finally found him out for the absolute bastard he was. There had to be sympathy, too. Myra had to be seen to have woken up to her own shortcomings. She had to be pitied as a sad, regretful and vulnerable woman who had been misunderstood and did not deserve to be condemned to live out the rest of her days in the grey hell that was prison. Finally, her campaign included just enough of a crusade to suggest a certain concern for others: she appealed for a review of the parole system, for more prison facilities, for a more supportive rehabilitation programme.

Myra worked all of these elements together to create a tremendously credible case for her own release. She played it brilliantly. Her denial of Brady was enthusiastic in the extreme, culminating in her assertion that if they had both remained at liberty, he might have tried to kill her. She stated in her writings:

I now realise the extent to which I was used and fooled by both Ian Brady and David Smith. One is free because society wasn't choosy about its victims, the other has dragged me down with him. And I have acquired a reputation more notorious than either of them. The irony is crippling.

It is even more crippling in the light of my willingness to sacrifice my own safety and peace of mind purely to protect Ian Brady from detection; that when he was given life imprisonment, I prayed that I would get the same because the world outside meant nothing to me as long as he wasn't in it.

For almost five years, I was an emotional slave and gave him love and loyalty without question. It has been said to me that under different circumstances, this misplaced loyalty would have been a virtue to be proud of. Love and loyalty are sins for which I have paid dearly, by anybody's reckoning.

I am not proud that I chose to defend him to my own detriment or willingly embraced the same fate as befell him. At that time, I acted true to my nature, according to what I believed and thought was the truth. Now, however, if I could turn back the clock, knowing what I do now, my defence against the charges would be far different to merely offering myself as another mouth-piece to his defence.

I always believed that Ian Brady did his utmost at the trial to exonerate me. But he only did this to the degree to which he was prepared to admit his guilt. Beyond that, to save his own face, he was prepared to sacrifice me to my fate. And what a fate it's been.

I know the extent of my guilt, and he knows it too. When I broke off contact with him, I knew that he would view this as an even worse betrayal than David Smith's. Had I anything to hide, any fear of anything Ian might reveal, I would have felt chained to him. As it is, I cut my bonds with impunity, safe in the knowledge that whatever his worst might be, my conscience was clear, my integrity intact.

Once my eyes had been opened, I could see what my blindness had obscured. All these long years in prison have taught me just how foolish and immature I was. Not only am I now some years older, I am thousands of years wiser.

I learned during the trial about the various conspiracies, admitted by both Ian and David Smith. Much later, I dared to strip away the veneer from my emotions and really examine what was underneath. I gave much deep thought to lots of things about Ian which I hadn't previously wanted to think about, things which my protective subconscious discouraged me from thinking about.

I now consider it quite possible that my own life would have been in jeopardy if we'd carried on together, that I would have finished up as a 'victim'. In the light of what I now know about Ian Brady and David Smith, I realise that I was becoming a liability, that I was becoming involved in perhaps too many things for me not to have eventually become dispensable and therefore done away with.

In all of her campaigning, Myra had to present herself as someone quite different from the hatchet-faced blonde the public knew and hated. She blamed her trial-by-newspaper for the cartoon character that was her public image, and she blamed that image for her unlikely chances of parole. As she stressed in her statement to the Home Office:

It's no exaggeration to say that I've been an unwilling scapegoat for the press and public for years now. I have been crucified time and time again remorselessly, by those admiral denizens of the 'popular' press.

Since my trial in 1966, there has emerged a myth based on what the press have labelled the Moors Murders, which has escalated over the past years out of such proportions as to almost totally obscure the actual facts of the trial, the charges and convictions . . . .

From the [trial] verdict, based on the prosecution's flimsy case, I have become a child murderess, evil incarnate and God knows how many other similar labels. Described as I always am as the Moors Murderess gives the impression that I committed wholesale murders on my own account. Surely what is contained in this statement, and evident from trial transcripts, gives quite the contrary view?

Myra informed me that she had had psychiatric tests during her years in prison, and none had found any symptoms of the madness people still seem to think of at the very mention of her name. Her statement continued:

I have now worked through the painful process of sorting things into some kind of perspective. And I find it almost impossible to relate in any way at all to the mythical Myra Hindley which vivid imaginations have created. Yet it seems I will never be divorced completely from the 'monster myth' . . . .

I cannot conform to such a picture, but this is the picture which the general public has embraced and clung to jealously along with all the other mythical fragments which their imaginations have painted and which they have framed into something as enduring as a Victorian sampler.

I'm afraid their picture bears little, if any, resemblance to me as I actually am. But I suppose even if confronted personally with the truth, to experience it with their own eyes, people would still be loathe to part with their illusions. I know this from experience.

Myra was always taking a swipe at the public for preferring the cartoon to the reality. She said this was why general opinion about her was so 'blind and bloodthirsty'. She told me she was 'living all the time with the crippling knowledge that public opinion is perhaps the major factor which keeps me in prison and denies me the hope of release and of leading a normal, fruitful and fulfilling life.' This was why, she said, she felt compelled to write her lengthy statement to the Home Office. She wanted to protest at the way in which she felt the parole system failed notorious prisoners like herself. And she claimed she wanted to make her own case for a parole review – whether or not she had any realistic chance of release. She observed:

A life sentence at its 'best' does have milestones on an otherwise empty road in the form of these reviews. They give the prisoner some grounds for hope that the next review, which is automatic after the first one, may be the one that yields a date, thus providing a goal of some kind to work towards, a straw, even, to grasp at when one is at a low ebb.

But my particular life sentence contains no such goals or straws or milestones, just an empty, endless road stretching into nowhere, with no hope in any shape or form to provide the vital incentive to keep on keeping on.

She added:

At this moment in time, the negative aspects of prison life are beginning to outweigh the positive ones, and I feel I have reached the point where continued imprisonment could only bring a deterioration, not only in the sense of increasing institutionalization but, more crucially, an irreparable erosion of the spirit and morale which have served me in good stead for so long and enabled me to persevere in spite of crushing odds.

Denied the hope of eventual release, I can only see myself losing that vital reserve to keep on keeping on.

Myra used every opportunity, including her 'novel' to the Home Office, to complain about the numbing monotony, trivial restriction and humiliation of prison life. 'Over the years,' she remarked, primly, 'amenities have not improved to any extent, and deprivations remain – the stodgy, starchy, boring, uninspired prison food, and the countless hours of confinement in often over-crowded, unhealthy confines.' She protested at everything: the 'minuscule' cells and windows, the jug-and-bowl washing facilities, the ban on using proper toilets from early evening until next day, the lack of warm water first thing in the morning, the allocation of only one hour of exercise, the absence of greenery, the three-a-week limit on sending letters, and the fact that she could only have one visit a fortnight. She wrote:

For years, I did the same thing practically every day. I was incarcerated in Holloway Prison with countless thousands of other women passing in and out of my life, some of whom were guilty of crimes as bad as, if not worse than, both those of which I am allegedly guilty and those of which I am actually guilty.

Yet those women are gone, long gone, released back into the society which perpetuates my imprisonment.

The hours spent queuing for everything she needed, and the longer hours she spent locked away in her cell, got Myra down like mad. So did the regular cell and body searches, which she saw as a real invasion of privacy. 'I have been existing in a regime which has denied me even basic responsibilities, robbed me of virtually all initiative,' she carried on. She couldn't half whinge when she wanted to.

Every decision pertaining to everyday life is made for me. I am told when and what to eat, when to go to bed, when I must stop reading. My light switch is controlled by others. I am limited in what I wear, and how often I can change my clothes. Even my freedom of speech is curtailed, for if I say something wrong, I can face disciplinary charges . . . .

Nothing can convey the mental and psychological aspect of prolonged imprisonment, the years and years of the suffering, the repressing of natural emotions, the degradation.

She hated living with the threat and reality of violence, and with the 'poor, sick, tortured minds' of other women around her. Myra insisted that she had survived her years in prison only through using the educational facilities. She had studied German, French and Spanish and was following a six-year BA course in Humanities with the Open University. But she claimed she had nearly exhausted her options, and she felt that learning opportunities should be expanded. She stated in her writings:

It has been a constant struggle to avoid contact and infection from the dangerous and negative aspects of all prison existence, the pervading aura of disturbed mentalities and unhealthy minds, the crushing weight of mindless boredom and dangerous lethargy and the overall stultifying atmosphere of prison life.

It has been all too easy to succumb and sink below their Lethean waves, but I've always managed to struggle above them again and with characteristic resilience, move on to attempt some new educational advancement. Through education, I have achieved an intellectual development to a greater degree than otherwise possible, but it is becoming increasingly difficult to continue to develop.

Myra Hindley, in her pages and pages of typewriting to the Home Office, was not merely pleading for a parole review. There was an underlying motive. She was carefully beginning to present herself as a person who could safely be released back into society, and, in some suitably short passages, she dealt with this in so many words. She announced solemnly:

Where the concepts of atonement and retribution are concerned, both have been fully extracted. I have atoned, and society has had retribution. There is absolutely nothing more to be gained by continued incarceration from anybody's point of view.

Whenever the question of whether I have 'reformed' is posed, there is really quite a simple answer. Up to the age of eighteen years, I was an ordinary, average teenager, brought up in a working-class district by an honest, hard-working family. Like them, I had never been in any kind of police trouble, never out of work since I left school, and had I never met Ian Brady, would no doubt have married my fiancé and become the mother of children.

But I did meet Ian Brady, and during my formative years, when I was impressionable and vulnerable. Because my infatuation for him undermined everything else, I lost completely my faculties of criticism and learned to smother my natural curiosity to the point that it became dormant . . . .

I am guilty of two anti-social acts – two crimes. That I regret my participation in the matter of the photographs is an understatement. It is not something I regret or feel remorse for because I was found out and sent to prison. I regretted and was filled with remorse right from the beginning.

What I did was completely out of character and something that will never happen again under any circumstances. As far as the accessory charge is concerned, I have learned probably the most bitter lesson.

It hardly seems necessary to say that never again will I become involved in any unhealthy relationship, let alone one anything like the one that I shared with Ian Brady, or as blindly intense, and certainly never again will I ever be involved in anything in any way criminal or unwholesome.

I do not have a criminal mind nor, in spite of past lapses, do I have an unwholesome nature.

I was once a person in my own right. For some time after meeting Ian Brady, I became a different person, acting out of character. Now I have reverted back to a much maturer, wiser version of my earlier self. I am ultra-aware of my faults and failings, which I have worked at correcting, simply to become at harmony with myself. I am also aware of how much blame can and should be attributed to myself, for allowing myself to be so easily overwhelmed and so blindly infatuated.

But I can say with total certainty and conviction that in the light of all that has happened, it is simply out of the question that I will ever put myself in such a position again. Not only have I lost the most precious of things, freedom, but I have also lost my self-respect, been an object of hatred and loathing, the focal point of contempt, become, for others, the personification of evil and have been crucified almost beyond endurance.

Out of the wreck of my life, I have salvaged my self-respect and my integrity, and in spite of the battering over many years, I feel I can hold my head up before God and man. I am at relative peace with myself and have ample confidence in myself to sustain me whatever happens, a peace and confidence based on many years of self-analysis and deep and critical introspection . . . .

If anything, I have been harder on myself than have my adversaries, but, as a result, I can say I have purged myself of many mean and petty qualities which are incompatible with a harmonious nature and spirit. I feel I have more than paid my debt to society and I feel equally that I shall not be any kind of burden on society as such.

She added with a strange certainty:

Once I am released, I have my own plans to begin a new life, so much so that society will not be admitting Myra Hindley into its ranks, either by name or reputation.

The myth never did have anything to do with me, was not of my making. I shall continue to disassociate myself from it in much the same way as I have always done. I have served society in good stead as scapegoat and whipping boy for far too many years now.

Confronting the idea that it might not be too safe for Myra Hindley to be let loose again in the outside world, to put it mildly, she commented:

It has been mentioned to me that a further problem concerns the question of my protection and my future plans – in other words, what will happen to me upon release.

I have no illusions about the possibilities of disturbed people's quest for vengeance. But I am confident that once I am released, by degrees, and with the help of many willing people, I will be able to lead an unobtrusive and normal life.

My future plans are many and various, with a number of equally suitable alternatives. I am quite sure that I can adequately fulfil the standard prerequisites for release on parole – a home and employment, acceptably sound finances, staunch support from family and friends, and no possibility whatsoever of encountering any environmental or personal contact which is undesirable in any way.

In short, if I were released tomorrow, in a short space of time I could be listed among the many thousands of 'parole successes'.

At the time, I happened to agree with her, along with all the other people she converted to her cause. Well, so much for the amateur psychology. In years to come, she would prove to me that her stories, her fancy words, her flowing prose, her tearful innocence, her begging for understanding, amounted in total to just one thing: a load of bollocks.

CHAPTER TWELVE

Obsessions

She didn't fall in love with me overnight. She'd fancied me something rotten from the first day she saw me, but the 'deep' stuff didn't come until later on. The very fact that she was Myra Hindley meant that she couldn't even start to think about trusting someone until she knew them really, really well. And the very fact that she was Myra Hindley meant that I couldn't even start to think about trusting *her* until she'd proved to me that she deserved my friendship. So the relationship developed slowly, one step at a time, while we circled suspiciously around each other, while I asked, and she answered, while I agonized over her claims of innocence.

When, eventually, I decided in her favour, she was thrilled to bits. She had an ally, somebody who could help her, somebody she could trust with her confidences. She talked more freely to me than to any other person, and she started showing me a lot of her personal poetry and prose. I was amazed, at first, at her melodramatic style of writing, full of overblown emotion and airy-fairy imagery. But it was a fascinating insight into the mind of the Moors Murderess. A typical essay was one titled 'The Intimate Revelations of Myra Hindley in Prison for Life'. I'll never forget how it opened: 'What is life for? To die? To kill myself at once? No, I am afraid. To wait for death until it comes, I fear that even more. Then I must live. But what for? In order to die? And I cannot escape that circle.'

The general theme of the piece was her own imprisonment, the prospect of a future 'too awful to contemplate', filled only with identical days and the consequent fear of impending madness. Central to it all was the idea that 'I don't really live, I merely watch.' She illustrated the idea of unbearable boredom with the introduction of a clock, referring to the 'tick-tock of time', the 'twitching of the hands' and their 'eternal repetition' at regular intervals throughout the composition. Interwoven were details of Myra's more specific preoccupations. In one part, she wrote of a familiar worry: 'I wondered if I would be very much surprised on rising each morning to realise that my hair had turned white. I have felt it turn white so often under the intolerable burden of my thoughts and my sensations. Yet it remains as brown as ever.'

I was particularly fascinated by two passages, these concerning the only big relationships of her life. One was about Ian Brady and the other was about Trish Cairns, the lovely prison officer who'd fallen for her and tried to help her escape. Brady she presented , as usual, as her idol, the man she worshipped 'more blindly than the congenital blind'. She went on to submit that she finally saw the god fall off the pedestal. This happened, she claimed, when she rediscovered the real God. She stated: 'God decided that though I had abandoned him, he refused to abandon me and leave me to my own blind devices any longer, and he gave me back my faith, but not my young childish faith now – a new, enlightened and mature faith which grew and bloomed slowly but steadily like a flower, straining upwards to the sun for very life.' The bringer of this enlightenment, she said, was Trish Cairns, ex-nun and 'instrument of God's grace'.

At this point, the essay went really over the top. Myra drooled, 'Her fingers touched my soul and awakened it from its long sleep and her voice, her words of encouragement, of quiet conviction, penetrated the very core of my heart, and many beautiful seeds grew and flourished in the newly awakened warmth.' According to Myra, Trish took her hand and led her 'out of the wasteland into the sunshine and birdsong of life.'

Describing Trish as her soulmate and reason for living, she then decided she wanted to live, not just exist, and that's when she did it: 'I asked her to escape with me.' Myra continued:

I had told her before, when we formerly planned a life after release, that life with me would be a dangerous hazard that she would have to share.

I told her the way is suspicious, the result uncertain, perhaps destructive. 'You would have to give up all else. I alone would need to be your sole and exclusive standard. Your motivation would even then be long and exhausting. The whole past theory of your life and all conformity to those around you would have to be abandoned.'

But she was willing to make the sacrifice then – because she loved me and wanted to help me.

Towards the end of her composition, Myra had to admit: 'The result is more destructive than I ever envisaged. She, too, is in prison.' She said, 'I can't bear the thought of her being in prison, branded, scarred and so vulnerable.' But at the same time, her feelings were more wrapped up with her own sense of loss than with Trish's predicament.

I can't endure this intolerable separation . . . if only we could keep each other going by being allowed to just correspond with each other. Her letters were a source of joy and comfort to me. Mine to her were a means of expression I can never achieve in letters to others.

I feel stifled, trapped, inhibited, bound up and chained within myself for want of expression, for the need to commune not just spiritually with her, but to communicate even in written if not spoken words.

For she is my anchor, my safety, my rest and my peace, and hope would grow again, and I would no longer feel so impotent, so helpless to help her.

Myra went on and on, in her familiar way, about this 'God-given' love she had for Trish, 'a pure, a deep, a beautiful, unsoiled love'. She ended her piece with a prayer, telling God that she was 'frightened' and 'hurtling downwards into the pit of black despair'. She concluded spiritedly: 'So I keep up the struggle not to go down and if I must go down, I'll go down fighting.'

So much for the God-given, pure, deep, beautiful, unsoiled love she had for Trish. Quite apart from the flippant comment she'd previously made to me about Trish being putty in her hands, she showed the strength of her feelings for the officer she'd ruined by continuing with her poetry, her prose and her extravagant romantic declarations. But the loved one was no longer Trish. It was me.

The intimacy of the friendship I'd established with Hindley, the intensity of our conversations, had sent her into fits of adoration. She seemed to have forgotten all about Trish; in fact, she refused to have anything to do with her for years after Trish's 'betrayal', when she handed Myra's illicit letter in to the prison authorities at Styal. Before long, it was the talk of Holloway: Myra Hindley was deranged over Janie Jones.

I'd had a load of love notes from lesbians in there, and I'd paid no attention to them. There's no way I would have had an affair with anyone inside, no matter how desperate I might have been. I wasn't interested. But where Hindley was concerned, I couldn't just ignore the situation, because we were friends. Or so I thought at the time. I was never in love with her in a million years, but I did feel a bit sorry for her. I said to myself, Well, she's convinced me she's innocent of the murders, and she's doing life inside. If she's madly in love with me and it's making her happy, elated to the sky that I'm her friend, well, it's not doing any harm.

At the same time, I told her, 'I am your friend, you know, but you can forget any other ideas you might have. You can worship and idolize me as much as you want, so long as you do it from a distance.' In a way it amused me. I suppose I was getting my jollies out of it, because she was used to getting people under her spell and manipulating them. She had a few girls under her thumb in Holloway, but it was definitely me she had the big thing for, and I wasn't going to let her take me over like she'd done with the others. It was me who had my finger on the button.

She was mesmerized by me. She said I had a magnetic personality, and I agreed with her: 'I know I have. It's part of show business.' She loved the way I used to sing on the wing and in the Christmas concerts. She liked singing, and I started coaching her. I made such a good job of it that she won a talent competition in the prison, and I, as a professional singer, had to be satisfied with second place!

Myra also loved to ask for my advice about her appearance, especially when she was getting ready for a visit. She often borrowed my denim skirt, and once she wore one of my dresses for a visit from Lord Longford, her long-time supporter. She told me, 'He's in an important position to help,' and she always wanted to look her best for him. Eventually, she wanted more assistance. She said, 'I can't do make-up, because it's been so long. Will you do it for me?' And I used to put her face on for her, every time she had a visit from Lord Longford.

It wasn't long before she started getting jealous of any of the other women who wanted to be friendly with me. And from there, she became genuinely obsessive. This was partly to do with the environment. By its very inward-looking nature, its lack of distraction, the prison existence can intensify every emotion, turn a simple infatuation into the grandest passion in the whole world. Added to that was the fact that I had all the qualities most likely to enrapture Myra Hindley. She saw me as a celebrity, which endowed me not only with a certain glamour but also with the potential to bring her freedom campaign to a wider audience, should I feel inclined. She regarded me as a woman of the world, someone who might more readily accommodate her 'confessions'. I was known to be a compassionate listener, and she would therefore stand some chance of sympathy and emotional support from me. Finally, I entertained her. It wasn't often that Myra Hindley had a good old laugh in prison . . . until I turned up.

As she grew more besotted, I started to notice her eyes. They never left me. She watched every little move I made, which was a strange feeling. She really wanted to possess me. I was made what was known as a red band for the welfare department at the beginning of August 1976. This meant that I had joined a group of trusted convicts who were given extra responsibilities and greater access to various parts of the prison. I had the right to work overtime if I wanted to, and I often did. I'd take over other women's work so they could free themselves to receive visits. I'd feel sorry for some of them, because they'd be going through marriage break-ups, or they'd be missing their kids, and they'd need every visit they could get.

Myra had no such understanding. She'd be shouting and screaming like a raving lunatic every time I was late coming back on to the wing. I've never heard anything like it. She'd be hanging over the balcony, in hysterics, watching for me or pacing up and down like a bloody panther.

This amused the screws no end, and they used to love winding her up. When they knew she was having a tantrum over me, they'd deliberately keep me downstairs to make coffee for them, which was one of my duties as a red band. I couldn't refuse to do it. I'd go back upstairs and Hindley would be in a terrible state. I'd say 'Look you can perform as much as you like, but you know I can't refuse to make coffee when I've got the band on. You're a selfish, self-centred bastard.'

I used to take the mickey, too. I'd say, 'I know you're mad about me and all that, but you're not going to take me over. I own myself. Nobody takes me over. I had the Crank who tried, and he was strong, but not even he could succeed. I told him I'd rather do life inside than have him back. So if you're going to kick up all this fuss, you can get stuffed. I'm just going to say "That's it. Don't come into my cell any more."'

And she'd be stamping her feet, wailing, 'No, you don't understand . . . .' She'd say she'd been afraid of being attacked, or she'd needed to talk to me about something. She often used to tell me, 'Every minute that you're not here feels like a lifetime to me. Every minute is precious. And it's so important to me, but you don't seem to care.'

I'd answer, 'I'm a red band, and you can rant and rave till you're blue in the face, but I'm going to stay with the girls who need me, when they need me.'

She'd back down then. She'd say, 'It's just that I miss you when you're not there. You make me laugh, and you're so much joy to me.' 'Yeah,' I'd agree, 'and I'm a joy to a lot of other prisoners too.'

When she wasn't throwing one of her scenes, Myra was very shy and nervous around me, almost in awe. She would never put her feelings for me into words. The only way she could ever do that was in her poetry and her letters. She never, ever approached me in any physical way. I'd get hold of her and kiss her on her cheek, and she's kissed me on the cheek, but there was nothing sexual about it. It would happen on a birthday, or if one of us were going to a different part of the prison for any length of time. Nothing more than that ever took place between us, no matter how much she wanted it to, or fantasized in her writings that it would.

Various articles and books have stated that Myra had a string of affairs in prison. It would have been quite difficult for her to organize. It was easier for the women who were sharing cells. If they wanted, they could snuggle under a blanket together in the night. But Myra had her own cell. However, determined women could always find a daytime hideaway, like the bathroom. Myra could only hope to snatch the odd ten or fifteen minutes here or there with willing partners. She might even have had the occasional liaison in the church, where she was rumoured to have had sex with Trish Cairns. I do know she had some long-standing and passionate affairs with other prisoners.

Some of the lesbians used to be absolutely brazen. We used to roar with laughter. They used to sneak under the beds together, and hide from view by draping a blanket from the top of the bed to the floor. Then they'd have to crawl out sharpish when they heard the screws yelling for them, wondering where they were. One girl told me about her most memorable experience below the bed. She said she'd been in there for about ten minutes when she heard an officer yelling her name. She raised her head and got her hair tangled in the bed springs. She ended up tearing out half her hair in her hurry to get back out before the screw found her.

I happened to tell that story to a journalist 'friend' of mine who came visiting. He changed the names of the participants to Myra Hindley and Janie Jones and published an article about it, which devastated me. I was horrified. It was like the end of the world. During the visit, this man actually suggested that I could make a fortune by claiming to have had an affair with Myra. I said, 'You could offer me the crown jewels, but I wouldn't lie about that.'

The 'love affair' was conducted only by Myra and only in writing. She used to pen poetry about how she felt about me, and how I was like a butterfly, and it just went over my head. It didn't mean a wank to me. I'd show it to my cell-mate Jenny, and we'd scream with laughter. We'd spare a thought, at the same time, for poor Trish Cairns. There she was doing six years' porridge for the love of Myra Hindley. And here was Hindley pouring out page after page of adoration for me.

Each poem or letter ended with the words 'I love you' and two 'X's, and each was memorable for a far-fetched passion that Myra, in person, would never have been capable of admitting. In one moment of divine inspiration, she likened herself to a 'bowl of kisses', which, she went on to claim, she was offering to me! This basic idea was enough to send her careering off into a world of feverish lust, with lines like these:

> *You make me feel the peak of desire, pitching me headlong over into foaming seas of satiated passions whose waves gently bear my shuddering body to tender shores of fulfilment . . . .*
>
> *Revive me with your kisses, your caresses, your nails raking my back and my shoulders, let me bury my burning face in your moist and supple flesh, feeling my teeth biting into you as you would a heavenly ripe peach.*

She went on to invite me to be the bush to her flame, she wanted to consume me in a holocaust of liquid fire, she was determined to drink the honey from my lips, and she begged to sink into my arms with shuddering sighs. I don't know what she'd had for supper the night she came up with that one! Much to my relief, she assured me in other poems that desire was merely one of the many feelings she had for me. Mainly, she wrote screeds about love and tenderness, and waffled on about 'the swansdown cushion of sleep' and 'the perfumed depths of my dreams'. She felt like 'a teenager in love for the very first time', she declared, which was disconcerting in the extreme. I'd never been likened to Ian Brady before, and I hope I never will be again!

The comparisons were seemingly endless and always ridiculous. Myra thought I was like a blossom drifting from a bough! At other times, I was a rainbow-coloured butterfly drifting through the islands of her mind on gossamer-light wings! I was a fountain of perpetual delight, and I was a sunlight shower! I was a dove, a hearth, a steadfast land! Once, Myra was emphatic that I wore a beautiful, tender mask which had something to do with heather-clad mountain-tops and lonely shepherds! At times, she'd abandon her fanciful outbursts to pursue a more solemn course. She wrote typically:

> *I wish I could tell you how much and how deeply I love you, but I can't. Words have not yet been invented to describe such feelings of such capacity and depth in such a short space of time. (Yet I feel it has been written across the face of fate even before the concept of time evolved.) You have become central to my existence, so that I cannot*

envisage life without you.

The hours we spent apart in prison were hellish enough, she assured me. She ached for me, dreamed of me. But when we were together, something altogether stranger happened to her. 'I can hear our hearts in silent communication, beating in perfect unison,' she announced. I must say I'd never noticed. Her writing continued:

I can feel the silent coursing of the blood in our veins moving like twin rivers towards the one same source . . . .

You pierce the innermost depths of my being with the sweet and wholesome pang of your love, and from sheer melting joys of you and desire of you, my soul even faints with longing, yearning for you, asking only to be with you for all time, all sweetness and delight.

My heart hungers and feeds upon you. Let me ever thirst for you, my flood tide of pleasure, my own treasure house. Let my heart and soul be set on you, firmly and unmovably rooted in you until the end of recorded time, for yours, my love, is the right human face I, in my mind, had waited for this long, seeing the false and searching for the true, then found you as a traveller finds a place of welcome suddenly, amid the wrong valleys and rocks and twisting roads.

Obviously, I'd never invited this frenzied level of devotion, and, just as obviously, I could never pretend to return so much as a fraction of it. Instead, I did the biggest thing I possibly could for Myra Hindley. I saved her life.

Josie O'Dywer was a young girl, probably in her early twenties, when I first met her in Holloway. She was tall, and looked fantastic – a bit like James Dean, with big, blue, piercing eyes and curling hair. She never wore any women's gear, only men's. She also suffered extreme mood swings. Part of her problem stemmed from her family background. She used to tell me how much she despised her father but had loved her mother dearly. One day, in the heat of an argument, she yelled at her mum, 'I wish you were dead!' The mother subsequently did die, and Josie was convinced that it was her fault, that she'd uttered the words that killed her.

I'd always reassure her, 'No, you didn't. It wasn't your fault at all.'

But she was so distressed she couldn't see reason and could fly into the most violent tempers without any warning. I've seen five or six screws barely able to hold her down on the floor. She had the strength of a lion, Josie. It was absolutely incredible. She could be very sweet at times, especially when it was to her own advantage. She hated the screws, but she made a point of hanging around them, getting them to feel sorry for her, fascinating them. She once spent an hour just chatting with the assistant governor in her office. I'd always got on very well with Josie. I thought it was a shame that, in her condition, she was in prison at all. She should have been having care in some other establishment.

During the course of her years in and out of institutions, Josie had made best friends with Mary Bell, the notorious child killer. Ironically, she loathed Britain's other infamous child murderess, Myra Hindley, stating simply that Myra was 'different'. Our contrasting opinions of Myra never caused trouble between us until one Sunday morning in May 1976, when I returned from church to be accosted by Josie. 'Janie Jones, you friend of that murdering bastard!' she screamed, shaking with rage. I was shocked. Josie had always been all right with me, yet here she was now, giving me all this abuse in front of a bunch of officers. She then started yelling, 'I'm going to fucking kill that bastard Hindley.' If I'd been an officer, I'd have taken Josie back to her cell immediately she started issuing threats and locked her in until she'd calmed down. No one did.

I hurried off to my cell and found Jenny trying to placate Myra, who was lying on my bed crying her eyes out. The *News of the World* had dragged up the Moors Murders again, commemorating the tenth anniversary of the trial, thus reminding Hindley that her crimes had not been forgotten and never would be. They would haunt her for the rest of her life. The prison staff had taken the precaution of cutting the articles out of the papers, so as to avoid inflaming feeling against Myra among the inmates, but somebody had obviously gone to the trouble of showing the cuttings to Josie O'Dwyer.

Myra asked at the prison office for permission to stay in my cell with Jenny and me because she felt very upset and depressed. She was told that her request would be passed to the governor. While she waited for the decision, she remained unlocked in my cell. All of the other prisoners had been banged up for the lunch-time period, except for the 'carriers', including myself and Josie, who ferried the food trays to and from the kitchens and the cells. We were always locked up last. Myra started to get impatient about the lack of news from the governor, so she decided to enquire again at the office. I listened to her footsteps echoing along the landing, and suddenly my psychic flashed on. I knew something was about to happen.

I rushed outside in time to see Josie O'Dwyer jumping on to Hindley from the recess, one hand grabbing her by the hair, one fist punching her and one great big bovver boot kicking her right in the face, over and over again. She was like a wild woman. Two screws standing nearby merely watched. The recess was the area containing a large open toilet where we slopped out our pots in the mornings. Josie was trying to get Myra over the wire mesh at the top of this recess. Had she succeeded, Hindley would have gone crashing down from the very top landing to her certain death on the ground floor, far below.

Most people, if they were being attacked, would try to defend themselves somehow, even if they were scared to death of their assailant. But Myra did nothing. Absolutely nothing. Her blood was squirting all over the place, she was being kicked and punched senseless, but she simply swayed around limply as she took every blow. She didn't lift a finger to help herself. So, in I charged. I grabbed the hand that Josie was holding Myra's head with and dug in my nails as hard as I could. At the same time I ground my heel into the foot Josie still had on the ground. These actions, together, had the desired effect. Josie released Myra – but not before she'd broken her nose and kicked out the cartilage in her leg. There was blood everywhere.

By this time, somebody had pushed the alarm bell, and the heavy mob came rushing in. Josie was taken down to a punishment cell. She wasn't very heavily punished, though. Everybody knew she was enjoying special treatment down there. The screws were bringing in everything she wanted. She was getting loads of cigarettes, and she was having her shirts ironed for her. She was very well looked after. There was no doubt that she'd been used by the officers to beat up Myra Hindley. They couldn't attack Myra themselves, but they could easily wind up a very violent, disturbed young girl enough to do it for them.

I realized that Josie had merely been the pawn in a bigger game, so when the visiting court came to Holloway to sit in judgement on the incident and called me as a witness, I left out some of the details. I knew Josie shouldn't have assaulted Myra, but then there was once a time when I would've done the same thing myself if I'd had the chance. So I admitted only that I saw the punching and kicking. I decided not to mention that Josie had tried to force Myra over the top of the recess. I reckoned she'd be in enough trouble for what she'd done.

In the end she lost a bit of remission. That was all. As for Myra, she suffered six weeks of agony. Knowing what I know now, I can cheerfully say she deserved it, although I'll never regret stopping Josie from pushing her over the landing. If Josie had killed her, she'd have been as bad as Hindley. And if I'd allowed it, I'd have been as bad as both of them. A quick death would have been too good for Hindley, anyway. She deserves to suffer in prison for the rest of her life. Back then, though, a Hindley convert, I was concerned for Myra as she waited, in pain, for around six weeks to have her broken nose reset and the cartilage in her leg fixed up. She was tended to in the downstairs prison hospital, but she could not be properly treated until a place became available in an outside hospital.

Just before she went, I said to her, 'Look, you've had your nose broken. This is your opportunity to get it reshaped.' I was remembering conversations we'd had in the past where she told me she intended to have plastic surgery so as to become unrecognizable, in anticipation of being released. She duly took my advice and had the famous nose job – and I hate to admit that I'm responsible.

Myra was booked into the hospital under the name of Susan Gibb so that none of the doctors and nurses would realize the identity of their patient. She was accompanied by a couple of screws and a detective, who guarded her round the clock. The detective was posted outside the ward, where he sat disguised as a doctor, complete with the white coat. His one mistake was to forget that doctors don't usually while away their working hours reading the *Police Gazette*! Hindley was in fits of laughter about the telling-off he got from the screws over that one.

While Myra recovered from her injuries and her ordeal, Josie O'Dwyer showed no improvement. She was in and out of punishment regularly for attacks on other women, and throughout the rest of my time in Holloway, she persisted in sending me threatening messages, telling me she would 'get' me. Luckily, she never did.

Violence was very much part and parcel of prison life. It was an absolute jungle in there. I used to watch in amazement. The atmosphere was volatile anyway, with the women shouting and screaming all the time, for all sorts of reasons – anything from suicidal depression to the frustration of confinement in a tiny cell to temper tantrums connected with PMT (pre-menstrual tension). I was pretty lucky not to suffer from PMT, although many of the women had loads of trouble from it, and the prison authorities simply refused to acknowledge the condition.

A good few of the prisoners had serious personal problems, which added to the general tension. They couldn't see their kids as often as they wanted to, or their families were in financial difficulty, or they were worrying about what their husbands were up to outside and imagining all sorts of things. Patience became even more strained when the weather was hot. Then the tiniest thing could spark off a violent outburst. Someone might run out of tobacco or find something stolen from their cell, or say the wrong thing to the wrong person. Wham! There would suddenly be an eruption. There would be noses bleeding and women grabbing each other by the hair and bells ringing and screws rushing in to see what was going on.

The heavy mob would grab the offenders and put them down into punishment, give them an injection and knock them out. When they woke up, they'd find themselves locked in a cell where they would stay for the foreseeable future without money and without recreation, probably without visits and with the likelihood of the loss of remission. The yelling and wailing, the effing and blinding, in the punishment block had to be heard to be believed. The women would be flinging their pots up against the walls, doing everything in their power to create havoc. And when they were returned to the prison mainstream, they were usually as highly strung, as liable to aggressive behaviour, as they were before they left it.

I was once attacked myself, although it didn't amount to much, and I can't even remember what set it off. I didn't get hurt in any way. A woman tried to push me, but I made it clear I would defend myself. I wouldn't let anybody get the better of me without putting up a damned good fight. I never showed fright in front of anyone in prison. It would have been the worst thing I could do. Generally, though, I was well liked and not usually picked on. I got on with nearly everybody because I used a bit of psychology and tried to understand individual personalities and problems, so I could relate to each person in the appropriate way. Quite a bit of power-play went on, which would often explode into fighting. Women would be at each others' throats over who was top dog, or who was chief tobacco baron, or who was the ace wheeler-dealer.

The lifers tended to walk about like something extra-special. They had perks, you see. They were permitted three or four changes of clothes, and they could have certain items such as tape recorders and radios in their cells. They could have their own bed covers sent in, as well as china plates, a teapot and a kettle. All this accounted for the resentment towards them of the rank-and-file prisoners who had no such privileges. Myra Hindley was one lifer who did indeed feel important in Holloway. More than that, she considered herself a superstar. She'd grown up in the north, a little nobody, and now she was really somebody. She was a name.

One woman of our acquaintance, Bernie Harwood, had been in and out of prison all her life since childhood. She must have been fifty-something. She liked to think of herself as the Duchess, and she swanned around for all the world like number one. She detested Myra Hindley because she believed that Myra considered herself to be the boss inside and was therefore challenging her position. She was also nursing an old wound regarding Myra, which dated back to the days before my arrest. She had resented the fact that the then-Governor of Holloway, the popular Mrs Dorothy Wing, had taken a special interest in Hindley. Mrs Wing had been so convinced of Myra's potential for rehabilitation that she drove her out of the prison, one day in September 1972, for a walk on Hampstead Heath. Although she was entitled to do this for any category B prisoner, the fact that her charge was Myra Hindley caused a national outrage when the story somehow exploded all over the newspapers.

Bernie Harwood later told me that she had personally leaked the information to cause as much trouble as possible for Hindley. She only felt guilty later on when she realized how much distress she'd created for Mrs Wing, who was publicly rapped by the Home Office for having made an error of judgement. I don't know to this day if Bernie Harwood was telling me the truth. I do know that she continued to threaten to 'get Hindley', and although things never actually came to blows, she went out of her way to make Myra's life awkward whenever she could.

There were all sorts of personal jealousies simmering away below the surface of life in Holloway, and these gave rise to regular flare-ups. There were women who were jealous of each other for any one of a hundred reasons. Some were jealous over girlfriends within the prison. Others were jealous over officers' favouritism. I was aware, from time to time, of some of the convicts being jealous of me over my so-called glamour and also because of my record for good behaviour. A few of them tried to lead me into trouble, tried to get me helping them out with various devious things, but I never fell for anything like that. I didn't mind risking my parole over some little scheme I might have engineered myself, but I certainly wasn't going to risk it for anyone else's amusement. Mostly, I was a model prisoner.

I simply ignored any suggestions I didn't like. I accepted jealousy, in all of its manifestations, as a fact of life in jail, went about my business as usual, and kept my eyes open for the next punch-up. One day while I was in Holloway's hospital unit – as a patient and also as a helper – I saw one girl pick up an urn of tea and throw it all over another woman. They grabbed each other and started to fight. I don't know what caused it, but they were quickly separated and that was the end of that. Or so I thought. Later, the same night, one of the women tried to set fire to herself. I was one of the first to smell it, because I was in the cell right next to hers. It was a hell of a hot summer, 1976, and there was very little air, so the smoke from the fire had me choking within seconds. I opened my window, and I was yelling out for all I was worth. I thought I was suffocating. Luckily, the alarm bells brought help in time to save the girl, as they did again when other women tried the same thing.

But more often than not, when the bells went, it was a false alarm. Some of the women in the hospital were unstable, and they used to delight in ringing the bells to create a panic, especially since they knew there was a shortage of staff. This used to infuriate me, especially since I'd had a premonition that something serious was going to happen. I'd say, 'You know there are hardly any nurses down here, and you get them running around in circles for nothing with your piss-balling about. You're just taking the mickey. If you don't stop it, they're not going to take the bells seriously when there really is an emergency.'

Most of the nursing staff were lovely, and they bore up to the nonsense with amazing good humour. My favourite was Sister Jean Frazer, an adorable coloured woman, and I also liked Sister Clifford who was strict but had a heart of gold. She did everything she could to help the prisoners. One night, however, we had a very aggressive nurse on duty. Again, the hospital was short-staffed, and again the bells were ringing and ringing. The nurse raged, 'If those bells ring any more, I'm going to have them switched off.'

The women's response was to keep on ringing. And then there was silence. The nurse had done as she'd threatened. Next thing, I sat up in my cell in horror: 'God! Somebody is on fire!' The most dreadful stench of burning flesh was coming from the direction of the padded cells. These were where women were taken if it was feared they might try to harm themselves. I shouted as loud as I could to everybody, 'Bang on the doors! Bang! Bang!' By the time the message got through and help arrived, the girl had burned to death.

My most personal experience of fire was when one broke out in my cell. I didn't light it, I hasten to add. It was started by another prisoner in the most serious and misguided fit of jealousy I would ever suffer in prison. It all began in the spring of 1976 when I received news that my house had been burgled – hardly an enviable situation in itself! I was permitted to leave Holloway for a day and return to Campden Hill Road under escort, to make a list of everything that had been stolen from the house. It had been lying empty, ready to be sold or, failing that, rented out as a means of raising the money to pay my trial costs.

In a way, I'd rather not have seen what had been done to my home. It was heartbreaking. I cried my eyes out when I walked in and saw the state of the place. Loads of stuff had gone missing including televisions, a beautiful set of six early Victorian French chairs worth about £5000, a lovely porcelain collection and a box of valuable jewellery. It was a very dubious burglary. There was no sign of a forced entry, and no clue that the intruder(s) had had trouble moving the bulky objects out of the house. Several people had keys to the front door, to my knowledge, but I couldn't accuse one without accusing them all, and I didn't have grounds to suspect anyone in particular.

On 26 March 1976, I was let out of my cell at 1.30 p.m. I was asked to take some cans back to the kitchens and while I was there, I was held back by another inmate who insisted on having a chat. She was a strange character, so desperate to be admitted to an outside hospital that she kept trying to injure herself. On one occasion, she blacked her own eyes, which was too much of a minor complaint to warrant more than a cold tea-bag from the prison nurse. On another occasion, I stopped her pouring boiling hot toffee over her hand. After this conversation, instead of returning to my cell, I went straight to the regular group-therapy session. The prison had brought in a therapist to talk to women who needed emotional help. Many of the prisoners really did have problems. Others went to the sessions because it was a way of getting out of their routine work and, as an added bonus, they could smoke too. The doctor didn't mind. In fact, he used to offer round his own cigarettes.

I used to enjoy the meetings because I would learn so much about the other women. I'd always been fascinated by what made people tick. Typically, it was me who had to start the ball rolling every time. The very first day we attended a session, I looked around and saw thirty people gazing into space, none of them prepared to break the ice. 'Right,' I announced, 'it looks like I've got to start it off. I'm a sex expert!' I told them all about men and their different fantasies – everything from their more usual fetishes, such as nurses' uniforms, to the more specialist tastes of those who liked to be tortured and trodden on with big high heels. For fun and informality, I mentioned the wealthy chap I knew whose major kick was girls with feathers up their bottoms shouting 'Cock-a-doodle-doo'.

I went on and on about the parties and the two-way mirror and the half-time swapping sessions. And finally, I described the genuinely disturbing cases of child abuse and violence that I'd come across. This was enough to trigger a series of confessions from the women in the meeting, some who'd been abused by step-parents, others who suffered from agoraphobia. I felt that week by week the therapy was achieving more.

On the day I was referring to – 26 March – we were only a few minutes into the session when a woman called Chris noticed the smell of burning. She thought it was herself at first and patted her jacket to make sure she hadn't set light to it accidentally. I though it might have been something to do with the doctor, since he'd just put out a cigarette, but I was wrong. Meanwhile, the smell was getting stronger. We went to investigate the kitchen, thinking someone may have forgotten about something cooking. Wrong again. The smell got worse.

Suddenly, I looked up and saw the officers on the top landing kick open a door and rush in with a fire extinguisher. I nearly died when I realized it was my cell. All of my clothes were burnt black. There was my £15,000 mink coat, my grey pin-stripe trouser suit, my velvet suit – all the changes of clothes I was allowed to have. I was left with what I stood up in. The newspapers had a field day with the 'mink coat' angle.

A couple of the officers cried when they saw the wreckage of my belongings, and I ended up having to comfort them. 'Don't worry,' I told them. 'It's only clothes. I can always get more. The main thing is that no one was killed or harmed.'

What upset me most was the fact that one of my fellow-prisoners would think of doing something like this to me. Although there wasn't evidence enough to name the culprit, everybody knew who it was, including the screws. They were sure enough of their feelings that they moved the woman off the wing. She was the same woman who'd kept me talking in the kitchen, just before I went to the therapy meeting. The flames were probably already licking around my clothes at the very time I was standing chatting to her.

She'd only recently been brought on to our wing from the mother and baby unit, and the prisoners had been warned to watch her carefully. Her own baby had been taken away into outside care after other children were found to have been scratched by pins, allegedly by her. She'd also been suspected of starting a small fire in the unit. After the removal of her own kid, she became desperate to find her way out of prison so they could be reunited, hence her efforts to get herself hospitalized outside the gates. She was obviously mentally disturbed. Most of the women hated her, would have loved to kill her, but a few of them delighted in winding her up. My day away from prison, sorting out the burglary, had been a gift for them. They had taunted her, 'Look at that. You can't go out to see your baby, but she can get out and go home because she's Janie Jones. It's all right for her.'

And so I had the burglary to thank for the misfortune of the fire. But it wasn't the only problem my house would give rise to during my imprisonment. Only four months later, I was told that squatters had moved in, alerted by the 'For Sale' sign I'd had put up. They remained in Campden Hill Road for the rest of the year, and they had the audacity to talk to the press about their occupation. In September 1976, they posed for photographs at the window. They told reporters that 'the two-way mirror doesn't mean anything to us because we're completely uninhibited about such things.'

They refused to move from the house, and an application for legal aid to evict them was made in court. They wouldn't leave my premises until they had to, ten days before Christmas. I'd felt absolutely helpless about the situation, all the way through. But I'd have felt a whole lot worse if I'd known what a shocking, disgusting pigsty they'd made of my home. That I wouldn't discover until my release.

The first time I ever set foot in Styal Prison, Cheshire, I felt it straight away. There was a ghost in there, and it was something really, really evil. I immediately told the first officer I could find. She asked, 'Why do you say that, Janie?'

I replied instinctively: 'I don't know, but I feel that someone's died a tragic death here, and I can hear a child crying, and there is somebody shouting out.' 'That's weird,' the screw said. 'This used to be a children's place in the wartime.' She also confided, 'Some of the officers have to sleep downstairs now and again, and I've never liked to do that. I hate it. I feel this cold thing coming past me, and I'm scared stiff. Like you, I experience a sense of something evil.'

Before many days were out, I'd seen a vision, a woman in a long grey robe walking past me with a child who was screaming and shouting. I was even more convinced that something terrible had happened in this building. 'That's quite possible,' agreed the screw, when I told her. 'I'm sure there's a lot of history in this house.'

The accommodation at HMP Styal comprised a number of houses built on a high-security estate. But despite all of its careful landscaping, the views of gardens and trees and flowers that I'd missed for so long, I wanted nothing more than to return to Holloway. Styal was vile. My loathing of the place wasn't simply based on my psychic feelings, which alone would have been enough to warn me I would never be happy there. I had various other reasons for urgently wanting to leave. To begin with, I was moved from the first house into another one full of murderesses, personifications of the devilish atmosphere that surrounded me on that very first day and that never left me. There was so much hate in there, it was unbelievable. I longed every night to be banged up in the safety of my cell in Holloway, with the big lock on the door. As an added incentive to get out of this hell-hole in the middle of nowhere, I had received a threat to my life from an inmate named Billie, a bullying, butch woman from whose clutches I was always trying to protect the young and more naïve arrivals at the prison.

The front door of the house would be locked at night. Inside, you could wander around at will – at any time to leave the dormitory you had to share with the most despicable women imaginable and to walk into any other dormitory you chose, full of similarly ruthless prisoners. The frightening thing was that they could also walk into yours. I suffered from all sorts of illnesses, apart from the obvious anxiety, while I remained in that place. A leaking ceiling, which I reported six times without result, gave me a cold, chest trouble and cold sores on my lips. I suffered more frequently from migraine and sickness, lasting up to four days non-stop. My weight plummeted to around six stone. Another problem was a drastic reduction in my visits, due to the inaccessibility of Styal. And I was allowed only one weekly letter. Finally, there was the exhaustion caused by constantly travelling to and from London in the never-ending battle to unravel my legal and financial affairs – themselves a cause of constant worry and tension.

From the beginning of my sentence through to the early part of

1977, I was a person of no real fixed abode: the authorities kept shuttling me between Holloway and Styal. Sometimes I remained for months in one, sometimes for a similar length of time in the other. During my stays at Styal, I was regularly whisked off south for a night in Holloway and then returned to Cheshire the next day. The trips between there and London were monstrously expensive. No wonder: I was driven in hired cars. The press raised a fuss about this unnecessary extravagance, and I must admit, I agreed with them.

The *People* ran a headline on 13 February 1977, declaring: PRISON SHOP-BY-TAXIS SHOCKER. That story, about Styal, revealed that 'taxis used to take prisoners on 400-mile round trips to London.' On one such occasion, my car broke down. It was reported with glee in the papers that I sat there in all my glory, ordering the screws to get out and push. Did I? Well, I can only say that if they were prepared to take the instructions, of course I would give them. I enjoyed giving instructions! It was also stated that when a replacement car arrived, a Volvo, I sailed off with the driver, looking a million dollars in my low-cut dress, leaving the prison officers to find their own transport. It was unbelievable. What actually happened was that when the car died, another one, a Volvo, was sent out. It had nothing whatsoever to do with my personal preferences, and we carried on with our journey, all together.

I had to appear before Bow Street court every couple of weeks to explain the continuing non-payment of my thousands of pounds' worth of trial costs. The trouble was that I couldn't raise the money until I sold the house. And I couldn't sell the house without a permanent base in a London prison where I had proper access to my various advisers – solicitors, estate agents and so on. I was often miles away when my representatives were trying to deal with a multitude of problems, from small but important details to the major headache of the squatters. In Styal, my hands were tied.

By the New Year of 1977, I'd started campaigning earnestly to be accepted into Holloway as a full-time resident. I went on hunger strikes, I appealed to the Home Office, I wrote to my MP in London, I rallied support from Lord Longford and various other luminaries, and I once walked voluntarily into the punishment block at Styal after refusing to go to London and Holloway without the whole of my belongings. I just did not want to return to that houseful of murderesses.

At the same time, I was writing letters and drumming up support for my protest at the rejection of my parole applications. Now not only was I watching violent and poisonous criminals walking out of the prison gates way ahead of time, but I was also reading reports of sentences passed in court that made a mockery of the savage seven years I'd been handed. A madam called Pearl had walked out of court with a suspended sentence after being charged with activities involving 124 call-girls. Another lady collected a suspended sentence for her part in a drug-trafficking offence involving £1 million.

And as all my appeals for justice and for manageable living conditions continued to meet with little response, I started wondering if somebody, somewhere, had some pull and some strings and was simply interested in making me suffer a little bit more. I believed that some higher authority was trying to grind me into the ground. I just couldn't understand why my appeals for parole were thrown out so decisively. I could not fathom why it would be in anybody's interest to keep me in Styal Prison as opposed to Holloway. I asked myself, 'Is there somebody very high up, somebody like the Lord with the "schoolgirls" and the teddy bears, trying to tread me down because they are frightened about what I can say when I come out? Is there someone really trying to give me a nervous breakdown?'

Then, all of a sudden, a light appeared somewhere in the middle of the tunnel: the new Holloway Prison building was about to open, and Myra Hindley and myself were among those taken to see round it. We were both told that we would be moving in, and we were shown our cells. Myra's was going to be opposite the office. The new place was heaven after what we'd known before. It was luxurious by comparison with the big, old, draughty, freezing Holloway castle. The cells had en suite toilets and wash basins, and you could look out of the windows and see little bits of greenery. It was wonderful.

But just as suddenly as our hopes had been raised, they were dashed. Myra and I were informed that we were not now going to the new Holloway. Hindley was to go to HMP Durham, which was described by prisoners who'd been there as 'a morgue', the very depths of hell. She went hysterical. She caused ructions. She had already been to

Durham for a time and she knew that you were never allowed to leave your wing, that you were watched day and night by cameras so you couldn't get away with anything, and that you could hear the men on the other side of the prison. My cell-mate Jenny had been there for a little while too. She said, 'Darling, it is absolutely diabolical.'

Nevertheless, Myra was packed off to Durham, and from there to Cookham Wood near Rochester, Kent. For my part, I was informed that I would be going to my 'allocated' prison, Styal, where I would remain on a permanent basis, barring my necessary appearances in London. In a letter from the Home Office, I was told that while my disappointment at the allocation of cells in the new Holloway was 'accepted', I had been permitted to stay in London for extended periods only to help me resolve my 'complicated private, business and legal affairs'. I was required to go back to Styal 'as soon as [my] presence at Holloway was no longer essential to putting [my] affairs in order'.

My affairs of course, were nowhere near in order; they were becoming more confused as they went along. But I was, nevertheless, transferred to Styal full-time, according to the authorities' wishes and despite the bitter opposition I put up myself. In the end, I would be returned to Holloway to finish my sentence, in the new building. But, for now, I had somehow to keep my chin up as I prepared to share – and trust – my life with some of the most vicious women in the country. For the time being, I also had to forget about Myra Hindley because the rules forbade correspondence between prisons. There would be no further contact between us – for some years anyway.

CHAPTER THIRTEEN

Welcome to the Jungle

Every female jail has its share of nut-cases. They are the convicts who believe that they have nothing left to lose and are therefore entitled to barge through life doing exactly as they please. They are ruthless bullies, women who can find no use for conscience and compassion except as 'weaknesses' in fellow-prisoners. They can then intimidate and prey on the 'flaws' in these women – using whatever means necessary and for whatever ends.

Outwardly less frightening but equally dangerous are those inmates who are mentally disturbed, who should be receiving psychiatric help rather than custodial containment and who are liable to fly into violent frenzies for no apparent reason. Then, at the other end of the scale, there are some inherently decent women who have ended up behind bars by accident, by set-up, for love or through dire financial necessity.

The middle ground contains a colourful collection of all-sorts. The petty offenders spring to mind. So do the addictive criminals, the con merchants, the lovable villains, the well-to-do thrill seekers . . . . and the scum of the earth, the ones who have not been ashamed to scavenge or batter a few lousy pence out of ordinary folk who can least afford it.

Every prisoner has to find her own place in this strange society, her own way of dealing with the people who surround her, her own means of distinguishing the forgivable from the unforgivable, and her own ability to make real friends while not inviting enemies. The secret of my own survival in the jungle was the combination of several particular abilities: I could mask any fear I may have been feeling; I could see the funny side of life; I could rebel against any problem and rise above it in the end; and I could communicate with even the most difficult women, because of my genuine and insatiable interest in other people.

A small percentage of lifers had committed such stomach-churning crimes that I would have nothing to do with them. I'd look them in the eyes but remain at arm's length, knowing the dangers of courting or antagonizing amoral people. Other less savage cons, whose murders I could still never justify, I tended to view as numbers to begin with. Only on that basis could I co-exist with them in prison and go forward into any kind of relationships. Anna Mendleson and Hilary Creek, the Angry Brigade terrorists, were among this number. They were both serving ten-year sentences for their parts in a bombing campaign when I met them in Holloway. Neither bore any resemblance to the traditional image of the terrorist as grim-faced fanatic.

Anna was stunning to look at. She was taller than Hindley even, six foot something, and very pretty and elegant with it. She had a lovely, humorous nature. University-educated, she was talented musically, singing along in a beautiful voice when she played the guitar. Once I had accepted her purely and simply as a captive, same as myself, I could allow myself to think about the crime she'd committed. I asked her, 'What did you blow places up for? What made you do that?'

She told me she was influenced by the boyfriend she loved, and she added: 'I was young and stupid, but I'm not saying I don't deserve to take my share of the blame.' She shared a cell with Myra Hindley for a time, apparently at the time of the escape plot, and they always got along well together, probably because Anna, like myself, became convinced of Myra's innocence. Myra, however, used to hate Anna's friend Hilary Creek and say the most terrible things about her. Hilary was smaller than Anna Mendleson, with mousey-blondish hair and a little upturned nose.

I wasn't one of Hilary's biggest fans. I disliked the way she curried favour with the screws. She got away with loads of things. For instance, she was informed at the same time as I was that she would be transferred to Styal Prison. She had enough pull within Holloway to wangle her way out of this arrangement, and so she stayed where she was. Yet, while I had every reason in the world to remain in a London prison and had put heart and soul into my campaign of official and rational protest, I was moved.

Some prisoners I took an instant liking to, and my instincts served me well in these cases. I remember my Holloway cell-mate Jenny with great fondness, and I'm in touch with her to this day. She's working on helping prisoners, having taken her degree in sociology. Jenny was massive at the time I met her, really big and jolly. She used to have me in hysterics. She had a religious Catholic background, but ended up serving two or three years for her part in some major fraud involving a franking machine. The ringleader was a gay friend of hers, Jimmy. She made a lot of cash, but she didn't really see any of it because she was always pissed out of her mind, having a ball. She'd tell me, 'Oh, yes, I was up to my neck in the fraud. But I haven't got any money left at all. I used to give it all to Jimmy and his boyfriend.'

Jenny was neither a hard nut nor an idiot. She was a generous person, one who wanted to enjoy her life to the best of her ability, which was something we had in common. We also shared a tremendous sympathy for the underdog, the woman who could never even dare to dream of happiness. That woman is more often the murderess than the rampaging psycho so beloved of Hollywood scriptwriters. Crimes of passion, murder committed through the snapping of a mind profoundly damaged by others – these were the crimes that fascinated me in prison and their perpetrators, almost without exception, responded to my natural curiosity and concern. They began to talk.

I've always had the knack of bringing people out of themselves, just through showing interest, and understanding emotions and problems. At the same time, I'd speak my mind if I thought they were wrong. I never patronized anybody. When I was a kid, my father once said of me, 'She's lived another life. She's like a tiny little thing with a mature head on her shoulders. She's always asking questions. She wants to know.' I never changed.

It was as a teenager working in the Three Counties Hospital, the mental home in Bedfordshire, that I discovered my special talent for relating to irrational and sometimes bloody-minded people. One woman patient had refused to talk to anybody in years. Yet, within a week, I had her chatting and confiding in me, purely because I'd guessed her underlying problem and confronted her with it. Another lady, who'd been resident for four years, was well enough to be discharged after pouring her heart out to me and learning to look at her troubles from other angles.

Prisoners in Holloway responded to me in exactly the same way. I was like an agony aunt in there. I used to have a mile-long queue of women outside my cell door, coming to see me for advice. They were worried about their relationships, or their kids outside, or their visiting orders. I knew everybody's background, and what they were in for. I was also regularly approached by remand prisoners, asking me what to do about different aspects of their trials. It was exhausting. And it wasn't just the convicts who took advantage of my counselling services. In the most ironic twist of all, the doctor in charge of the women's therapy sessions once summoned me for a private consultation – to ask me what to do about his love life!

There were all kinds in there. On one occasion, I was warned by the screws about a young kid, an arsonist, who had come on to the wing. They said, 'She gets all these funny turns, and she gets violent when she takes her period.'

I said, 'I'll take charge.' Venturing into her cell, I saw a beautiful, red-haired girl peering at me with one eye while she covered the other half of her face with a sheet. It was a habit of hers. I often felt it signified that she liked one half of herself and hated the other half. I knew that she was schizophrenic and had claimed to hear voices. I told her, 'I used to be a nurse, so I know about the voices. Some people can hear voices that other people can't, and I know these voices can say awful things. What do yours say?'

'They tell me to cock my leg up and piss against the wall,' she replied.

'Oh,' I said, 'That's an awful thing to have to listen to. Just ignore them when they start saying silly things like that.'

The more we talked, the more she started opening up, and I could get to the nitty-gritty of what was happening. As a youngster, she'd lived at her aunt's house and was sexually abused by one of her aunt's many boyfriends. Eventually, she was put into a girls' institution where she started fires because she hated it so much. She had a very low opinion of herself. No matter how many times I complimented her, she'd reply, 'I'm ugly. My mother used to say so.'

I told her, 'You've gotta try and pull yourself together. You need medical treatment, there's no doubt about it, but you can be put right, and you can leave here and get married.'

'Who'd want to marry me?' she whined.

'Lots of men,' I assured her. 'You're a beautiful girl. You've just had some sort of breakdown.'

I took her under my wing, kept her occupied and looked after her that bit more than usual, made allowances for her when she was on a period and the voices seemed to be at their worst. She started helping me with my coffee-making duties in the welfare department, after I'd promised to take responsibility for any fire she might start. I told her, 'I'm taking you with me on trust. If you set anything on fire, I'm the one who's going to end up with the punishment.'

'Oh, I won't,' she said. 'I'm happy with you.' And I had no trouble from her. After three or four months, she'd improved immensely. Everyone said she was like a changed person. When she did throw a tantrum, it was thanks to a couple of sadistic screws who'd say stupid things to her, just to set her off. I'd say, 'Look, don't rant and rave about it, or they'll stop you coming with me on the coffee duty.' That would calm her down.

I was subsequently moved to Styal Prison full-time, and I didn't see her again until I was returned to Holloway at the end of my prison sentence. I was horrified to walk into her cell in the prison hospital and find her back at square one, lying on her bed with a sheet over half of her face. Sister Clifford, the nurse with the heart of gold, could only do so much. She told me, 'It's one of those things. You know I'm short-staffed. I haven't got enough nurses to give her the care she needs.'

That was why they liked me being down in the hospital when I was in Holloway. I voluntarily took on care work, which would otherwise not have been done because they were being forced to operate on a skeleton staff. They were run into the ground there. Nurses would be working double shifts, and it would sometimes make them niggly and nasty. They were dealing with potentially violent people, so they had a lot to put up with.

I used to enjoy mixing with the mentally disturbed people. I'd do their make-up, hair and nails, pluck their eyebrows and try to make things more pleasant for them. One woman I was told to be wary of had a habit of battering people. I talked to her. She told me, 'I hammered my brother-in-law over the head.' I asked why. Her reply I reported to the nursing staff as she said she'd heard voices telling her that the brother-in-law had been trying to take her house away from her. She was one of the fortunate ones. She was transferred to another institution where she was able to receive psychiatric help.

I saw so much pain among the other prisoners, and I used to live their pain. I used to fight for the women inside all the time, if I could. I'd run backwards and forwards, trying to sort out their problems with visits, or whatever else I might be able to help with. Where I could I would attempt to fight the system to get the wrongs of our lives put right or at least made more bearable. There was, however, one woman in Holloway that I wouldn't have crossed the landing to help. She was the murderess of my old friend Bob Geddes, the journalist who liked to buy and sniff ladies' knickers. She told me, 'I stabbed him and the blood flew many feet up into the air, but I'll get away with it, because I'm his common-law wife.' She wasn't his common-law wife. That was a lot of bollocks, and I knew it for a certain fact: I knew all about this woman through Janice, my first and only female lover, who was a friend of a friend. The truth was that Bob had been letting her stay at his flat because he felt sorry for her. She showed her gratitude by stabbing him to death. She was absolutely screwy. But her claim to have been his common-law wife was believed by the authorities, and she was released from prison on her first parole application. Six weeks later she was back, for arson on her brother's home.

When I moved to Styal more or less permanently, I found myself once again in demand as an adviser. Women made it their business to seek me out with confessions and appeals for help, and those I regarded as acquaintances, I'd do my best for, as ever, even if it only meant listening. One of the first prisoners I met told me the A to Z of how she battered her father to death. She was a little bit retarded, but it was obvious she'd loved him and deeply regretted what she'd done. Her background was that, as a little girl, she'd looked after her bedridden mother, whom she idolized, and also cooked and cleaned for her father. When she was thirteen or fourteen, her mother died. Her father then insisted that she should be around at all times to look after him.

Several years later, she started going to the pub where she met a married man and became his lover. She killed her father for £500 of his savings, which she intended to give her boyfriend. After the murder, she threw the hammer into some water near where she lived and phoned the police. She told them there'd been a burglary. But she didn't even bother washing her father's blood off her clothes, so when the cops turned up she was arrested straight away.

She used to cry her eyes out to me. She'd weep, 'Oh, I killed my daddy, and I loved him. Why did I do it?' Yet, she refused to accept any specialist help in prison, so I became her substitute analyst. I had a great deal of sympathy for this woman. She was another one who should never have been in a prison but in an establishment geared towards helping the mentally backward.

Crimes of passion I also understood, and I spent many hours discussing them with the perpetrators. One such woman was Mary Scanlon, who became quite a good friend of mine in Styal. She was in for life. Her story began when she fell in love with her Indian boyfriend and moved into a fourth or fifth floor flat with him. Soon after, Mary's brother brought a teenage girl to the flat for sex. She didn't leave the next day. She didn't have a home to go to. She'd taken a liking to Mary's flat, and a couple of nights later, she was still there. One night, Mary went to bed after having had quite a bit to drink. Suddenly, she awoke to see that her boyfriend had left the bed. She found him having sex with the brother's girl. In an instant of fury, she picked up a knife and stabbed him, then walked all the way down the stairs to the ground floor and called for the police. She never moaned about her sentence. She'd tell me, 'I deserve to be in here,' but I never agreed. It wasn't as though she was the sort of woman who would walk out of the prison gates and suddenly take off on a killing spree. I believed that the circumstances of her crime were most unfairly reflected in the sentence she was given.

I had no such sympathy, however, for another 'passion killer', a strait-laced, church-going schoolteacher called Isabel. She had embarked upon married life with every reason to look forward to a happy future. She had two children and a husband she adored – but her downfall was that she adored him too much. When he started going out with another woman, she not only put up with it, but she also pretended to be his sister so that he could bring the mistress home without any embarrassment to her.

One day Isabel was having sex with her husband when the mistress's little child blundered into the room and caught them. The husband didn't want the kid to tell his lover that he'd been screwing his 'sister', so he ordered Isabel to murder the child. She did, to 'show her love' for her husband. And she ended up serving time while he was out in the free world doing God knows what. I wondered what kind of a person she was, really, to have got herself involved in something so sickening. If I hadn't know her history, I'd have thought she was an unbelievably nice woman. She told me over and over again, and very matter-of-factly, that what had happened, happened because the devil had come to her. But, devil or no devil, she never stopped loving her husband, and she carried on seeing him on prison visits.

On a happier note – for the intended victim – one would-be murderess just couldn't get it right. Lesley Lord, a nondescript, blondish woman, who was in her mid-to-late thirties when I met her in Styal, was determined to kill her husband because she felt abused by him. She tried. And she tried again. And again. She succeeded only in getting herself arrested and earning a nickname in the press: the Bungling Assassin.

Lesley told me that her marital problems set in when the husband started making her pose for nude and pornographic photographs against her wishes. He then forced her into wife-swapping sessions with other couples, which she didn't like either. She got thoroughly fed up.

Her father-in-law used to come and stay at their home quite often, and she ended up confiding everything in him. One thing led to another. She fell in love with her father-in-law and decided to murder her husband.

She told me, 'Once I went out picking poisonous mushrooms. I chopped them up, I put them in his food, I watched him eat them – and nothing happened. Another time, I tried to electrocute him by tying various wires together, but that didn't work either. I tried all sorts of things, to no avail. Finally, I crushed up some very strong sleeping pills and spiked his dinner. He dropped down on the floor, and as he lay there, I banged him over the head, and I kept banging. Then he got up.' She was sentenced to something like seven years, and the father-in-law served time inside as well. Yet even after all that, the husband would visit her in prison and ask her to come back to him.

Yes, there's nowt so strange as folk, to paraphrase the old northern saying. But some of the folk in Styal Prison were more than strange. As I said earlier, there were some very nasty pieces of work in that place, and I did my best to avoid any contact with them. Unfortunately, this wasn't always possible. I had to share a dormitory in one of the jail houses with a con called Pat, who was convicted of murdering her own child because the kid had disturbed her while she was watching television.

There were sixteen or eighteen women living in different dormitories in the house the day a knife went missing from the kitchen. The inside doors were never locked, and when night fell, Mary Scanlon, who also slept in the same room as me, kept urging, 'Let's barricade ourselves in.'

She managed to whip up a vote of agreement, but I had to hide my terror. I was sure (and much later I heard I was right) that we were barricading ourselves into a dormitory with the woman who had the knife: Pat Benson. She worked in the kitchen. She was definitely disturbed. She was capable of doing anything with the knife. She was a lifer, and another murder would make no difference to her sentence. I don't mind admitting that I spent a sleepless night, lying in bed with my eyes closed for appearances' sake, but listening out carefully for even the slightest rustle in the dark. Mercifully, it didn't come.

A delightfully entertaining conversation took place one morning between myself and a group of new arrivals at Styal, young girls who were
anxious to learn the ropes as quickly as possible. They wanted to know,
'What's the regime?' and 'What are the screws like?'

'Well, it's prison. You're locked in, and that's it. But if you behave
yourself, you'll be all right,' I replied.

One girl then turned to me and said, 'I hope we don't meet Janie
Jones.'

'Why's that?' I enquired.

'Oo,' she said, 'she's evil, she glares, and she puts a spell on you.
You've got to be very careful. She ran the prison in Holloway, you know.'

'Oh, really?' I smiled. 'What do you think of me?'

'Oh, you're nice,' returned the young girl. 'I like you very much.'

I persisted: 'What does this Janie Jones look like?'

'Oh, she's very big and tall, and she's got long blonde hair, and
she's got these big eyes that hypnotize you and scare you . . . .'

At this point, Mary Scanlon, who was waiting with me in the queue
to see the doctor, started killing herself laughing. She asked the girls,
'Do you know who this is, then?'

'No,' they chorused.

'She is Janie Jones.'

They couldn't believe it. They kept saying, 'Never! A little thing
like you?' It all ended in hugs, with the girls telling me how ridiculous
they felt.

I said, 'Don't you worry your heads about me. But if you take my
advice, you'll steer well clear of several women around these parts, and
particularly Mary Bell. She is evil on two legs. She is the devil.'

Mary Bell killed her first victim, four-year-old Martin Brown, on the
eve of her eleventh birthday in her home town of Newcastle. Two months
later, she struck again. This time, she picked on another local infant, three-
year-old Brian Howe, puncturing his body with scissors after his death and
carving the letter M on his stomach with a razor blade. In December 1968,
she was sentenced to detention for life for the manslaughter of both boys,
after the jury accepted a plea of diminished responsibility. She was sent

first of all to a special unit in an approved school where in 1970, one of the masters was accused of indecently assaulting her. He was subsequently acquitted in court, after the judge suggested to the jury that the allegations were a total fabrication on Mary Bell's part.

She was still only eighteen or nineteen years old when I first met her. She had lovely black hair, beautiful blue eyes and a face like a little angel. A very intelligent girl, she had lots of charm and smarm. She tried her best to make friends with me at first, even asking me if I would read her poetry, but I quickly gave her the message that I wasn't interested. I'd been getting strong vibrations from her, and I could feel that she was wicked through and through.

It didn't take long to find out just how wicked she was. She would be very sweet and nice when the officers were around, because like every other woman in there, she wanted to get out. She did bewitch them, too. Well, most of them. They believed she was as innocent as she looked, and they let her get away with blue murder. She knew all the fiddles, all the ways round the rules and regulations, and even the governor was quite sympathetic to her. But the screws only had to turn their backs for a moment, and she'd be cutting up the other girls' clothes, using scissors. She'd be telling threatening tales of black-magic rituals to scare the women into handing over their tobacco and other possessions. She be laughing as she stuck pins into photographs of their children on the notice-board, or smeared them with blood.

She used to boast about all sorts of cruelty connected to her satanic rituals. She bragged that she cut the throats of pigeons and of some little kittens born within the prison grounds. Women would often come running to me, screaming and crying about what Mary Bell had done to their kids' photos, but they were far too scared of her to even look her in the eye, much less do anything about it. I used to stare at her. I'd say, 'I can see straight through you because I'm psychic. I know you're evil, but you don't frighten me.' Once, I asked her if she ever felt remorse about the poor little kids she'd killed.

She replied, 'I only feel sorry I was fucking caught. I'll not get caught the next time.'

I shot back, 'Ah, so there will be a next time, if you ever get the chance.'

Not long after this, I wrote the following entry in my diary:

Today, Bell has topped it all. She was on about evil fucking Hindley murdering kids. What a nut-case. I can't believe my ears. I remind her that she's killed two little, sweet boys who will never live to give their mothers pleasure, and all she can do is laugh like a drain.

I told her: 'You need a bloody good psychiatrist, and I doubt if even the best one in the world would be able to put you right.' I said this as contemptuously as I possibly could. I didn't want her to keep hanging around me. I didn't want her in my presence. If she came into the sitting room, I'd walk out. I hated her. She was always showing off to anyone who would listen about her experiences in the approved school, which was mixed. Many times, I couldn't help but hear her trumpeting:

'Cor, I used to go round with no knickers on and get all the boys at it. They were so simple, I had them all round my little finger. I could get them to do anything I wanted.'

One person who would not do what she wanted was the master who ended up in court. She informed her friends, 'I used to tell him that I wanted chocolates or I was going to report him and say he had been having sex with me. I scared the life out of him. But in the end, he stopped bringing me the chocolates, the bastard, so I did report him. Pity it didn't work. Usually I can manipulate any man. I have a power over them.'

She planned to use this power when she was released to con some mug into giving her a child of her own. In fact, this is exactly what happened. In October 1988 the papers reported that Mary Bell had gone into hiding with her four-year-old daughter. She had originally dumped the child, leaving her with her father when she ran off with his ex-best friend, a 'witchcraft weirdo'. Probation officers subsequently handed the little girl back to Bell. What's happened since, I wouldn't like to guess.

The art of survival in Styal Prison was more difficult for me than it had been in Holloway, not only because of the black atmosphere generated by so many of its inmates but also because I vehemently objected to being there. I had private worries, too, about the health of my dear sister, Beatrice, who was heartbroken, who cried and cried when I was sent to prison and was crying still. My mother was also ill during this period. She'd always visited me, and she was very supportive, but she couldn't understand why I was in jail in the first place. By the time I'd been transferred to Cheshire, she had literally worried herself sick. At one point, I received a letter telling me that she was dying, but the authorities refused my request for a day's leave to see her. It's a ruthless system.

I still did my best to keep up my spirits. I carried on singing, of course. When I spent time in the workroom, I'd be examining the clothes that were being made there, but inside my head, I was somewhere else. I was in a recording studio. I'd be listening to the radio and letting my imagination run wild. Something that was very important for morale was the illusion, at least, of femininity. I would have been lost without my make-up, which I bought from the canteen shop out of my earnings, and my Pond's cold cream for removing it.

Hair care, too, was vitally important to almost all of the women. Some of them used to get suicidal when their black roots or grey hairs started showing through. They'd be wailing, 'Look at this, I can't possibly go on my visit next week.' They talked about the 'humiliation' of not being able to have their hair done, and how it dented their self-respect. I'd always managed to get my bleach smuggled in, any way I could. Usually I'd offer another inmate piles of big cigarette ends if she would arrange for one of her mates to bring my bottle in on a visit and hand it over secretly. Each time I'd use it, I'd see the screws looking at my blonde roots, thinking, 'She's had her hair done.' Then I knew I would have a cell search, followed by a strip-search. They went through everything with a fine tooth-comb. Naturally, though, I'd already got rid of the evidence.

Once, I was sent before the governor. She said, 'Right, Janie. Your hair is beautiful. How do you keep the roots so marvellous?'

I looked her right in the eyes and said, 'Well, madam, I go to church every Wednesday and Sunday. I get down on my knees and say, "Please, God, strike me with a flash of bleach," and when I wake up, there it is.'

The screws who were with me started laughing, but I was docked two days' pay for my cheek. I used to tell other prisoners that I treated my roots with a mixture of early-morning piss (for the ammonia) and Steradent, which had to be mixed together to form a thick paste. A lot of them believed me and passed this 'information' on to the screws. I thought it was ridiculous that women had to suffer so seriously over a few grey hairs, so I bombarded the Home Office with a series of petitions, demanding hairdressing facilities for the prisoners, which we would pay for from our wages. After several disappointments, the governor received the reply I wanted:

If you are able to find a hairdresser who is willing to come to the prison each month to cater for the women who are for one reason or another unable to meet their own requirements, and if women are willing to pay for the services of a hairdresser, there is no objection to this being arranged.

I notified all of the prisoners, so when the governor started dragging her heels over the introduction of the service, claiming she did not have a spare room for the hairdressing sessions, there were near riots. Before long, we had our crimper, and women all over the prison were walking around with their hair done beautifully, no longer ashamed and living in dread of visits from their men.

Visits, of course, were a crucial part of the survival scheme, along with letters. I received stacks and stacks of fan mail. Usually, I'd glance through it and throw it away, but on two occasions, I invited a correspondent to come and see me. I was never allowed more than one visit every two weeks, and in Styal, I was even more restricted, so I had to be very selective with my invitations. Mostly, they went to family members or solicitors. But a letter I received one morning from a man called Theo Saunders intrigued me to the point at which I decided I had to meet him. He was a happily married man with a daughter who had simply written to offer his support and express his outrage at my sentence. I replied with a note of thanks, and he wrote again, assuring me that if I ever needed any help I only had to ask.

He duly came to visit and turned out to be a very sweet man; we built up a wonderful friendship over the ensuing months and years. He campaigned and petitioned on my behalf and was tireless in his efforts to help me whenever he could, without ever asking anything in return. I

WELCOME TO THE JUNGLE

last saw him four or five years ago when he was passing through London to visit a sick sister in Reading. He didn't look at all well. The following Christmas, I noticed that he hadn't sent his usual card, and I haven't received one since. Loath to upset his family in any way by ringing up to enquire about him, I remain no wiser, although I fear he may have died. I thought the world of him, Theo.

The second letter that inspired me to arrange a prison rendezvous with a stranger was from a crank, a teacher called Ron. He was such an out-and-out nut-case that I simply had to meet him. I wrote to him for some time beforehand, and his letters became more outlandish as they went along. He swore his adoration, devotion and willingness to become a complete slave; he sent flowers to me at the prison, and he said he'd 'very gladly' supply me with anything I wanted. Anything at all.

Just for fun, I replied to him, saying that as a 'very strict mistress', I needed an expensive pair of leather boots from a certain shop in Knightsbridge. I added that if he were a good slave and made sure these boots were delivered to me in prison within three days, then, of course, I would allow him to visit me. I was laughing with the other girls, saying, 'He ain't gonna send the boots in.' But I was wrong. He did. And they were beautiful. So I had to grant the visit.

Come the day, we were all in stitches. I assured the other girls that I'd give him a good kicking under the table with my new boots, and when the hour arrived, everyone in the visiting room was watching and giggling, including the screws. He turned out to be a little chap, about forty-five, who beamed with pleasure at everything I said or did. Each time I kicked him, he said, 'Oh, yes, yes, I deserve that. Wonderful, wonderful. I need another one.' I was in fits of laughter for the rest of the day over Ron.

Weeks later, though, I was getting a bit fed up with the correspondence, so I wrote a letter that I felt sure would discourage him. I told him that I wanted him to give me the financial backing for a project I was planning to launch when I came out of the nick. I wanted to buy a restaurant and call it Cranks Anonymous, I explained. It would be decked out like a prison, with side-cells containing dining tables. The security staff would be kitted out like judges. The waitresses would be dressed as screws, and I would be the whip-wielding manageress – the governor. A selection of whips and canes would also hang on the wall. Any customers behaving badly or complaining about the food would be frogmarched to the roof gardens and tied to a cross for punishment.

Punishment would be a pelting with custard pies, sold to other diners for a couple of quid a bag, or for more serious offences, a belting with whips and canes, again by anyone else who just happened to be in the restaurant. It was just a fantasy, a crackpot idea, but, like many of my other frivolous schemes, it served to help me laugh my way through many a cheerless day in prison.

CHAPTER FOURTEEN

A Bit of What You Fancy

Any trivial incident could suddenly brighten up the deadening monotony of the nick. A silly practical joke or a comedy on the telly could have us all cackling our heads off, such was our desperation for an antidote to the gloom that surrounded us. So the opportunity of a little illicit pleasure – a sexual encounter, a glass of booze or a smoke of pot – was seized upon by many of the women as a glittering prize; the ultimate highlight.

I couldn't blame them. I'd always been opposed to drugs, so I never condoned that particular activity in jail or out of it, but I raised my cap to those prisoners who managed to get away with anything else in the name of vice! To be imprisoned was to be treated like a robot, to be watched at all times of the day and night, to miss the simplest pleasures more than anything – like a quiet hour alone, or a walk in the park in springtime, or a plate of lovely, hot chips for lunch.

I could only ever eat little bits of prison food, which was greasy and cold. It was an absolute luxury to be able to make a flask of hot tea to take to the cell, although it was a rare one. Tea-bags had to be bought out of our tiny prison earnings. I spent practically every penny I made on tea-bags, powdered milk and, of course, my hair. I refused to become institutionalized like some of the characters around me who grew, mentally, into the robots they were expected to act like. They had free food, no rent to pay, they were exempt from any responsibilities except their menial prison chores, and they were perfectly content. They didn't want to go home, a lot of them, which I found pathetic.

But if prison bred a lot of sheep who were happy to be herded around from morning to night, one year to the next, it also produced a lot of enthusiastic young criminals. It was a teaching ground for crime. In Holloway, first offenders were flung in with hardened cons. Young girls who'd come in for something silly like shoplifting, who'd never been in trouble in their lives before, would suddenly be hearing all about the money to be made from burglary or drug dealing. And so instead of leaving jail vowing, 'I'm never going to go back there,' they'd be thinking, 'Yeah, maybe I can go out and make some easy money.' It was a bloody snakepit.

I used to have words with these youngsters. I'd say, 'If you listen to all this talk, you'll end up like the old lags, in and out, in and out.' And some of the old lags might not have been in and out, in and out, quite so frequently had there been any efforts made towards proper rehabilitation. The prison system doesn't really give you anything to turn to – a trade or a course that would help with employment upon release. People are simply chucked out at the gates with a bus pass or a train ticket.

I'd recommend the establishment of a network of huge, half-way houses in the countryside where prisoners can serve out the end of their sentences while receiving employment training and advice. I think it's important to teach people who offend, recognize their talents, try and give them a new start in life, rather than throw them out with no money, no hope and no prospects except for a life on the dole. My own plans involved a return to my great love, singing and entertaining, as well as a new ambition to work for prisoners' rights and the homeless. In fact, I later managed to combine the two when I gave a benefit concert in a London pub for Women in Prison.

Nobody could begin to know what it's like in jail unless they've been there. I wanted to go home more than anything. I couldn't stand the grey, daily grind of Her Majesty's institutions. I couldn't stand the lack of stimulation, I couldn't stand the fights and the constant threat of violence, and I couldn't stand a lot of the screws.

Some – usually the married ones – were very nice indeed, kind and caring and as helpful as they could be. Some were lesbians who were interested only in finding girlfriends. Some would bring their personal problems into the prison and take them out on the women. And then there were the out-and-out bastards, the sadists who derived a great deal of pleasure from the job. They were the ones who loved the idea of locking us up in cells, sneaking on any little thing we might do, ordering punishments and generally causing as much pain and distress as they could. In my experience, at least three out of ten were getting their jollies from it.

The male warders, who staffed Holloway's padded cells because they had the strength to restrain violent prisoners, if necessary, would occasionally take their devotion to duty a touch too far. I saw one woman, the sister of a solicitor, coming out of those cells with black eyes. I'd always hated cruelty against an unwilling victim. Back at the Three Counties Hospital, I used to hit the roof if I saw any employee treating a patient roughly, and I'd always report it. In general, prison life would have been so much easier for everybody if the more aggressive screws had tried to pacify instead of antagonize. They had so much hate inside them. Then again, they were on the receiving end of a fair amount of abuse from various prisoners, so it all went round and round in a vicious circle.

The memories come flooding back to me really vividly at times, even now. If I flick on the telly and chance upon the Australian cult soap opera *Prisoner: Cell Block H*, I'm right back in Holloway or Styal. Not that I think the series is particularly true to life – *Behind These Walls* with Googie Withers was much more like it – but certain story-lines and characters remind me of my days behind bars. Lizzie, the prisoner with the little old wizened face, is typical of what you'd see inside, and Bea

Smith, the redhead, is very good. Some of the screws have been quite convincing, too, especially 'Vinegar Tits' (Vera) who has now left the cast. She was the evil one with the scraped-back, mousey-coloured hair and the hang-ups, the dramas of her mother's death and her boyfriend problems. She was a powerful character.

To me, though, the whole thing seems too soft and lovey-dovey. As I've already described, there are some very vicious individuals in women's prisons, and many of the inmates have personal habits which would shame an animal. Some girls used to throw their dirty sanitary towels out of their cell windows. Others would go to the toilet on a piece of toilet paper, wrap it up and throw it out of the window. Then an officer would have to walk round the outside of the building with a prisoner carrying a pointed stick to pick up the 'shit parcels', as they were called. The officer would be yelling, 'You dirty, filthy load of swine and bitches!' while the prisoner carried on picking up the parcels. It was a disgusting job, and it was usually the butch women who ended up doing it. They thought they were like men doing men's jobs, so it wouldn't turn their stomachs.

No one could ever find out which inmates were responsible for these parcels. They were usually slung out at night. It was one thing to have a pee in your pot. But anything more and your cell-mate would object to spending the rest of the night in the same room. It would be, 'Oh, God, don't. Can't you wait until the morning?'

I hated the indignity of the pot. Sometimes I'd be desperate for a pee, but I'd hang on in agony if there was any imminent chance of being let out of the cell to the proper toilet. I couldn't escape the odd emergency in the middle of the night. But as for going to the toilet properly in the cell – I would have killed myself rather than do that. I'd wait until my door was opened. And that's probably why I started suffering from haemorrhoids, like a lot of the other girls in there.

If the things made that made life bearable were the visits, letters, laughter, learning and therapy sessions (which were also available at Styal), then the icing on the cake was the scandal! There was nothing more thrilling than a juicy piece of gossip in a place that was supposed to prevent the opportunity of anything gossip-worthy happening. And there was no greater sense of achievement than to carry off something naughty, right under the noses of the screws. My own contribution was the time I had three bottles of booze smuggled into Holloway.

One day in December, my fun-loving cell-mate Jenny happened to remark to me, 'Oh, Christmas is coming up. I'd like to have something to drink.' I answered that I wasn't that fussed. 'Oh,' she said, 'think about it. We could all get pissed together, and Hindley could have some brandy.'

Myra was clapping her hands with excitement. 'Oh yeah,' she nodded eagerly. 'I haven't had any for years and years!' Myra had her own ideas about how we would get it, too. 'I know one of the guys in the admin office,' she said. 'He likes big bristols and low-cut clothes – and he can turn a blind eye to anything.'

Shaking my head, I said: 'No. I'm not gonna do it that way. I know a prisoner who can get it in for me in exchange for a load of tobacco.'

I didn't ask too many questions, but the girl I knew did somehow manage to have three full-size bottles of spirits brought into the prison building. My instruction was to collect them from the kitchen, where I found that the brandy, whisky and gin had already been transferred into bottles that had once contained cordial. Small amounts of fruit juice had been left inside to disguise the colour of the liquor. I took my booty from the kitchen to my cell in a plastic pail, which I usually carried milk bottles around in, with a few dusters thrown on top. As Jenny and I walked through the centre, we saw a procession of screws coming towards us. I walked past the whole lot of them, smiling and saying, 'Good-morning.' Jenny went as red as a beetroot and shook, scared out of her life.

'How can you do it?' she whispered.

I set the bottles on my outside window sill, and they were still there when a little Irish screw called Willie Walker came into my cell after arranging for me to pluck her eyebrows. She was hilarious, always scurrying around the prison trying to catch people breaking the rules, and nosing around the cells. She sat down while I fiddled around finding the tweezers, and then suddenly sniffed.

'I'm sure I can smell brandy in here,' she announced. Jenny nearly had a heart attack.

I said, 'Brandy? What are you on about? Here I am plucking your eyebrows for free, and that's all you can tell me, you silly old cow! The only brandy I've got is in a bottle of essence from the canteen, for the Christmas cake.'

'Ah yes,' she said. 'I knew I could smell something.'

I joked, 'Look, I've got a cucumber too, and I'm going to give it to one of the birds, merrily, this weekend!'

'Oh, you filthy little monkey,' she retorted, mock-disapprovingly. I used to delight in giving her the shock treatment and winding her up, and I loved getting one over on her even though, on that occasion, I was on a real knife-edge.

I didn't partake of any of the Christmas cheer Willie Walker had so nearly found. I didn't dare, because I knew a couple of glasses would set me off. In another way, it's just as well I abstained: at the time I had no idea that the stresses and strains of prison had made me allergic to alcohol. Half a dozen women, including Myra, shared the whole lot between them in the cells and then went flouncing out into the recreation area. They were pissed out of their minds. Hindley was in another world, dancing and laughing, twittering, 'Oh, how wonderful!' The screws were coming in to find out what the noise was, and couldn't believe their eyes. They demanded to know what the hell was going on.

I managed to stifle my laughter and asked them, 'What do you mean?'

'These women are drunk,' they asserted seriously.

'Are they?' I asked. 'Well, if they are they've gotten rid of the evidence. And I haven't got anything. You can search my cell if you like.' Of course the screws were too late. The drink was finished and the innocent, empty bottles well washed out.

Although booze was not an unobtainable commodity in prison, marijuana was far more plentiful, and many of the women found that it alleviated the stress of their sentences. Myra Hindley was one of them; I've seen her smoking it a few times.

I tried it once myself, but only to placate the other prisoners. This happened near the start of my sentence, before anybody knew me very well. I'd been sitting in a cell where there was a bit of pot-smoking going on, and they wanted me to have some too for their own security. The reasoning was that if I'd been involved myself, I wouldn't go telling tales to the screws. As an anti-drug fanatic, I was horrified at the proposition, but I nevertheless agreed for the sake of harmony on the wing. I had two little puffs, I giggled for the rest of the evening, and I had a headache the next day. It was horrible. And it was the one and only time I ever touched the stuff. I told the women: 'If you get any more of that, and you're going to smoke it, just don't invite me into the cell. There's no way I'm going to do that again.'

Little Willie Walker used to run around in circles looking for pot, and this gave us ammunition for a few practical jokes. Prisoners working in the gardens would pick up handfuls of grass after mowing the lawn, and they'd put it inside some envelopes. I'd say to Willie, pretending to tip her off, 'There's somebody on this wing with some grass.'

She'd reply , 'I know. It's disgusting. If I could only find it.' One of the other girls would walk past a few minutes later and drop an envelope. She'd pick it up, open it and start sniffing: 'What's this?'

'It's grass, Willie,' I'd tell her, with a big smile. 'Grass from the lawn.'

Another similar prank we played on her was intended also to annoy a prisoner on the landing below ours, an out-and-out bitch who had all these potted plants in her cell. One day, within Willie's earshot, I told another con that this woman we disliked was growing marijuana under the bed in her cell. We saw Willie clocking this, we saw her little feet trotting off, and the next thing we were all locked in our rooms. Jenny and I were looking out to see what was happening below. All of a sudden, this prisoner I'd mentioned was brought out, her cell was searched and all of her plants taken away, the whole bit.

Inside, Willie was looking under the bed for the marijuana plant, and, of course, there was nothing there. We screamed with laughter. Her little ears were always wigging. She said to me, 'You're always one step ahead of me, Janie Jones, you know what's going on all over the wing, but one of these days I'm going to catch up with you, you little monkey.' She was a great little officer. I loved her. She was around fifty, and we knew she was a tartar, but she really wouldn't do any harm. She treated everyone equally. She was quite a religious woman, she was single, and looked quite butch, but she wasn't a lesbian. She told me, 'I once had a boyfriend I was going to marry. He was very nice, but in the end, I couldn't go through with it. Maybe I should have. But I'm quite happy in my own way.'

Unfortunately for Willie, she never did find any drugs on her never-ending searches, though I'd have been delighted if she'd discovered some of the stronger stuff that was coming into the prison. The authorities tried their best to tighten up, but whatever the women wanted, they would get in somehow or other. Visitors would pass stuff over, mouth to mouth, while kissing prisoners. There were all sorts of dodges.

Josie O'Dwyer, the con that beat up Myra Hindley, was wild for anything she could lay her hands on. Any way she could get stuff in, she would. She was like a lunatic when it came to drugs. Another girl called Linda, who came to Styal, was a heroin addict who screamed and cried during the whole withdrawal period. Her best friend in prison was the woman who'd sold her drugs when they'd both been on the outside, but the dealer had been smart enough not to get hooked. I used to hate her. I'd think, 'Yeah, you did it for the money. Misery-dealing. You deserve everything you've got.'

Linda went through physical cold turkey, but continued to dream about the fix, despite her disgust at the mess she'd been in while she was on heroin. I couldn't understand how a person could go through so much pain and suffering to come off a drug, could shrink with horror at the memory of her previous debauchery, but could still think lovingly of another fix. I was always worried that Linda would go back on it when she got out. Whether or not she did, I don't know.

The lack of sex in prison never bothered me too much. I firmly believed that the women were unwittingly dosed with some sort of drug, which calmed the urge. I had visits from male friends, but I accepted the situation for what it was. I was in there, there was no point in thinking of men in a physical way, and I had to make the best of it. I thought of most men as a load of bastards anyway.

Many women, however, were reluctant to give up on their sex-uality. At one time, there was a spate of dildos made from porridge, which they would collect at breakfast time and empty into the leg of a stocking. They'd let it harden and later use it for their own personal pleasure. The sudden popularity of porridge for breakfast mystified the kitchen staff for weeks! Little Willie Walker was soon on the case, of course, and she was immediately on the hunt for as many porridge dildos as she could find.

Then she became alerted to the fact that some porno mags were circulating round the wing. 'Filth and pornography!' she'd shriek. 'It's disgusting! Where is it?' Invariably, she'd find one of the offending magazines right under her nose. She could never bear to look at it.

Magazines were one thing, but a few women of my acquaintance found they didn't have to stop there: they picked up their own real, live men – right in the middle of prison. The dirty deeds that were possible in Holloway came to light when an inmate got pregnant! The father was one of the male wardens who were regularly called in from other jails to staff the padded cells when it was thought some restraint of prisoners might be necessary. The girl in question was a little backward and had been in a padded cell at the time of the incident. The story was that she screwed this reportedly handsome warder in return for tobacco.

In Styal, the opportunities for sex were probably greater. While I was there, one male officer was having it off with at least two of the lifers. They'd do it in the church or hidden from view in the gardens. He was a very nice, middle-aged officer – not particularly good-looking, but he had a nice personality, full of jokes and laughter. He and his wife lived close to the prison, and because his wife had had an operation of some sort, she couldn't have sexual relations with him. He wasn't the type to take advantage of anybody. It would have had to be a woman who made the first approach, a lifer who wanted her oats and moved in on a vulnerable man.

Personally, I got on very well with him. He helped me look after my potted plants. On one occasion, I asked his advice about a plant of mine, which was infested with greenfly. He told me to bring it out to the gardens and he'd look at it. I got the plant, and I walked all the way across the gardens with it, watched by two prisoners who didn't like me. They reported me to a particular screw they adored, claiming they had spotted me trying to make an escape at the far end of the grounds, by the front gate. After that I was accompanied by an officer everywhere I went.

One of the women who was knocking off the warder was Lesley Ford, the Bungling Assassin. She used to work in the church, cleaning the silver and so on, and the man regularly took flower arrangements from the gardens into the church. They used to go off and hide inside big, plastic tunnel-shaped constructions, which were placed around the grounds and used like greenhouses. Lesley would come back from their sessions bragging that he'd given her fruit, cigarettes, perfume or miniature bottles of spirits.

I wrote in my Styal diary one day: 'Bell's shouting her mouth off again about the male officer.' Anything Mary Bell could do to get somebody else into trouble, she would. Mary Scanlon, my friend who'd stabbed her Indian lover, was another lifer who was screwing this warden. She also worked in the church, and she used to come back with stories of sexual exploits under the church altar. But the most bizarre story of all was one involving a woman called Carol Hanson.

When it all began, I wrote about it in my diary. I knew then it had the makings of a first-class scandal, but I could never have guessed at anything like its gruesome outcome. My scribbles said:

Carol Hanson is in for life. She and her husband murdered kids, cut them up and put them in suitcases. I will not have her sit behind me with scissors in the workroom.

She makes my skin creep. She's got an ugly, spotty face and glasses, with a big sickly grin. She loves to try and get me into conversation. She always touches me while she's talking, and I can't bear that. I have to keep telling her to stop.

She's a red band and she acts all goody-goody. She sucks up to the officers, all sweet and nice and innocent. She seems to be into witchcraft. She keeps on about her husband, and how he makes churches with matchsticks. She's a weirdo.

Her stomach is very big and swollen. She feels she is pregnant. She is going to an outside hospital for examination, and when she comes back, she will tell me what happens.

When she did come back, I couldn't believe my ears. My diary continued: ' She told me they took a big ball of hair from her, with eyes and teeth and a mouth. It's awful.'

I told her, 'I don't believe you.'

She said, 'It's the truth. They called it a phantom pregnancy.'

As far as I'd ever understood, a phantom pregnancy happens when a woman wants so much to be pregnant, she develops the symptoms. So I assumed that Hanson was giving me a load of crap, and I asked an officer about it. I said, 'Carol Hanson is telling me that she's had a ball of hair with teeth in taken out of her, and that it's something to do with a phantom pregnancy.'

'Well, I certainly wouldn't have mentioned it unless you'd asked,' replied the officer, 'but since you have, I am telling you that it's true.' I could still hardly believe it. But strange things do happen, things they can't explain, and that was certainly one of them.

Obviously, the vast majority of sexual enterprises took place between women prisoners. It was less easy for cons to have affairs with screws. Some of the inmates were lesbians to start with. Some were heterosexuals who were merely looking for gratification, and while most would go straight back to men after they were released, others would walk out of the gates as converted gays.

I've seen women coming into the nick as straight as dies, going round the bend with worry about whether their husbands were having it off with someone else, tearing their hair out – 'Oh, if I ever caught him what would I do?' Then the lesbians would get to work on them, turning them against the husbands, and the next thing they were telling their old men they didn't want anything more to do with them. Naturally, lots of relationships do survive the wife being inside, but an equal number don't. I've know of women leaving prison only to find their husbands with mistresses and their marriages in ruins. They've gone back to crime specifically to return to prison because they 'couldn't see any point in anything' after that.

Known lesbians were often allocated cells together, to keep peace and quiet, and a lot of the screws loved to peer through the spy holes at night and watch what was going on. The warders at Styal used to put all the gays – the big, butch Berthas and their girlfriends – into one house opposite the one I was in.

Most of them were harmless, but some of the tougher ones were dangerously calculating. They'd watch for new, young arrivals on the wing, and they'd pounce. They'd make a big fuss of these unwary women, make passionate declarations of love and fleece the girls for tobacco and money – or possessions, which could be turned into either. One great big lesbian woman pretended to adore her victims and would drop them as soon as she'd got something as sacred as their wedding rings off them. Then she'd get her visitors to sell them. Another put her girlfriend on the game, from behind bars, when the younger one left prison. I was always warning the kids to beware of women who 'fell in love' with them.

It was because of this that I was threatened with violence by a lesbian called Billie who was furious with me for always guarding the girls and tipping them off about the wedding-ring racket. One day, I wrote in my Holloway diary:

> *Butch lesbian Billie has just jumped on her next victim, Linda, a young married mother with a little girl, giving her the same line as the rest: she's fallen in love at first sight. Linda is only eighteen years of age, and Billie will soon have her gold wedding ring with at least six or seven others, ready to pass out on her next visit . . . . Now she's got permission from a butch screw to share a cell with Linda, to comfort her. What a sick joke. Because of the shortage of officers and the constant overcrowding, they just seem to do anything for peace. We are locked in sometimes twenty-three hours a day – out for meals and banged back in.*

I had lots of bloody love-letters sent to me. I used to attract them like bees round a honey-pot. I don't know why. Some of the straight women developed crushes on me, maybe because they thought I was glamorous or amusing. And the lesbians used to be after me too. I had to destroy the letters straight away because I would've got into trouble for having them. And I'd tell the authors, 'Look, it's just one of those things, but I love men.' They'd be trying to persuade me, 'Oh, you don't know what you're missing,' and all this crap, but I'd take it with a pinch of salt. I'd get on all right with them but I didn't want to get too friendly in case it started aggravation. They were always trying to sit somewhere near me in the workroom, so I used to have to make sure I was surrounded by my own friends.

A load of the screws were lesbians, and I couldn't resist a little joke every now and again. One day, coming out of a visit, I was told by two screws, who were lovers, that I had to have a routine strip-search. 'Oh, great,' I said and started singing the tune of 'The Stripper'. I did all the bumping and grinding as I took my gear off, and they were so embarrassed. They couldn't wait to get rid of me!

They weren't my biggest fans, those two, but I did have some screws among my admirers. There was one in Holloway, mousey-blonde, attractive and quite shy. She was having an affair with a principal officer in the same prison, a real harridan who ruled her with a rod of iron and, according to rumour, used to give her 'punishments'. This PO was insanely jealous because her girlfriend had the big thing about me, and she did her utmost to make my life hell. I had a go at her once. I said, 'Don't you dare try and make things difficult for me, just because your friend likes me.'

But she kept on creating stupid inconveniences. For instance, one day, as one of my red-band duties, I was taking a group of women from one part of the prison to another, through the grounds. It was pouring with rain, and I was carrying a broken-down umbrella, which had been given to me by one of the women in the welfare department where I made the coffee. The governor had seen me with the umbrella and passed no comment. But then the PO noticed me and took it away.

She said, 'It could be a dangerous weapon.'

I replied, 'Yeah. It could be a dangerous weapon to give you some stick with.'

She snapped back, 'You're no different from any other prisoner, and you're not having it.'

She was such a different personality to her girlfriend, who was popular with all the prisoners. She was really kind-hearted, and she used to shriek with laughter when I told her about my celebrity sex parties. We had quite a lot in common, including the fact that we both used to be nurses, and we became good friends. She used to bring in wool for me, and I knitted a couple of things for her. Willie Walker, the little Irish screw, used to say, 'She's going to get herself into trouble hanging around with you, Janie Jones.'

I used to hoot with laughter: 'Oh, Willie, you silly old cow, she's not doing any harm. She comes round to see me because she likes me. What are you carrying on about?'

At the Christmas party, she came over to dance with me in front of her lover, the PO. I couldn't help getting them both going a bit. While we danced, I scratched my nails into the screw's hand, because I knew she liked a bit of pain. She was getting all excited, saying, 'Oh, you're wicked doing that, what a wicked girl,' while the PO stood fuming on the other side of the room.

But the attentions I received from that smitten screw were nothing compared to what happened in Styal. An officer there became absolutely obsessed with me. She looked quite butch, with her waist-length hair pulled up neatly on top of her head, and she was quite an amusing woman. She used to follow me all over the place, never taking her eyes off me. Later, when I was accused of trying to escape from the grounds through the front gate, she was ordered to go everywhere with me. Of course, she loved that. I used to get my jollies out of winding her up, knowing the other officers were aggravated that she was deranged over me. Yet, for all of her devotion to me, she never allowed me any special privileges.

It was the talk of the prison. When the other girls saw her, they'd start shouting, 'Janie, oh my love, I love you,' and all she could do was glare back. Before long, she was transferred to another house, well away from me. She was very upset over that, because she hadn't done anything unprofessional, she did her job properly and she was a very hard worker. She fell in love with another inmate eventually, and when that prisoner left Styal she handed in her notice and went too.

There was, however, one prison officer who I did develop very strong feelings for, purely in the way of friendship, and she was called Denise. We're still the very best of buddies today. We didn't get off to the best start when I met her for the first time in Holloway, close to the start of my sentence. I was with a group of women who were carrying trays to the kitchen. On my tray was a massive container full of sugar.

Denise went past with some prisoners from her wing, and she noticed one of my mob taking a scoop out of my sugar with an empty coffee jar. She assumed that my container was loaded with coffee, and she decided that the other prisoner and I must have been conspirators in some scheme to steal kitchen supplies. She tipped out my bag, which contained only a hanky and a few girlie bits and pieces, looking for contraband coffee. Of course, there wasn't any. I went absolutely spare. When I returned to the wing, I reported the incident to the PO who said, 'Yes, I know about it. The officer concerned has already phoned. But take no notice, it's all right.' From that day on, I called Denise the 'Coffee Queen'. And then I discovered she was moving on to our wing.

At first, she gave me a hard time. She had me scrubbing the steps and doing all the worst jobs there were. But, eventually, something clicked. We started playing table tennis in the recreation area, and we gradually became good friends. She had a heart of gold, and everybody liked her, but she went by the book. She wouldn't let anybody away with anything, including me. I remember one day, I saw her eating some mints, and I said, 'Here, give me one of those.'

She replied, 'Oh, no, you've gotta stick by the rules.'

Our friendship finally became very close indeed, although not physically so, but it didn't stop all the other screws from gossiping. In the end, Denise was told that she was being moved to another prison. As an officer, she was not allowed to carry on any real friendship with any of the prisoners and there would be no question of her continuing to see me when I was released. Her reaction was to reply: 'I will carry on seeing Janie because she's my friend and I admire her,' and she left the prison service. It was an enormous sacrifice and testament to our friendship. I looked forward to joining her one day on the other side of the gates.

CHAPTER FIFTEEN

Chimes of Freedom

VICE QUEEN JANIE FREED! screeched the *Sun* on 30 April 1977, informing the nation that I was going to be released the next week. That the newspaper had this information came as quite a surprise to me. Far from being given the customary six to eight weeks' notice, I'd only just been told myself, and no more than a handful of close friends knew. I suspected that one of the screws had leaked the story for a quick few quid. I had recently been sent back to HMP Holloway, and when the day arrived, the prison was besieged by reporters, photographers and television cameras. I'd never seen anything like it. Luckily the authorities had anticipated all this and had arranged for my friend David Yallop to drive into the prison grounds to collect me. He arrived in a little battered Mini. I got into the back and hid under a blanket. We headed towards the gates at normal speed and passed the unsuspecting crowds of press who paid no attention to David's car, much to my amusement. They were obviously expecting a limousine, a fanfare and a dramatic, quote-a-second appearance from yours truly.

I didn't really know what to think or say as we drove out of sight of the building, into my uncertain future and a doomed renewal of my friendship with Myra Hindley. I can hardly remember anything of the journey apart from mixed feelings of excitement, confusion and relief. David was a very understanding companion. We'd known each other since the sixties, when we'd met in a television studio. David was the floor manager and I was appearing on a show singing 'Witch's Brew'. He'd since become an author, and I'd made good friends with his first and second wives, Marie and Anna.

David drove me to his place nearby in Crouch End to rendezvous with my best friend Denise. She was waiting with her car to take me up north to Durham to see my mother. We switched on the radio as we set off, and only moments later, I heard my very own chimes of freedom. They weren't the great, peeling, jubilant bells of my dreams. They were the rough and raucous thrashings of punk-rock band the Clash, with a track called 'Janie Jones' from their recently released début LP. I didn't know what was happening. I hadn't heard anything about it, and I thought it was some sort of attack.

I said, 'What the hell is this? I can't believe it. I've just gotten through the bloody doors of the nick, I haven't been out five minutes, and I hear some bloody punk group having a go at me. I'll have to find out about it.' In Durham, I went to visit my nephew and I asked him, 'Who are the Clash?'

'Oh, they're out of this world,' he replied. 'They're fantastic.'

I bought the album, and I listened to it, and when I realized the song was quite the opposite of the character assassination I'd imagined, I was thrilled to bits. It boosted my self-esteem and self-respect no end, at a very vulnerable time. In October that year, when I was back in London, political activist and rock journalist Caroline Coon got in touch with me. She said that the Clash would like to meet me, and asked if I'd be willing to have my photograph taken with them. I said, 'I'd be honoured.'

I met them in a pub, and we had a great time, just chatting. They told me they thought my sentence was disgusting and had realized the hypocrisy of the system. They felt I'd been used as a pawn in a game of chess. So I told them a lot about what had happened, and we got on really well together, all of us. Joe Strummer, the lead singer and guitarist, and his fabulous girlfriend Gabby lived quite near to me in west London, and we kept in regular touch after that.

In the early eighties, they invited me to a Clash show at Brixton Academy and to a party afterwards. I was stunned by the thousands of people packed into the hall, going mental. I walked into the party feeling a bit self-conscious because I didn't know anybody. There were loads of guests in the room, but Joe walked straight over to me and sat right at my feet chatting. He was so lovely. He was, and is, an unusually genuine bloke. One day I asked him to write a song for me. A week later, he personally posted a tape through my door with a message. The song was called 'House of the Ju Ju Queen', and I loved it. It was brilliant. I knew, though, that it wouldn't stand a snowball's chance in hell of getting played on the radio because of its lyrics. There were lines like: 'Listening to the bishop banging on the door/The nuns are locked up and the choir boys are sore.' But I really wanted to do it.

Joe offered to produce it for me, so we went into the studio together. Joe, Mick Jones (guitarist) and Paul Simonon (bass player) from the Clash all played on the recording, along with a drummer called Charley Charles and a keyboard player, Mickey Gallagher. We did a version of James Brown's 'Sex Machine' for the B-side, and the single was released on the Ace label in December 1983 under the name of Janie Jones & the Lash!

Immediately I came out of prison, I went into hiding. When I arrived at my mother's, I told her, 'I don't want anybody to know where I am. If they ask, tell them I've gone to Singapore, anywhere, but I'm not here.'

She took me quite literally. One day I heard her telling a journalist, 'Janie's gone to Singapore, but she'll be back tomorrow to sign on with the probation officer.'

It was so hard to adapt to real life again. I didn't want to go anywhere. I was nervy of everything. I didn't want to move from the house because I felt scared of the traffic. I just wanted to lock myself in: old prison habits die hard. I'd spent the last four years treating all my fellow-convicts with the greatest suspicion. Now, on the outside, I didn't trust anybody or anything. I believed there was always somebody plotting and planning against me, and I felt I had to be careful about every little thing I did. I would wake up thinking that someone was going to open my door or look through a spy hole at me, and then I'd remember that I wasn't in a cell any more.

It was all a big novelty, just to walk around without being watched, to go and make myself a cup of tea when I felt like one and to sit alone in a room, in tranquillity. It was almost like a new concept to me that I could do something or go somewhere without having to get the governor's permission, and that my letters would reach me unopened. It was like getting used to a new world.

I'd intended to stay at my mother's for two or three weeks, but I was persuaded back to London after only a few days by my old friend, the television producer Mike Mansfield. He sent a telegram asking me, as a personal favour, to come down and appear on the *Russell Harty Show*. Russell was prepared to turn the whole programme over to me, where, usually, he invited more than one guest. I said OK and returned to the city. That was traumatic enough, but on top of that, I had to face the prospect of performing live on telly without so much as a rehearsal. Dressed up beautifully in my black wedding dress, I looked as nervous as I felt. I talked about prison and about Myra Hindley, telling Russell Harty – and every living room in the country – that the woman was innocent of almost everything she was accused of, which was what I believed at the time. With unknowing and bitter irony, I sang 'You Took Advantage of Me', along with the Edith Piaf classic, 'No Regrets'.

After that, I stayed in London full-time. I had to face all the problems with my house. It hadn't been sold because of the internal damage the squatters had done, and, for the same reason, I couldn't live in it. There was shit from top to bottom. Denise had offered to help me clear the wreckage and clean the place up, a task which would take us a full six months and innumerable bottles of Dettol. I wouldn't have minded the squatters if they'd really been homeless and looked after the house, but they'd gutted it. They'd ripped out all the doors. They'd taken the two-way mirror. They'd smashed the light fittings, the shower doors and the bidet. They'd broken everything in the kitchen. Hardly anything in the house was left intact. They'd used the floors as toilets, and they'd left dirty needles all over the place, from drug abuse.

Denise would dash over every evening after work to help me make my house habitable again, and then she'd have to travel all the way back to Kent, where she lived with her parents. It was exhausting for her, and hardly a lot of fun, but that's the sort of friend she was. I was living in a three-bedroom flat in Harley Street, central London. It was rented from a doctor by a Fleet Street journalist called Chris Hutchins, who invited me to stay there until my own place was in order. I'd known Chris for years. At weekends, Denise would stay there so that we could get over to Campden Hill Road early in the morning to carry on with our scrubbing. Chris lived a little further out of town with his wife and kids, but he kept the flat on because it was convenient to the West End, should he need it. He wasn't usually there. I was still at Chris's flat on 12 June 1977 when the *Sunday People* ran a sensational story with the headline: JANIE JONES AND HER EX-WARDRESS. It claimed that Denise had been chucked out of the prison service because of her friendship with me; it implied that there was a lesbian element to our relationship; and it stated that Denise was about to move into my house in Campden Hill Road. (In fact she later did. It saved her commuting between Kent and London, where she worked for the Civil Service.)

Denise was devastated by the article, but it wasn't only upsetting for her. It was upsetting for her parents, who were great pals of mine. I felt dreadful, more for Denise than myself. She was an ordinary working person who went to church coffee mornings with her mother. She was a very moral woman, and she'd given me the most tremendous help out of pure and loyal friendship. Now she was being publicly pilloried for her own generosity. I tried to placate her. I said, 'Well, it's done. We've just got to accept it. They'll be eating their fish and chips out of it in a few days' time.' Chris reassured me that he had had nothing to do with it and genuinely didn't know where the story came from. I stayed on at his flat until my own home was ready for occupation. During this time I agreed to appear on *Brass Tacks*, a Manchester television chat and phone-in show, speaking on behalf of Myra Hindley, along with her sister Maureen and Lord Longford. Denise came with me on the train. So did Lord Longford and Chris. We arrived in Manchester to meet Myra's sister for the first time. She was fairly nondescript, really, like a girl next door. She'd experienced David Smith's violence and divorced him after the trial. Later she'd remarried. On this occasion she seemed very, very nervous, which was a shame, because it didn't help her delivery on television. She'd become convinced, over the years, that Myra was innocent. In fact, she'd been brainwashed, same as everyone else close to Hindley. The programme itself was powerful and controversial, to the extent that we had to be hustled out of the back doors of the television studios afterwards.

My social-security payments were £23.57 a week and would be for the two years I needed support from the state. With this fantastic income, I was obviously unable to make any contribution towards my debt of £16,000 court costs. I wanted to arrange some sort of payment by instalment, pending the sale of the house, and I needed a solicitor. Towards the end of 1977, I contacted a man I had known years before in the Georgian club. We'd never kept in touch, but he remembered me and agreed to do what he could on my behalf.

He started to sort out my affairs in a professional capacity, but before long he'd fallen for me, head over heels. It was purely affectionate, father and daughter, without any sexual aspect at all. He was quite an old guy, and he was lonely. He was unhappy at home with his wife and family, and by the time I came along with my housing problems, he was a manic depressive who smoked like a chimney and drank Guinness like there was no tomorrow. He became a very good friend. If it wasn't for him, at times, I don't know what I would've done. He was so understanding. For my part, I cheered him up and made him laugh. He came to my house every single day and went home every night without fail, until the end of his life.

I could confide anything and everything in him. I told him about Myra Hindley – why I was writing to her and visiting, and why I believed her side of the story. He was behind me all the way. He said, 'You're bringing kindness and humanity. The girl may have done wrong, but there is a possibility that she's telling the truth, that she was just involved to a small extent, and only then because she was in love with a violent man. You yourself knew the violence of the Crank.'

The solicitor had a little cottage in the Orkneys, out in the wilds. It was idyllic. You could watch the seals and the birds for hours and never see another soul. Myra, he suggested, might like to use the cottage as a retreat if and when she were released from prison, so nobody would find her. That's what kind of sweet man he was. He looked after everything for me. He settled my £16,000 debt so that I could keep my house. He said: 'I don't want you being humiliated going backwards and forwards to court. I'm going to pay it all off.' In him, I had found someone I could trust implicitly, which was a rare joy for me. He only ever asked for one thing in return and that was for me to avoid publicity – which meant steering away from anything at all that might generate it.

I received some offers of work in television and entertainment, but I turned them down because of him. He wanted me to be like a possession, but I thought it a small price to pay for the care and help he gave unfailingly to me.

One day in 1978, I was walking along the platform in Notting Hill Gate tube station when I saw a familiar figure coming towards me. I stopped and looked straight into the eyes of my old friend and house-mate Eric, who'd sung about me so sweetly, and so outrageously, in his statements for the trial. 'Ee . . . .' he said hesitantly.

'Don't you "Ee" me,' I said. 'Ridiculous, Eric. I told you to make a statement, not write a novel.'

'Ee,' he said, 'I'm sorry. You're the best friend I ever had.' It turned out he'd been spending a lot of time around Notting Hill since my release, hoping to bump into me and make up. I couldn't hold anything against Eric, really. The pressure he was under from the police and prosecution to come up with evidence to help put me away would have been all too much for a person of his shy and nervous temperament. I invited him round to the house for a cup of tea. After that, he came visiting every day, travelling over from his rented room in Acton. My solicitor friend liked him very much and eventually suggested that Eric should move back to Campden Hill Road, now that my house was secure again.

We spent our days quietly enough, the three of us, with a strange assortment of characters passing in and out of our lives as lodgers. Two of the loveliest people I ever had the good fortune to meet were Caroline and Julie. When they first came to see round the house, they told me, mysteriously, that 'someone else' would be paying their rent. I didn't like the sound of this. I thought, Oh, no, I'm not having any of that. I'm not going back to prison for anybody. I told them, 'I have to know who it is.' Finally, they revealed that they were training to be Carmelite nuns, and they'd been afraid to tell me in case it would put me off. I roared with laughter.

Their 'boss', Father Matthew, came round to see the house, and I confessed to everything that had happened in it in the past. I wanted him to hear it from me first, just in case there should be any publicity in the future. His reaction was to bless the house from top to bottom. Father Matthew became a regular visitor at the weekends. I told him all about Myra Hindley, and he gave me a book on theology to send her. Lots of Caroline and Julie's Carmelite friends used to visit too, and they were beautiful people. They wanted only to give their lives to God.

The exception was Caroline. I knew she wasn't right for the church. She liked music, and she missed being able to go out and about at nights. She told me that she'd once been in love with a man who was an alcoholic. They were engaged and almost on the way to the altar when they suddenly decided against marriage. She fell into a pit of depression and started eating a lot. She'd look in the mirror and imagine she was ugly. But, she wasn't ugly. She was very pretty, with gorgeous red hair. And she still wasn't certain that she and her ex-fiancé had made the right decision in calling off the wedding. I told her, 'You could still get happily married and have children. I don't think this Father Matthew thing is for you.'

It was for Julie, though. She was married to the church. She just wanted to be there all the time, praying and singing. She had a voice like an angel. She looked like one too. I'm sure she's now a fully fledged Carmelite, thrilling someone, somewhere, with her beautiful singing. Six or seven months later, though, Caroline left the church, found a boyfriend and went back up north to her hometown to become a nurse.

Shortly after the trainee nuns' departure, I found a 'slave', a young chap called Gary who was working in a fish and chip shop round the corner. He used to wave out the shop window at me, and I'd bump into him in the street from time to time. He was in a sorry state, drinking a bottle of booze a day, and he had been given six months to live if he didn't stop.

I felt so sorry for him. I took him in, on condition he stopped the booze. He was fascinated by my notoriety. He used to say, 'I want to be the mistress's slave,' and I jovially referred to him as such. He stayed for some time, but I always encouraged him to think about moving on and finding a girlfriend of his own. He took my advice and is now very happily married to a nurse. He still keeps in touch.

Gary was the last of my house-guests – except, of course, for Eric who is still with me, as a friend. With the house to ourselves again, Eric and I settled into a cosy domestic routine with daily visits from my solicitor friend. But it was a contentment we had learned not to trust fully, for, as the eighties had dawned, so had a string of disasters that would follow each other with frightful regularity.

In June 1980, I was informed of the death of Mary Hamilton MBE, who'd been the senior probation officer at Bow Street court, and had given me enormous comfort during my time in Holloway Prison. We became very friendly, and she gave me her phone number so we could keep in touch when I left prison. After a period of illness, she was taken into St Bartholomew's Hospital, London. I went to visit her several times. On one occasion, she said to me, 'You should have been here fifteen minutes earlier.'

'Why?' I asked.

'Well,' she said, 'Mr Barraclough was sitting on the other side of my bed.' Mr Barraclough was the man I was up in front of every two weeks, hearing why I couldn't pay the court £16,000!

Then in April 1983, my world was ripped apart by the death from cancer of my dear, motherly sister Beatrice at her home in London. So much for a happy new year. On 1 January 1983, an X-ray result showed up a shadow in Beatrice's chest. From then, her decline was terrifyingly swift. She was in hospital for a while, but all she wanted to do was go home. I battled with the hospital authorities and took her back home, where I moved in. Beatrice's husband couldn't stand the idea of pain, so I shared the double bed with my sister while he slept in the next room. Her daughter and I took turns at tending her through the night.

On 6 April 1983, I had a flash in front of my eyes. I said, 'Beatrice is going to die on 7 April at nine o'clock or 9 April at seven o'clock.' Her husband told me not to be so ridiculous. On 7 April, I called for the doctor early in the morning. My sister was in agony, and I had her sitting up. By the time the doctor arrived, her eyes were rolling around in her head. He had the mixture in the syringe, and he was just about to jab it into her vein, when I realized.

'Don't inject into a dead woman,' I told him. 'She's gone. She's gone.' It was nine o'clock on the dot.

Many years before this, I'd said to Beatrice: 'I love you so much. If anything ever happens to me, I'll try to get a sign of some sort to you, and if anything happens to you, I'd love you to do the same.' I never had to move. Just after she died, I saw the shape of a cross on her chest. It looked as though it had been burnt in and gone white. It had never been there before. When I went to see her in the chapel of rest it had gone.

Russell Harty, with whom I'd made my first public appearance on my release, died in June 1988. Eric's mother passed away in hospital in January 1989, followed by his sister who was suffering from a rare blood disorder. This was only months after the death from old age, in hospital, of my solicitor friend on 9 September 1988. He was seventy-three. He had been ill and weak for some time, and Eric and I had been visiting him in hospital. One day, during such a visit, he told me, 'When I die, I want you to come to the church.'

I said, 'It's too awkward. Your wife and family will be there. I'll come to the funeral, but not to the graveside.'

He replied, 'That's all right. You'll know that I'm with you, because I'll appear as a robin.'

His funeral, in Chingford, did him proud. I parked my car under a tree, with branches overhanging my front windscreen, in a spot where I could see mourners around the graveside. I was just sitting thinking about his wife and children, all fighting over the spoils, when a robin appeared on a branch, right in front of my eyes. Another friend had gone; another two, in fact. For I had severed all links with Myra Hindley, after finding her out for the scheming liar she was – and still is.

CHAPTER SIXTEEN

Hindley: With Hindsight

'Do you have a spare hairdryer you could send in to me?' asked Myra Hindley in a letter dated 5 December 1983, from Cookham Wood jail in Kent. 'There isn't one to be found in the prison, and it could be a while yet before they get one. Do you also have a couple of terry tea-towels? I've got a couple of cotton ones, but they don't dry dishes properly and they're not much good.'

I was running round in circles doing things for Myra after I came out of prison and therefore free to re-establish contact. I still considered myself to be her friend as well as a supporter who spoke out publicly on her behalf whenever possible. I corresponded with her regularly, visited her from time to time and sent in clothes, stationery and various practical articles that would help make her life a little bit easier. She reported in her next letter sent on 13 March 1984:

> *Janie, I had to laugh when you said you hoped the hairdryer was all right. I thought I'd see if it worked all right and plugged it in down in reception. Small bang, bright blue flash and smoke pouring from the front! The orderly leapt across the table and pulled the plug out. The officer looked at my blood-drained face, laughed (I wasn't hurt, just totally shocked – not electrically) and said, 'Are you sure she's a friend of yours?!' The electrician tested it for me and said the motor had blown, and it would be cheaper to get a new dryer than to replace the motor.*
>
> *Before I forget, thank you for the tea-towels and really lovely nightdress. Was it one of yours? It still retained a light scent of perfume or talc.*

Her letters were dotted with little smiley faces, indicating that she'd cracked a joke or was telling me about something that pleased her. They were also full of chat about visits – reminiscing over our last one or inviting me to come on another. When I had first agreed to go and see her, it was on condition that my real name wasn't used. I wanted it to be a private visit, not a publicity exercise, which could cause damage beyond our control. She wrote me a letter of confirmation, promising her lips would be sealed and agreeing that 'since you're on the outside, you can do without publicity even more than I can, and I need it like I need a hole in the head.'

I hadn't seen Myra for more than seven years. At the time of my release, she'd been in Durham – an impracticable journey from London. She'd been transferred to Cookham Wood in March 1983, and now, exactly a year later, I was walking back into her physical company. It felt unnatural to be meeting her again under such different circumstances. I was sure that the relationship would have been more comfortably pursued by letter, but I thought, Well, poor sod, she's been in all those years, and what's half an hour? It'll soon fly by. I drove to Kent, and, when I reached the prison, I put on a headscarf and a pair of dark glasses. I wore them until I was safely installed in the cell room where the visit would take place.

At one side of the room sat an officer. Directly opposite me was

Myra Hindley. She grabbed hold of me when I went in, kissed me on the cheek and shook my hand, all excited and elated. 'Oh, it's lovely, wonderful to see you,' she gushed. 'Oh, God, it seems years and years since I saw you. It seems like a century.' I'd taken in some chocolate bars and crisps for her, but, as a non-smoker, I'd forgotten to bring any cigarettes, and she went round the bend about that. She did have her roll-ups with her, but prisoners look forward immensely to visits where they are allowed to share – although not take away – the filter tips brought in by their guests. 'Oh, don't tell me . . . .' she wailed, disconsolately.

We couldn't really talk about anything too serious or too personal because the screw was there all the time, so it was mostly a lot of waffle, but I did make a list of bits and pieces that she wanted me to send in. What struck me most about Myra was that she looked completely and utterly different with her hair tinted a dark blackish shade. I told her at the time, 'I don't like the colour of your hair. It hardens you. I prefer it auburn.' She soon sent me a letter about that!

> Yes, I know my hair wasn't a suitable colour for my skin, but it's a long story. Briefly, I always used Clairol's 'Nice 'n' Easy' Natural Deep Auburn, not too dark, and after the first wash, it looked like my natural colour instead of a dye. But the cretins took it off the market and replaced it with – you won't believe this – Vibrant Burgundy! Now that may be fine for some but no way was I walking around with vibrant burgundy hair.

> So what we did, my hairdresser and I, was to mix it with a Clairol Rich Brown. It came out better than I thought it would, but was too dark. So I switched to Revlon Deep Auburn. Still too dark, so next time, quite soon, I'm going to get a lighter auburn. Can't remember the exact shade, but I think it will do the trick.

Clearly not too wounded by my criticism, she invited me back when she next had a free visit.

I went several times, in all, although there were months between each visit simply because Myra, like any other prisoner, was strictly rationed, and she had other people to see besides me. The conversations we had were always trivial, not only because there was an officer present but because prisoners, protected from the major dramas of life in the real world, do tend to make mountains out of molehills.

Eventually, Myra decided to stop taking visits in the small cell room. She disliked the fact that these 'private' visits were restricted to a mere half-hour, whereas prisoners entertaining their guests in the crowded public hall could look forward to much longer. I wasn't happy about this arrangement, but I went along with it anyway when I next agreed to see her. On arrival, I took my place with the many other friends and relatives of inmates and listened to the screw's announcements. When Myra Hindley's name was called, and I stood up to walk forward, I saw every head turn, and I could feel every pair of eyes in the room staring, glaring, at me, and I cringed. I was wearing the dark glasses, of course, but I still felt paranoid.

The prisoners sat in one long line, and their visitors sat in another line opposite. You could hear everybody else's conversation, and they could hear yours. In my case, they did their damnedest. I was under constant scrutiny from the moment I went in until the moment I left. I had brought my young lodger, Gary, with me. 'This is the slave,' I told Myra.

'Pleased to meet you, Gary,' she replied, laughing at what she considered to be an outrageous introduction. 'Oh, he's nice,' she carried on. 'Do you think he would get me some crisps?' And she was telling him what to buy from the refreshments counter, and he was running backwards and forwards for tea and coffee and everything else she wanted the whole way through the visit.

Afterwards, he was thoroughly excited about having met a murderess. He said, 'Cor, she didn't look like one, did she, mistress? I didn't expect she'd look so sweet and nice, and she was pleased to meet me!'

I called on Myra one more time in Cookham Wood. Again, we were under such close observation by the other prisoners and their visitors that I vowed I was never going back, at least under these circumstances.

Hindley's writing was neat and small. She crammed as much as she could into the four small sides of prison paper that were allotted per letter. She wrote about everything that was on her mind, from trivial, routine gossip to bigger topics such as her educational studies.

Myra was still very much a target for attack, and when anyone succeeded in getting at her, she'd tell me in a letter. For instance, she once wrote:

> I was assaulted by a sewer-rat who took me from the back in my room – it was so unexpected and such a shock I couldn't do a thing – just as well; there's nineteen years of pent-up everything inside me, and I dread to think what would've happened had I seen her coming.
>
> I don't like violence of any kind, not even verbal violence, and I stopped fighting after I left primary school – except to beat up great bullies who terrorized my sister – and I'd hate to soil a nineteen-year record of non-violence but – it was as well for both she and I that she did it the way she did.
>
> No bones or anything broken, but she slapped me around the face and head with her shoe (she pinned me in a corner on the floor with her ton of weight kneeling on me, so I was helpless, my right arm and leg pinned underneath me) and tore out a chunk of hair. Head ached for a while, and a stiff shoulder and neck, and a very tender scalp, but I'm a fast healer and what bruises and scratches did show soon faded.

Myra had never recovered from the brutal attack by Josie O'Dwyer, which I'd witnessed. She often mentioned it in her letters, referring to Josie as J. O. D. and adding something like, 'I hate to soil the letter with her name' or, 'End of unsavoury subject'. On one occasion, she stated:

> I have to forgive her (although I don't really, honestly believe I have, yet) if I want to be forgiven my sins, but I can't forget, and God forgive me, but I loathe her. I'd like to meet her – or I would, were I as violent and vicious as she is, or maybe was – and I'd give her something to be frightened of me for.

Myra's letters were a catalogue of illness, although she continued to pride herself on a healthy constitution! She'd write to me with a 'really grotty virus', then swollen glands and a sore throat, then a weight problem – 'I'm not going "officially" into a size fourteen!' – then a nervous tummy and loss of appetite, then heavy and irregular periods necessitating a fifteen-minute D&C operation, then heartburn, then flu again, and, finally, a glimpse of the change of life. She told me:

> *Unfortunately, I'm suffering from very hot flushes, regular ones, which are both extremely uncomfortable and embarrassing – when I'm talking to people, especially men! I had a blood test but my hormone level, or whatever it is, is normal . . . . Men are so bloody complacent about periods and the menopause.*

She added this with reference to the doctor.

There was also her insomnia. Myra lay awake at nights thinking about her plans to write a book, agonizing over each new piece of 'garbage' printed about her in the press, worrying about her mother's declining health and fuming about 'that parasite of a step-father of mine', who, according to Hindley, 'drinks his money away'. Typically, Myra also continued to fret about her own appearance, attractiveness and age, as she always had done when we were in prison together. In one letter she said:

> *I still have to get someone to do my make-up for me like you used to do. I try myself sometimes, but it never looks the same – only eye make-up; can't be bothered with anything else except maybe a touch of blusher.*

Later, she managed to find a willing helper, and she wrote to me asking me to send her a make-up bag! She explained, 'A girl here put my eye make-up on for a visit on Sunday, and so many people said how different it made me look, I've decided to wear it more often.' Her letters, however, displayed a bravado that she, in reality, had often lacked, with her recurring nightmares of white hair and wheelchairs.

I once wrote to her of the day my solicitor friend fell out of a tree and busted his ribs. Myra responded:

> *So you were furious because he shouldn't be climbing trees at his age (though I hope I'm able to climb a tree, too, at that age – I refuse to grow old and decrepit – old, maybe, but no way decrepit, and since one is as old as one feels, well, I think it will be a long time before I feel old).*

She echoed the sentiment some months later when she wrote asking me to send in some small- and medium-sized plastic rollers and hair grips. She claimed,

> *One day, please God, I'll be able to buy you a present for a change –*

*the b******s can't keep me forever, and I'll still be together and raring to go if it's twenty more years (I hope it isn't!).*

The prospect of release was never far from Myra Hindley's mind and it joined her other preoccupations in keeping her awake at night. One jokey comment of mine provoked her into this reaction:

I'm not sure that I like being referred to as a 'sinking ship'. I may well be on an ocean with nothing but horizons and no land in sight, but I think I keep afloat pretty well considering all the shots I've taken in the bows.

As far as her freedom campaign was concerned, Myra identified three main enemies. One was a public conditioned to react against her in a certain way by the familiar press caricature. The second was the Conservative government. On 8 August 1985, after being told that her case for parole would be not be reconsidered for another five years, she declared that she hoped the Tories would be kicked out by then because she didn't stand a chance with 'that bunch of heavies' in power. In the same correspondence, she spoke of the third thorn in her flesh: the continuing publicity. She complained it had been virtually never-ending for months and was really wearing her out, though she kept 'plodding on regardless'. She wrote:

The most recent [story] has been in the Sunday People, *in which Ian Brady is alleged to have said I was involved in other matters, and he has information that could keep me behind bars for a hundred years.*

After some hesitation – because I was reluctant to become involved in a public slanging match – I sent a statement off to my solicitor, who gave it to the Observer, *saying that I denied his allegations, and if he does have information about other killings, then I wish he'd relate it to the police and end the speculation and the anguish of parents and relatives concerned.*

At the end of November in the same year, she heard that Ian Brady was being transferred to Park Lane, the maximum-security mental hospital in Liverpool, where he would be treated more like a patient than a prisoner. She contacted me within the week. On prison notepaper dated 6 December 1985, she neatly wrote:

So he's got what he's been after for the past sixteen years at least. This is why I'm reserving judgement about things. I don't think he's as mad as he's made the doctors believe he is, and that although he's obviously got problems, he's as shrewd and intelligent as he always was.

In February 1987, Myra Hindley confessed that she had been every bit as guilty of the Moors Murders as Ian Brady, even though she had played a different part. After years of lies, deception and pleas for sympathy, she finally told the truth to Detective Chief Superintendent Peter Topping who was in charge of the Greater Manchester CID. She had been aware of the murders of Keith Bennett and Pauline Reade all along, and she knew that their bodies were still buried on the moors. She also knew, roughly, where.

Prior to this, she had received a letter from Keith Bennett's mother, begging for information about the whereabouts of her son's body. Hindley had also been receiving visits from Peter Topping who had decided to reopen and solve the cases of the two children still missing. In December 1986, still protesting her innocence and her misfortune in having been a besotted woman holding on to the coat tails of an evil man, she was whisked out of prison, under heavy guard, and taken back to the moors. The visit, which provoked a massive public outcry, was ostensibly made so that Myra could guide the police to areas she'd visited with Brady. He had already made a confession – of sorts – to a Fleet Street journalist and was ready, he suggested, to reveal absolutely everything.

After Myra's excursion, Peter Topping continued interviewing her until she made her confession, following long discussions with her solicitor and a Methodist minister. She was quietly taken to the moors again, away from the glare of publicity, a couple of months later, just after her confession was made public. At the beginning of July 1987, as a direct result of Hindley's help, searchers found the body of Pauline Reade, still in the beautiful little party frock she was wearing when she disappeared all those years ago. The hunt for the body of Keith Bennett intensified, but despite Myra's co-operation, despite the efforts of Brady who was also taken to the moors amid storms of public protest, the small boy's grave has never been uncovered.

Hindley, for her part, followed her confession with extravagant claims of sorrow and regret, insisting that she'd been too afraid to tell the truth before because of what it would do to her family and to her own chances of survival at the hands of other prisoners. In my opinion, she confessed because she suspected that Brady was about to spill the beans properly, so she decided it was in her best interests to get in first.

I was devastated; absolutely gutted. I was as sick as a dog for a week when I heard. It had been Brady and Hindley all along, I realized. She was there for the murders, they were in it together, and they must have been getting their jollies out of it all. They were as sick as each other. She had tried to implicate David Smith because she thought his history of violence would count against him. She blamed Brady for everything, and yet she was worse than he was.

Brady was a mental case, no doubt about that. But he knew what he'd done, and he admitted most of it from the beginning. He might have been the scum of the scum, the dregs at the bottom, but at least he had the 'decency' to confess to many of the allegations against him during the trial, to say, 'Yes, I did do that,' rather than issuing blanket denials. He made no excuses. Hindley just carried on blaming Brady. She lied and lied and lied over all those years, and showed not one scrap of remorse, only a desire to gain sympathy for her own 'innocence'. She refused to come clean until twenty-one years later, when she had to.

What about those kids she watched him murder, kids who never had the chance to grow up, marry and have children of their own? If she had any real feeling for them, or their families, she would have told the truth years before. She was very clever, much cleverer than Brady in a lot of ways. She must have locked her version of everything into her brain, she must have rehearsed it over and over, and she must have forced herself to believe it so that she could persuade other people to believe it too. She plotted and she planned. She became the finest actress in the land, and she picked her confidantes carefully, either for the protection and goodwill they could offer her in prison or for their ability to help her campaign to get out.

She made fools of fellow-inmates, and she made fools of those influential people who committed the crime of offering compassion and humanity. She conned her sister rotten. She conned Lord Longford rotten. She conned her psychiatrist rotten. And she conned me too. I'll never, ever forgive her. I heard about her confession, and I felt huge, heaving waves of nausea as I realized how she must have been laughing at me while she manipulated my emotions, talked me gently, sadly, tearfully into believing her. I thought about all the crap she told me, just to get me fighting for her, and how she'd surely have gone through life forever weaving the same webs of deceit, if it hadn't been for Brady wanting to make his full confession.

By God, I felt humiliated. Not just because of my own gullibility, but because of all the things I'd done for Myra in the name of friendship – a friendship that she returned by wrapping me up in her tissue of lies and using me merely as a pawn in her fiendish game. I recalled the struggle I put up with my conscience when I first met Myra, my prayers for guidance, my lists of trick questions, my endless interrogations, and the cunning, gradual ease with which she eventually put my mind at rest. I remembered the comfort I offered when she was upset, the physical help I gave her when she was attacked, the thousands of words I spoke on her behalf inside and outside the jail. I reflected on my television campaigning, my visiting, my endless rounds of errands for her, and I burned with rage.

Then I thought of her current situation. I would have bet a million dollars that she was sitting there spinning more of her fairy stories, twisting the facts of her confession, cajoling the women into believing that it was still all Ian Brady. I could hear her plaintive voice telling them, 'Yes, I knew the bodies were there, but it was Ian that killed them, not me. I was just in love, and I was too scared to stand up to him.' Furious, I picked up a pen and wrote a stinking letter to Cookham Wood, telling Hindley what I think to this day: that she should rot in prison and then in hell.

Months passed by, and I began to get Myra Hindley out of my hair. She answered my letter with a pathetic plea for forgiveness and understanding. These things were obviously not forthcoming on my part, and the correspondence froze instantly and for ever. I couldn't help brooding about Hindley from time to time, but my anger and indignation, my pacing around the room like a raving lunatic, had given way to a manageable contempt, and I never expected my life to become entangled with hers again. But, unhappily for me, it was about to.

On 1 February 1988, a year after Myra's confession, the *Sun* was suddenly all ablaze with the revelation that Hindley and I had had a lesbian relationship in the nick. The article was the first part of a serialization of Jean Ritchie's book, *Myra Hindley: Inside the Mind of a Murderess.* I was outraged. I'd had two letters from Jean Ritchie, one dated 15 June 1987, and the other, 22 July 1987, asking me on both occasions for help with her research. I firmly refused, wishing to have nothing more to do with Myra Hindley. Before the confession, it would have been another matter: I would have been only too happy to contribute some paragraphs of support.

The next I heard of Ritchie's book was in a flurry of phone calls from people informing me of the horrendous allegations in the *Sun*. I was furious. Way, way back, before I married the Crank, I did live with a noted lesbian, Janice, as I detailed earlier. But I never have been a lesbian myself. I was always attracted to men. I like women friends, and I love beautiful women, but only in the same way that I love beautiful objects of any sort.

The newspapers had already involved me in one so-called lesbian scandal, which was my perfectly platonic friendship with Denise, the former prison officer. To be dragged into the middle of another gay controversy was intolerable, especially since my 'partner' this time was the treacherous Hindley – and since the topic of Denise was sensationally raised again. My solicitors whacked off a letter to Jean Ritchie, informing her that I was 'horrified to learn of the vile allegations you make against her in your book'. The letter added that, 'Miss Jones is not and never has been a lesbian and she was appalled to have this article drawn to her attention by friends.' I began to wonder if I were ever going to get shot of Myra Hindley. Yet, while I felt like this, there was one person would have done practically anything not to get shot of her: Patricia Cairns, the warder who ended up on the other side of the prison bars for trying to organize Myra's escape. When Trish came out of jail, she was as devoted to Hindley as ever. Even after the confession, when Myra's former circle of supporters had washed their disgusted hands of her, Trish alone flew the flag determinedly for the murderess she loved.

She remained hypnotized, forgiving, sympathetic. I realized this when I picked up my daily newspaper one day quite recently to learn that she'd been visiting Myra, and I immediately got on the phone to find out why.

My two-hour telephone chat with Trish, which I taped, confirmed only her unswerving loyalty to Myra Hindley. Some of my more vitriolic comments she'd answer only with a laugh. Others she'd ignore by changing the subject. And she answered most questions with the contention that she hadn't known about the murders when she first met Hindley, she hadn't subsequently discussed them with her, and she had assumed all along that Myra had had more to do with these crimes than she'd ever wanted to reveal – so the confession hadn't come as any great shock to her.

'I think you're crazy,' I told Trish, at the beginning of the conversation.

'I know,' she agreed.

I told her that I cut all my ties with Hindley when I heard about the confession. And I asked how she could possibly remain friends with Myra now that she had admitted to the very things she'd spent years denying all knowledge of.

'That doesn't bother me,' replied Trish. 'That doesn't come into it as far as I'm concerned . . . . You must have accepted, you must have realized that she was a party to it. That was obvious from day one.'

'Well, I thought she was mesmerized by Brady,' I retorted. 'I believed that he influenced her, and that she was madly in love with him and didn't realize what he was doing. That is the God's truth.'

'He probably did influence her,' said Trish. 'But she's not stupid . . . she's a highly intelligent woman, so as far as I'm concerned, she knew what she was doing. I've always thought that.'

I butted in: 'And you can still go in and see her, knowing that she knew where the bodies were? I can't understand that.'

'Was that the turning point for you?' asked Trish, deflecting my question.

'Definitely,' I answered. 'It was the biggest shock of my life. Before that, she had me believing that she didn't do anything, that she didn't know where the bodies were, that it was Brady and Smith. But when I found out the truth, I could not believe I had associated with her. I felt guilty. I felt dirty and unclean. I couldn't visit her again for all the tea in China, knowing what I know now.'

'But you saw her as she was at the time – you cared about her, didn't you?' argued Trish.

'Well, no, I didn't,' I said. 'Because she told me she was innocent of almost everything the prosecution accused her of. If I hadn't believed that, I would have stood back and let Josie O'Dwyer kick the daylights out of her.'

'I can't feel that strongly about it,' differed Trish. 'That came out at the trial, didn't it, the fact she was involved in it?'

'But she denied it emphatically!' I screeched.

Trish: 'She may not have killed them [the children] with her own hands, but she was definitely involved . . . and at least she's had the guts to admit it after all that time.'

'Only because she knew Brady wanted to confess,' I interrupted.

'Yes, I thought that was probably part of the reason,' conceded Trish, adding that she thought it must have been 'a very traumatic experience' for Myra to go back to the moors.

'Oh dear,' I said, 'that would have been a few days out for her, getting her jollies out of it.'

'Aren't you wicked, you,' chuckled Trish.

'No, it's quite true,' I ranted on. 'She thought she'd be goody two-shoes, trying to show them where the graves were . . . there's a method in her madness every time. She was as bad as whoever killed those kids. How the hell can you get involved after that? You've suffered enough pain, you've done six years, you're working hard on the buses, look what you've had to come down to and you're still hypnotized by her.'

'How can you say I'm hypnotized?' demanded Trish. 'You don't know. I've got my own mind, Janie.'

'You are hypnotized. You've gone back in to see her again. You're still mad about her.'

'I've seen her a couple of times since I came out of prison. That's all.'

Call me nosey, but I had to ask Trish what happened on her first reunion with Myra.

'I thought she looked older, and I'm sure I do too. She looked less

THE DEVIL AND MISS JONES

strong, sort of grumbly, not the same robust character – as though the sentence is getting to her. She was a shadow of her former self. I know it's understandable, but I always looked upon her as a really strong character. It really shocked me. It's not exactly breaking her, but it's taking an awful lot out of her. It's a horrible place, that Cookham Wood.'

'And when it came to saying goodbye,' I prodded, 'what did she say?'

'Nothing,' said Trish.

'Did she hold or grab you hand?' I persisted.

'No, just ordinary,' answered Trish. 'We were both a bit drained, really, and with officers sitting on top of me, you can't be natural, can you? It was just like me talking to you.'

'You can't love her after all that time, can you?' I asked.

'Well, in a different way,' hedged Trish. 'It's not the same as when you first fall in love, is it? Time changes people.'

'Yeah, well, I think you're a fool to yourself,' I commented. 'I think you should keep well away from her.' Trish replied that she was about to take a break from visiting Myra, essentially for the sake of her family's feelings, but fully intended to see her again at some point in the future. 'You just can't keep away,' I scolded. What was it about Hindley, I wondered, that had so infatuated Trish for all these years?

'She's a strange combination of things, really,' mused the ex-warder. 'I mean, I agree with you that there is an amount of cruelness in her, and there is a kind of naivety as well. A very complex person.'

'She's ruthless,' I announced. 'She manipulates people, and when they are no more use to her, she flings them over. Recently, I've read up on the trial and its aftermath – everything there is to read – and my only conclusion is that Hindley does what she does because all she wants to do is get out. You must realize that now.'

'Oh, yes, yes,' said Trish.

'I don't think she ever will get out,' I rattled on. 'And she shouldn't.'

'She may not,' said Trish. 'She's been in, already, a long time, twenty-six years or something like that.'

'She'll do anything she can,' I added.

'I'm not stupid,' flashed back Trish, suddenly annoyed. 'If I'd done twenty-six years in prison, and there was some light at the end of the tunnel, to use one of her phrases, I wouldn't use any means whatsoever but I'd certainly do anything I could to fight for my freedom. Wouldn't you?'

'No,' I returned. 'Not if I knew I'd murdered people. Not if, shortly after my confession, I'd been prepared to go into all the gory details of blood gurgling out of the throat of one of my young victims – to a former inmate I'd previously pleaded innocence to!' This was a reference to an emotional outburst Myra had made during a visit from a former convict friend of ours who was now at liberty and working for prisoners' rights. Allegedly, these gruesome reminiscences took place in front of another visitor at the same table: Myra's mother. Hopefully, she was as deaf as her reputation would have it. I told Trish that when I was told first hand by the ex-con about this conversation with Hindley I wondered again, 'Oh, my God, what type of a person is she?'

'I know, Janie, but don't you think you are a different person now than you were twenty-six years ago?' asked Trish, in another of her attempts to steer the debate away from the question in hand.

'Yes,' I replied. 'But I could never, at any point in my life, have watched or tolerated the murder of a little child. Never. I could be ruthless, yes, but I could never do anything like that.'

'I appreciate the strength of your feelings,' responded Trish. 'But the point is, you don't know what you would do if you were put into a certain situation like that. I think I could never hurt a fly, but in certain circumstances I could perhaps be cruel to somebody if I was pushed to it. You know what I mean – you just don't know.'

'Oh, well, there's cruelty and there's cruelty,' I disagreed. 'But that is murder and she [Hindley] got excitement out of it. They both got pleasure.'

'I'm sure they did,' said Trish, matter-of-factly. 'I'm not disputing that. All I'm saying is that it was twenty-six years ago.'

'It doesn't take away from what she did to those children and parents,' I stormed. 'I don't think she should ever come out.'

Since I've been out of prison, and this is the God's gospel truth, no sexual activity has taken place between me and anyone else, and I mean it – 'full stop'! These days, I'm into complete purity. This was why I welcomed the trainee Carmelite nuns into my house. Knowing them was to know something without blemish, and I loved that. It's what I'm interested in more than anything. I don't miss sex at all. I think what turns me on is getting my jollies out of springing shock treatment on other people, saying and doing outrageous things and watching their reactions.

Any man who changed my mind about the way I live now would have to be a very brave and strong person after what I've been through, especially with the Crank and his violence. I'd tell him everything. At the same time, confusingly, I could never spend a lot of time with anybody who wanted to be dominating. I like a gentle person. More than anything, I go for somebody with a nice nature rather than good looks or physique, someone with an interesting mind. Men who can answer to all of these descriptions are few and far between.

And so in Campden Hill Road these days, it's just me and Eric, the odd couple – the oddest couple – and probably the happiest with it. Since the death of my solicitor friend, I've started venturing out again. For the first time since I left prison, I feel able comfortably to ignore rude comments made to me in the local shops by people who know my background. And when it comes to night-life, my confidence is building month by month. It's been gradual but I've started to get used to restaurants and night-clubs again, spending the odd night in String-fellows for instance, or a show-business party and thoroughly enjoying it. Intriguingly, the West End seems to lack the glamour – the *je ne sais quoi* – of the sixties and the personalities of that decade.

I've bumped into Cynthia Payne, the 'luncheon voucher' madam, from time to time, and she treats me like some sort of heroine. For my part, I never thought it was particularly impressive that she ran all those services for geriatrics in wheelchairs. She was always dying to meet me, Cynthia, though I didn't really want to get involved. I feared that contact between us would just lead to adverse publicity for me. Anyway, I was with my solicitor friend at the time and he didn't like the idea of publicity.

One day, however, I'd been invited to a birthday party at Longleat stately home. Among the other guests was Cynthia Payne. It was a lovely party, hosted on the lawns. Suddenly, a familiar, raucous voice accosted me: 'Oh, 'allo Janie, lav, marvellous meeting you, lav.' I returned her greeting, but I just didn't trust the situation. Next thing: 'Oh, Janie, lav, would you like me to go and get you something to eat, lav?' The woman was determined to make some kind of impression, but I was chatting and singing and carrying on, and I never thought anything more about it. Later on, I spotted her going behind a tree with a camera, so I jumped up with my camera and took a photograph of her trying to take a sneaky one of me.

I said, 'Listen, you old cow, if you want to take a photograph of me, you don't hide behind a tree.' I then stood with her for a proper posed picture, and I told her, 'Don't ever sneak around behind my back again. I can't stand anything like that.' Next thing, it was all in the paper. 'Janie Jones was with Cynthia Payne at . . . .' Every time I've seen her since in a club, she's come over to me – but it's been an honour for her to gaze upon my beauty! She feels she should have been a superstar years ago because of all her fantastic talent.

My own talent I proved long before I went into prison, and now I'd like to go back to singing. I'd also like to make an album, and I've got a song I'd love to record as a single. It's a personal thank you from me to Joe Strummer for the encouragement he gave me just by being there when I came out of prison, for immortalizing me on the legendary first Clash LP and for being a wonderful friend ever since. The song, 'A Letter to Joe', was composed especially for me by a friend, the sixties songwriter Tony Waddington. I'd love to do the theme song for *Prisoner: Cell Block H* on the B-side. That would be the perfect song for me, I think. Even though 'Vice Queen Janie' is now genuinely 'Nice Queen Janie'.

INDEX